TWENTIETH CENTURY VIEWS

The aim of this series is to present the best
in contemporary critical opinion on major
authors, providing a twentieth century
perspective on their changing status in an
era of profound revaluation.

Maynard Mack, *Series Editor*
Yale University

THE BEOWULF POET

THE
BEOWULF
POET

A COLLECTION OF CRITICAL ESSAYS

Edited by
Donald K. Fry

Prentice-Hall, Inc. *Englewood Cliffs, N. J.*

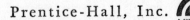

A SPECTRUM BOOK

Current printing (last number):
10 9 8 7 6 5 4 3 2 1

To Phyllis Peacock

Foreword

Beowulf criticism did not begin in 1936. Although J. R. R. Tolkien's *"Beowulf:* The Monsters and the Critics," first read in that year, completely altered the course of *Beowulf* studies, he built upon a broad foundation reaching back 121 years to Thorkelin's *editio princeps* in 1815. That this anthology excludes those pre-Tolkien efforts reflects not so much on their quality as on their emphases, for with Tolkien critical attention turned to the poem considered primarily as a work of art rather than as an artifact.

The general principle of selection in this volume is the representation of various critical approaches to the poem. The essays (and one poem) include studies of structure and unity, style, dramatic technique, symbolism, diction, realism (in the light of archaeology), religious evocations, themes, characterization, and even one general literary appreciation. The authors chosen have in my opinion written the best articles exemplifying these various approaches, and no effort has been made to include the most illustrious names in the field on the basis of their reputations. Hence, Professors Brodeur, Chambers, Greenfield, Klaeber, Malone, Pope, Sisam, Whitelock, and Wrenn are not found in the Contents, although they are amply represented in the Bibliography.

I have incurred many debts in compiling this collection, and I am most pleased to acknowledge them here. For encouragement and technical guidance, I wish to thank Fredson Bowers, David Bevington, Lester Beaurline, and Bob Regan. I was assisted with some of the knotty problems in the inserted translations by Bob Kellogg, Peter Nicolaisen, Bob Denomme, David Thelen, and Phil Rollinson; whatever errors slipped through, however, are my own. Alan MacDuff and Roberta Staples helped obtain some of the texts of the articles, and

Ed Kessler brought Richard Wilbur's poem to my attention. Of course I wish to thank my contributors, each of whom agreed personally to the inclusion of his essay.

Finally, my dedication expresses my appreciation to that teacher who started all this by channeling my interests toward the study of English literature. Perhaps I should also include John H. Fisher and Arthur Hutson, who later diverted me toward medieval studies and Old English respectively.

D. K. F.

Contents

Contents.

THE BEOWULF POET

Introduction:
The Artistry of *Beowulf*

by Donald K. Fry

Beowulf is the best surviving poem written in English before Chaucer. Prior to J. R. R. Tolkien's resuscitation of *Beowulf* studies in 1936, such a statement would have been met with derision; and Tolkien's thesis that *Beowulf* should be read as a poem, indeed as a masterpiece, has not been without its detractors. The tone of *"Beowulf:* The Monsters and the Critics" is defensive, and he overstates his case to disarm expected rebuttal. In the main, the battle has been won today, largely because Tolkien's pronouncement coincided with the beginnings of a general shift in literary studies from scholarship to criticism, from biographical, historical, and philological approaches to close examination of the text itself. For medieval scholars, Tolkien dealt the death blow to Matthew Arnold's pernicious "touchstones," a doctrine which could exclude Chaucer from the pantheon of great poets because he allegedly lacked "high seriousness."

The anonymous author of *Beowulf* was a master craftsman in the techniques available to every poet in any era. He clearly understood the need for structure and unity, both in the poem as a whole and in its individual parts. His descriptive passages reveal a knack for the telling detail, while his characterizations depend more on revelation than narration. His narrative technique is primarily dramatic, the product of both acute juxtapositions and gradual accumulation of detail. The pace is slow, befitting the sombre tone and theme. In the use of those particular advantages afforded the traditional formulaic poet (of Homeric Greece, Anglo-Saxon England, and modern Yugoslavia), he is unexcelled in English. His art never depends on the transcendence of tradition and the modern fetish for originality; rather he displays his mastery in exploiting to the full the potentials of inherited materials (plots and characters) and techniques (formulaic diction, themes and type-scenes).

Professor Tolkien describes the structure of the poem as "a balance, an opposition of ends and beginnings. In its simplest terms it is a contrasted description of two moments in a great life, rising and setting; an elaboration of the ancient and intensely moving contrast between youth and age, first achievement and final death." Such a structure unifies the poem. Actually, *Beowulf* depends on many structures as well as this balance, which is reinforced by such details as the burial scene at each end of the poem. The three monsters define a tripartite structure, with approximately two-thirds of the poem devoted to the Grendels, and the last third to the dragon. Or, as Joan Blomfield points out, the structure may be viewed as cumulative rather than as dynamically balanced. Another structure, familiar to the folklorist, is the "problem-solution" pairing, with the accompanying challenge to royal succession or national survival. One could view the structure as cyclic, in that the Danes' early loss of a king (Heremod) sets off at the beginning of the poem a chain of events which will eventually leave the Geats kingless in the end. Many have seen a unity of structure in the characters, whether in the person of the hero, or in Hygelac, or in kingship itself. Which unities are there by design cannot be known; all are operative on the reader.

Lately, some scholars have returned to the nineteenth-century notion of a multiplicity of shorter poems bound together into a poorly unified whole, with the corollary of multiple authorship. The poem does divide neatly at line 1998 (with Beowulf's account to Hygelac of his adventures) and at 2200 (when events leading to Beowulf's coronation are described), and Beowulf's report in lines 2069a–2199 does differ in some details from the facts presented by the earlier narrator. But perhaps the poet is using a technique best known in the novels of Lawrence Durrell's *Alexandria Quartet*, by which the same events are described in variant terms by persons with entirely different points of view. The narrator's emphases for his audience would naturally differ from those of Beowulf reporting to his king, who would need details of the Danish political situation and justification for the loss of his retainer Hondscioh. The result of the report is unity, by summation of the events in Part I. He uses the same technique in the dual narration of the Breca episode and the repeated oblique references to Hygelac and Heremod.

The imagery in *Beowulf* is relatively sparse, leaving most of the background to the audience's imagination, but providing enough significant details to stimulate and yet control the emotional impact of any scene or action. For example, by the time of the exciting moment of confrontation between Grendel and Beowulf, we know only that the monster walks, thinks, has a hand, a mouth, and flaming eyes. From these details plus his own fears and literary background of legends, the reader (or listener) supplies his own monster, which must inevitably be more frightening because of its personal tailoring. In a movie version of the fight scene in the hall, Grendel would remain in shadow if the director sought to play him for the maximum terrifying effect. The poet has an eye for significant and evocative image; when Beowulf and his troop set out from the shore to Heorot, the poet calls forth the splendor of a magnificent helmet such as the one found at Sutton Hoo with the mere mention of golden "boar-images" shining over the warriors' cheekguards (lines 303b–5a). To an audience schooled in the status and virtue represented by such helmets, this one detail would clothe the entire troop in heroic richness and power.

The poet's chief device for characterization is the formal speech, either by a person or about him. When the coastguard, challenging Beowulf and his retainers at the shore, says,

> Never have I seen a mightier noble on this earth,
> warrior in war-gear, than is one of you;
> that is no (mere) carpet-knight, dignified
> by weapons, unless his face, his peerless appearance,
>   should belie him, (247b–251a),

Beowulf is indirectly characterized by the observer's awe as one set apart from ordinary men by his size, nobility, and splendid appearance. Beowulf's first few speeches and the court's reaction to them characterize him as courteous, bold, proud, skillful, fearless, boastful, noble, and confident. His sardonic refutation of Unferth's account of the Breca contest reveals him as one not given to suffer fools gladly, but their subsequent reconciliation underlines his flexibility and generosity. Late in the poem, speeches by Wiglaf to the cowardly retainers and by the messenger to the Geats characterize Beowulf's subjects as weak and ultimately deserving of their impending doom, despite the virtues of their king and his heroic nephew.

The dramatic narrative technique functions in specific passages and over longer stretches of verse. The poet adds import and emotional tension to the three fight scenes by emphasizing a dramatic audience, whose survival depends on the outcome, a device connected with the almost cinematic "cutting" in the Grendel episode. Not only do the Danes act as spectators, but they also provide another point of view, far from the combatants, to which the poet may shift. Flashbacks add poignancy to scenes such as that preceding Beowulf's funeral by juxtaposing the past causes of events with their present or future consequences. They can also establish the credentials of the hero for a particular bout; for example, the Breca episode dramatizes Beowulf's expertise as a specialist in wrestling water-monsters even before Grendel or his mother emerge from their pool. Or the effect can be cumulative, as when the poet first reveals Hrothgar's genuine fear of Grendel's lake in the king's highly colored description of it, followed by the difficult march, the finding of Aeschere's severed head on the brink, and the slaying of the *nicor*. By then the audience is thoroughly apprehensive of Beowulf's leap into such a pool, and the Danes' despair at the surfacing gore is well prepared for.

The poet's consistency of tone reveals his mastery of texture and structure, mostly in the handling of digressions of various length. A long one, such as the Finnsburg episode, can set the grim past of the Danes into an atmosphere of treachery in Hrothgar's court. The overwhelming tensions of that long Frisian winter with its resolution by slaughter is emblematic and prophetic of the impending horrors of Hrothulf's revolt and the Heathobard feud. The occasional glances at the Heremod legends pose an example of the dangers inherent in royal pride, underscoring not only the lessons of Hrothgar's sermon to Beowulf, but also the instability of empires, especially one so weakened as Hrothgar's. Some very short digressions, such as those of the "last survivor" and the "sonless king," enhance the tone of gloom surrounding reflections on earth's transitory joys.

With few exceptions, critics of Beowulf in this century, regardless
of their estimates of the value of the plot, structure, or pace of the
poem, have praised the diction. As Arthur Brodeur states it, "the
majority of compounds in *Beowulf* are peculiar to this one poem,
and . . . a very great many of them are words which convey thought
or feeling more freshly and vividly than the powers of other Anglo-
Saxon poets ever compassed. They are, moreover, often used in
telling combinations, in which the various elements of the sentence
combine into a style more vigorous, stately, and beautiful than
that of any other Old English poem." The poet was capable of
using the diction with as much invention as it had taken to create
it, as in Beowulf's ironic thrust at the "Victory-Scyldings" (597b)
before he purges their hall of Grendel and *after* twelve years of
their not doing so.

In the early days of oral-formulaic studies, opponents of that
school feared that granting the oral premise would reduce the
diction to the level of clichés, which the poets (or singers) merely
shoved together to form lines. But with the introduction of the
formulaic "system," or basic diction pattern capable of generating
new phrases in metrical form, new possibilities for traditional yet
original diction were opened; today, critical respect for the *Beowulf*
poet's mastery of language has deepened as a result of formulaic
analysis, although only a few such articles have yet been published.

The poet also excels at the next level of poetic structure—that of
stereotyped sequences of narrative, or themes and type-scenes—
particularly in his awareness of the potential of the associations
inherent in patterns familiar to the medieval audience. For example, the messenger's prediction of the downfall of the Geats after
Beowulf's death closes with these words:

> Therefore shall many a morning-cold
> spear grasped by fists be heaved up in the hand;
> no sound of the harp will awaken the warriors,
> but the dusky raven eager over the fated ones
> shall recall much, tell the eagle how he fared at the
> feast, when he with the wolf plundered the slain (3021b–27).

With this bare mention of a spear and the Beasts of Battle tradi-
tionally included in combat scenes, the poet conjures up all the

terror and excitement normally associated with battles, without describing the battle itself. Sometimes he combines his awareness of multiple word meanings with a traditional theme to startling effect; for example, one very common pattern in Old English poetry is the theme "Banquet followed by Bed," which often symbolizes the bed of death after the banquet of life. In the Breca episode, Beowulf tells how the sea monsters dragged him to the bottom and intended to feast on his corpse. But,

> Naes hie ðaere *fylle* gefean haefdon,
> manfordaedlan, þaet hie me þegon,
> *symbel* ymbsaeton saegrunde neah;
> ac on mergenne mecum wunde
> be yðlafe uppe laegon,
> sweordum *aswefede*. (562–67a)

[They did not have joy of that *feast,* the wicked destroyers, that intended to partake of me, sitting around the *banquet* at the bottom of the sea; but in the morning they lay wounded by edges up along the shore, *slain* by swords.]

In the last line, the alliteration is furnished by "sweordum," and, therefore, the poet has a free choice of verbs for the second stressed element. He chose "aswefede" [slain] because its literal meaning, "put to sleep," fulfills ironically the banquet-bed sequence.

All of these techniques and skills embody the theme of the poem, which I take to be "heroism in a darkening world"; this differs only slightly from the usual statement of the theme as "good versus evil." The poem does concern "good and evil," but more specifically, how a hero, seen as the embodiment of the projected ideals of a heroic society, must perform in a world of ever-increasing evil and impending doom. Tolkien calls the resultant code "the creed of unyielding will," and best exemplifies it in one of his own creations, the noble Prince Aragorn of *The Lord of the Rings.* But, the real strength of this theme lies inevitably in the portrayal of Beowulf himself. In the earlier days of historical scholarship, the fact that the name "Beowulf" was attested nowhere else, plus the obvious folklore parallels to his personality and deeds, led scholars to call him an intruder into history from fairyland. Perhaps he was, but in this very isolation of the main character (nowhere better described than in Richard Wilbur's poem "Beowulf") lies the poignancy and emotional power of the theme. By the end of *Beowulf*, the reader is ready to share in the grief and praise so economically expressed by the mourning retainers riding in a circle around their king's grave mound:

> they said that he was of the kings of the world,
> the mildest of men, and the gentlest,
> kindest to his people and most eager for fame.

Beowulf: The Monsters and the Critics

by J. R. R. Tolkien

In 1864 the Reverend Oswald Cockayne wrote of the Reverend Doctor Joseph Bosworth, Rawlinsonian Professor of Anglo-Saxon: "I have tried to lend to others the conviction I have long entertained that Dr. Bosworth is not a man so diligent in his special walk as duly to read the books . . . which have been printed in our old English, or so-called Anglo-Saxon tongue. He may do very well for a professor." [1] These words were inspired by dissatisfaction with Bosworth's dictionary, and were doubtless unfair. If Bosworth were still alive, a modern Cockayne would probably accuse him of not reading the "literature" of his subject, the books written about the books in the so-called Anglo-Saxon tongue. The original books are nearly buried.

Of none is this so true as of *The Beowulf*, as it used to be called. I have, of course, read *The Beowulf*, as have most (but not all) of those who have criticized it. But I fear that, unworthy successor and beneficiary of Joseph Bosworth, I have not been a man so diligent in my special walk as duly to read all that has been printed on, or touching on, this poem. But I have read enough, I think, to venture the opinion that *Beowulfiana* is, while rich in many departments, specially poor in one. It is poor in criticism, criticism that is directed to the understanding of a poem as a poem. It has been said of *Beowulf* itself that its weakness lies in placing the unimportant things at the centre and the important on the outer edges. This is one of the opinions that I wish specially to consider. I think it

[1] *The Shrine*, p. 4.

profoundly untrue of the poem, but strikingly true of the literature about it. *Beowulf* has been used as a quarry of fact and fancy far more assiduously than it has been studied as a work of art.

It is of *Beowulf*, then, as a poem that I wish to speak; and though it may seem presumption that I should try with *swich a lewed mannes wit to pace the wisdom of an heep of lerned men,* in this department there is at least more chance for the *lewed man.* But there is so much that might still be said even under these limitations that I shall confine myself mainly to the *monsters*—Grendel and the Dragon, as they appear in what seems to me the best and most authoritative general criticism in English—and to certain considerations of the structure and conduct of the poem that arise from this theme.

There is an historical explanation of the state of *Beowulfiana* that I have referred to. And that explanation is important, if one would venture to criticize the critics. A sketch of the history of the subject is required. But I will here only attempt, for brevity's sake, to present my view of it allegorically. As it set out upon its adventures among the modern scholars, *Beowulf* was christened by Wanley Poesis—*Poeseos Anglo-Saxonicæ egregium exemplum.* But the fairy godmother later invited to superintend its fortunes was Historia. And she brought with her Philologia, Mythologia, Archaeologia, and Laographia.[2] Excellent ladies. But where was the child's namesake? Poesis was usually forgotten; occasionally admitted by a sidedoor; sometimes dismissed upon the door-step. *"The Beowulf,"* they said, "is hardly an affair of yours, and not in any case a protégé that you could be proud of. It is an historical document. Only as such does it interest the superior culture of to-day." And it is as an historical document that it has mainly been examined and dissected. Though ideas as to the nature and quality of the history and information embedded in it have changed much since Thorkelin called it *De Danorum Rebus Gestis,* this has remained steadily true. In still recent pronouncements this view is explicit. In 1925 Pro-

---

[2] Thus in Professor Chambers's great bibliography (in his *Beowulf: An Introduction*) we find a section, § 8. Questions of Literary History, Date, and Authorship; Beowulf in the Light of History, Archaeology, Heroic Legend, Mythology, and Folklore. It is impressive, but there is no section that names Poetry. As certain of the items included show, such consideration as Poetry is accorded at all is buried unnamed in § 8.

fessor Archibald Strong translated *Beowulf* into verse;[3] but in 1921
he had declared: "*Beowulf* is the picture of a whole civilization, of
the Germania which Tacitus describes. The main interest which
the poem has for us is thus not a purely literary interest. *Beowulf*
is an important historical document." [4]

I make this preliminary point, because it seems to me that the
air has been clouded not only for Strong, but for other more
authoritative critics, by the dust of the quarrying researchers. It
may well be asked: why should we approach this, or indeed any
other poem, mainly as an historical document? Such an attitude
is defensible: firstly, if one is not concerned with poetry at all, but
seeking information wherever it may be found; secondly, if the
so-called poem contains in fact no poetry. I am not concerned with
the first case. The historian's search is, of course, perfectly legitimate,
even if it does not assist criticism in general at all (for that is not
its object), so long as it is not mistaken for criticism. To Professor
Birger Nerman as an historian of Swedish origins *Beowulf* is doubtless an important document, but he is not writing a history of
English poetry. Of the second case it may be said that to rate a
poem, a thing at the least in metrical form, as mainly of historical
interest should *in a literary survey* be equivalent to saying that it
has no literary merits, and little more need in such a survey then
be said about it. But such a judgement on *Beowulf* is false. So far
from being a poem so poor that only its accidental historical interest
can still recommend it, *Beowulf* is in fact so interesting as poetry,
in places poetry so powerful, that this quite overshadows the historical content, and is largely independent even of the most important facts (such as the date and identity of Hygelac) that research
has discovered. It is indeed a curious fact that it is one of the
peculiar poetic virtues of *Beowulf* that has contributed to its own
critical misfortunes. The illusion of historical truth and perspective,

---

[3] *Beowulf translated into modern English rhyming verse*, Constable, 1925.
[4] *A Short History of English Literature*, Oxford Univ. Press, 1921, pp. 2–3. I
choose this example, because it is precisely to general literary histories that we
must usually turn for literary judgements on *Beowulf*. The experts in *Beowulfiana*
are seldom concerned with such judgements. And it is in the highly compressed
histories, such as this, that we discover what the process of digestion makes of
the special "literature" of the experts. Here is the distilled product of Research.
This compendium, moreover, is competent, and written by a man who had
(unlike some other authors of similar things) read the poem itself with attention.

that has made *Beowulf* seem such an attractive quarry, is largely
a product of art. The author has used an instinctive historical sense
—a part indeed of the ancient English temper (and not unconnected
with its reputed melancholy), of which *Beowulf* is a supreme expression; but he has used it with a poetical and not an historical
object. The lovers of poetry can safely study the art, but the seekers
after history must beware lest the glamour of Poesis overcome them.

Nearly all the censure, and most of the praise, that has been
bestowed on *The Beowulf* has been due either to the belief that it
was something that it was *not*—for example, primitive, pagan, Teutonic, an allegory (political or mythical), or most often, an epic; or
to disappointment at the discovery that it was itself and not something that the scholar would have liked better—for example, a
heathen heroic lay, a history of Sweden, a manual of Germanic
antiquities, or a Nordic *Summa Theologica*.

I would express the whole industry in yet another allegory. A
man inherited a field in which was an accumulation of old stone,
part of an older hall. Of the old stone some had already been used
in building the house in which he actually lived, not far from the
old house of his fathers. Of the rest he took some and built a tower.
But his friends coming perceived at once (without troubling to
climb the steps) that these stones had formerly belonged to a more
ancient building. So they pushed the tower over, with no little
labour, in order to look for hidden carvings and inscriptions, or to
discover whence the man's distant forefathers had obtained their
building material. Some suspecting a deposit of coal under the soil
began to dig for it, and forgot even the stones. They all said: "This
tower is most interesting." But they also said (after pushing it over):
"What a muddle it is in!" And even the man's own descendants,
who might have been expected to consider what he had been about,
were heard to murmur: "He is such an odd fellow! Imagine his
using these old stones just to build a nonsensical tower! Why did
not he restore the old house? He had no sense of proportion." But
from the top of that tower the man had been able to look out upon
the sea.

I hope I shall show that that allegory is just—even when we
consider the more recent and more perceptive critics (whose concern
is in intention with literature). To reach these we must pass in rapid

flight over the heads of many decades of critics. As we do so a conflicting babel mounts up to us, which I can report as something after this fashion.[5] "*Beowulf* is a half-baked native epic the development of which was killed by Latin learning; it was inspired by emulation of Virgil, and is a product of the education that came in with Christianity; it is feeble and incompetent as a narrative; the rules of narrative are cleverly observed in the manner of the learned epic; it is the confused product of a committee of muddle-headed and probably beer-bemused Anglo-Saxons (this is a Gallic voice); it is a string of pagan lays edited by monks; it is the work of a learned but inaccurate Christian antiquarian; it is a work of genius, rare and surprising in the period, though the genius seems to have been shown principally in doing something much better left undone (this is a very recent voice); it is a wild folk-tale (general chorus); it is a poem of an aristocratic and courtly tradition (same voices); it is a hotchpotch; it is a sociological, anthropological, archaeological document; it is a mythical allegory (very old voices these and generally shouted down, but not so far out as some of the newer cries); it is rude and rough; it is a masterpiece of metrical art; it has no shape at all; it is singularly weak in construction; it is a clever allegory of contemporary politics (old John Earle with some slight support from Mr. Girvan, only they look to different periods); its architecture is solid; it is thin and cheap (a solemn voice); it is undeniably weighty (the same voice); it is a national epic; it is a translation from the Danish; it was imported by Frisian traders; it is a burden to English syllabuses; and (final universal chorus of all voices) it is worth studying."

It is not surprising that it should now be felt that a view, a decision, a conviction are imperatively needed. But it is plainly only in the consideration of *Beowulf* as a poem, with an inherent poetic significance, that any view or conviction can be reached or steadily held. For it is of their nature that the jabberwocks of historical and antiquarian research burble in the tulgy wood of conjecture, flitting from one tum-tum tree to another. Noble animals, whose burbling is on occasion good to hear; but though

---

[5] I include nothing that has not somewhere been said by someone, if not in my exact words; but I do not, of course, attempt to represent all the *dicta*, wise or otherwise, that have been uttered.

their eyes of flame may sometimes prove searchlights, their range is short.

None the less, paths of a sort have been opened in the wood. Slowly with the rolling years the obvious (so often the last revelation of analytic study) has been discovered: that we have to deal with a poem by an Englishman using afresh ancient and largely traditional material. At last then, after inquiring so long whence this material came, and what its original or aboriginal nature was (questions that cannot ever be decisively answered), we might also now again inquire what the poet did with it. If we ask that question, then there is still, perhaps, something lacking even in the major critics, the learned and revered masters from whom we humbly derive.

The chief points with which I feel dissatisfied I will now approach by way of W. P. Ker, whose name and memory I honour. He would deserve reverence, of course, even if he still lived and had not *ellor gehworfen on Frean wære* upon a high mountain in the heart of that Europe which he loved: a great scholar, as illuminating himself as a critic, as he was often biting as a critic of the critics. None the less I cannot help feeling that in approaching *Beowulf* he was hampered by the almost inevitable weakness of his greatness: stories and plots must sometimes have seemed triter to him, the much-read, than they did to the old poets and their audiences. The dwarf on the spot sometimes sees things missed by the travelling giant ranging many countries. In considering a period when literature was narrower in range and men possessed a less diversified stock of ideas and themes, one must seek to recapture and esteem the deep pondering and profound feeling that they gave to such as they possessed.

In any case Ker has been potent. For his criticism is masterly, expressed always in words both pungent and weighty, and not least so when it is (as I occasionally venture to think) itself open to criticism. His words and judgements are often quoted, or reappear in various modifications, digested, their source probably sometimes forgotten. It is impossible to avoid quotation of the well-known passage in his *Dark Ages*:

> A reasonable view of the merit of *Beowulf* is not impossible, though rash enthusiasm may have made too much of it, while a correct and

sober taste may have too contemptuously refused to attend to Grendel or the Fire-drake. The fault of *Beowulf* is that there is nothing
much in the story. The hero is occupied in killing monsters, like
Hercules or Theseus. But there are other things in the lives of Hercules and Theseus besides the killing of the Hydra or of Procrustes.
Beowulf has nothing else to do, when he has killed Grendel and Grendel's mother in Denmark: he goes home to his own Gautland, until at
last the rolling years bring the Fire-drake and his last adventure. It
is too simple. Yet the three chief episodes are well wrought and well
diversified; they are not repetitions, exactly; there is a change of temper between the wrestling with Grendel in the night at Heorot and the
descent under water to encounter Grendel's mother; while the sentiment of the Dragon is different again. But the great beauty, the real
value, of *Beowulf* is in its dignity of style. In construction it is curiously
weak, in a sense preposterous; for while the main story is simplicity
itself, the merest commonplace of heroic legend, all about it, in the
historic allusions, there are revelations of a whole world of tragedy,
plots different in import from that of *Beowulf,* more like the tragic
themes of Iceland. Yet with this radical defect, a disproportion that
puts the irrelevances in the centre and the serious things on the outer
edges, the poem of *Beowulf* is undeniably weighty. The thing itself is
cheap; the moral and the spirit of it can only be matched among the
noblest authors.[6]

This passage was written more than thirty years ago, but has
hardly been surpassed. It remains, in this country at any rate, a
potent influence. Yet its primary effect is to state a paradox which
one feels has always strained the belief, even of those who accepted
it, and has given to *Beowulf* the character of an "enigmatic poem."
The chief virtue of the passage (not the one for which it is usually
esteemed) is that it does accord some attention to the monsters,
despite correct and sober taste. But the contrast made between
the radical defect of theme and structure, and at the same time
the dignity, loftiness in converse, and well-wrought finish, has become a commonplace even of the best criticism, a paradox the
strangeness of which has almost been forgotten in the process of
swallowing it upon authority.[7] We may compare Professor Cham-

---

[6] *The Dark Ages,* pp. 252–53.
[7] None the less Ker modified it in an important particular in *English Literature,
Mediæval,* pp. 29–34. In general, though in different words, vaguer and less in-

bers in his *Widsith*, p. 79, where he is studying the story of Ingeld, son of Froda, and his feud with the great Scylding house of Denmark, a story introduced in *Beowulf* merely as an allusion.

> Nothing [Chambers says] could better show the disproportion of *Beowulf* which "puts the irrelevances in the centre and the serious things on the outer edges," than this passing allusion to the story of Ingeld. For in this conflict between plighted troth and the duty of revenge we have a situation which the old heroic poets loved, and would not have sold for a wilderness of dragons.

I pass over the fact that the allusion has a dramatic purpose in *Beowulf* that is a sufficient defence both of its presence and of its manner. The author of *Beowulf* cannot be held responsible for the fact that we now have only his poem and not others dealing primarily with Ingeld. He was not selling one thing for another, but giving something new. But let us return to the dragon. "A wilderness of dragons." There is a sting in this Shylockian plural, the sharper for coming from a critic, who deserves the title of the poet's best friend. It is in the tradition of the Book of St. Albans, from which the poet might retort upon his critics: "Yea, a desserte of lapwyngs, a shrewednes of apes, a raffull of knaues, and a gagle of gees."

As for the poem, one dragon, however hot, does not make a summer, or a host; and a man might well exchange for one good dragon what he would not sell for a wilderness. And dragons, real dragons, essential both to the machinery and the ideas of a poem or tale, are actually rare. In northern literature there are only *two* that are significant. If we omit from consideration the vast and vague Encircler of the World, Miðgarðsormr, the doom of the great

---

cisive, he repeats himself. We are still told that "the story is commonplace and the plan is feeble," or that "the story is thin and poor." But we learn also at the end of his notice that: "Those distracting allusions to things apart from the chief story make up for their want of proportion. They give the impression of reality and weight; the story is not in the air . . . it is part of the solid world." By the admission of so grave an artistic reason for the procedure of the poem Ker himself began the undermining of his own criticism of its structure. But this line of thought does not seem to have been further pursued. Possibly it was this very thought, working in his mind, that made Ker's notice of *Beowulf* in the small later book, his "shilling shocker," more vague and hesitant in tone, and so of less influence.

gods and no matter for heroes, we have but the dragon of the Völ-
sungs, Fáfnir, and Beowulf's bane. It is true that both of these are
in *Beowulf,* one in the main story, and the other spoken of by a
minstrel praising Beowulf himself. But this is not a wilderness of
dragons. Indeed the allusion to the more renowned worm killed
by the Wælsing is sufficient indication that the poet selected a
dragon of well-founded purpose (or saw its significance in the plot
as it had reached him), even as he was careful to compare his hero,
Beowulf son of Ecgtheow, to the prince of the heroes of the North,
the dragon-slaying Wælsing. He esteemed dragons, as rare as they
are dire, as some do still. He liked them—as a poet, not as a sober
zoologist; and he had good reason.

But we meet this kind of criticism again. In Chambers's *Beowulf
and the Heroic Age*—the most significant single essay on the poem
that I know—it is still present. The riddle is still unsolved. The
folk-tale motive stands still like the spectre of old research, dead but
unquiet in its grave. We are told again that the main story of
Beowulf is a *wild folk-tale.* Quite true, of course. It is true of the
main story of *King Lear,* unless in that case you would prefer to
substitute *silly* for *wild.* But more: we are told that the same sort
of stuff is found in Homer, yet there it is kept in its proper place.
"The folk-tale is a good servant," Chambers says, and does not
perhaps realize the importance of the admission, made to save the
face of Homer and Virgil; for he continues: "but a bad master: it
has been allowed in *Beowulf* to usurp the place of honour, and to
drive into episodes and digressions the things which should be the
main stuff of a well-conducted epic." [8] It is not clear to me why
good *conduct* must depend on the main *stuff.* But I will for the
moment remark only that, if it is so, *Beowulf* is evidently not a
well-conducted epic. It may turn out to be no epic at all. But the
puzzle still continues. In the most recent discourse upon this theme
it still appears, toned down almost to a melancholy question-mark,
as if this paradox had at last begun to afflict with weariness the
thought that endeavours to support it. In the final peroration of
his notable lecture on *Folk-tale and History in Beowulf* given last
year, Mr. Girvan said:

[8] *Foreword* to Strong's translation, p. xxvi: see note 3.

Confessedly there is matter for wonder and scope for doubt, but we might be able to answer with complete satisfaction some of the questionings which rise in men's minds over the poet's presentment of his hero, if we could also answer with certainty the question why he chose just this subject, when to our modern judgment there were at hand so many greater, charged with the splendour and tragedy of humanity, and in all respects worthier of a genius as astonishing as it was rare in Anglo-Saxon England.

There is something irritatingly odd about all this. One even dares to wonder if something has not gone wrong with "our modern judgement," supposing that it is justly represented. Higher praise than is found in the learned critics, whose scholarship enables them to appreciate these things, could hardly be given to the detail, the tone, the style, and indeed to the total effect of *Beowulf*. Yet this poetic talent, we are to understand, has all been squandered on an unprofitable theme: as if Milton had recounted the story of Jack and the Beanstalk in noble verse. Even if Milton had done this (and he might have done worse), we should perhaps pause to consider whether his poetic handling had not had some effect upon the trivial theme; what alchemy had been performed upon the base metal; whether indeed it remained base or trivial when he had finished with it. The high tone, the sense of dignity, alone is evidence in *Beowulf* of the presence of a mind lofty and thoughtful. It is, one would have said, improbable that such a man would write more than three thousand lines (wrought to a high finish) on matter that is really not worth serious attention; that remains thin and cheap when he has finished with it. Or that he should in the selection of his material, in the choice of what to put forward, what to keep subordinate "upon the outer edges," have shown a puerile simplicity much below the level of the characters he himself draws in his own poem. Any theory that will at least allow us to believe that what he did was of design, and that for that design there is a defence that may still have force, would seem more probable.

It has been too little observed that all the machinery of "dignity" is to be found elsewhere. Cynewulf, or the author of *Andreas,* or of *Guthlac* (most notably), have a command of dignified verse. In them there is well-wrought language, weighty words, lofty sentiment, precisely that which we are told is the real beauty of *Beowulf*. Yet it cannot, I think, be disputed, that *Beowulf* is more beautiful, that each line there is more significant (even when, as sometimes happens, it is the same line) than in the other long Old English poems. Where then resides the special virtue of *Beowulf*, if the common element (which belongs largely to the language itself, and to a literary tradition) is deducted? It resides, one might guess, in the theme, and the spirit this has infused into the whole. For, in fact, if there were a real discrepancy between theme and style, that style would not be felt as beautiful but as incongruous or false. And that incongruity is present in some measure in all the long Old English poems, save one—*Beowulf*. The paradoxical contrast that has been drawn between matter and manner in Beowulf has thus an inherent *literary* improbability.

Why then have the great critics thought otherwise? I must pass rather hastily over the answers to this question. The reasons are various, I think, and would take long to examine. I believe that one reason is that the shadow of research has lain upon criticism. The habit, for instance, of pondering a summarized plot of *Beowulf*, denuded of all that gives it particular force or individual life, has encouraged the notion that its main story is wild, or trivial, or typical, *even after treatment*. Yet all stories, great and small, are one or more of these three things in such nakedness. The comparison of skeleton "plots" is simply not a critical literary process at all. It has been favoured by research in comparative folk-lore, the objects of which are primarily historical or scientific.[9] Another reason is, I

---

[9] It has also been favoured by the rise of "English schools," in whose syllabuses *Beowulf* has inevitably some place, and the consequent production of compendious literary histories. For these cater (in fact, if not in intention) for those seeking knowledge about, and ready-made judgements upon, works which they have not the time, or (often enough) the desire, to know at first hand. The small literary value of such summaries is sometimes recognized in the act of giving them. Thus Strong (op. cit.) gives a fairly complete one but remarks that "the short summary does scant justice to the poem." Ker in *E. Lit.* (*Med.*) says: "So told, in abstract, it is not a particularly interesting story." He evidently perceived what might be the retort, for he attempts to justify the procedure in this case, adding: "Told in this way the story of Theseus or Hercules would still have much more in it." I dissent. But it does not matter, for the comparison of two plots "told in this way" is no guide whatever to the merits of literary versions told in quite different ways. It is not necessarily the best poem that loses least in précis.

think, that the allusions have attracted curiosity (antiquarian rather than critical) to their elucidation; and this needs so much study and research that attention has been diverted from the poem as a whole, and from the function of the allusions, as shaped and placed, in the poetic economy of *Beowulf* as it is. Yet actually the appreciation of this function is largely independent of such investigations.

But there is also, I suppose, a real question of taste involved: a judgement that the heroic or tragic story on a strictly human plane is by nature superior. Doom is held less literary than ἁμαρτία [hamartia: tragic flaw]. The proposition seems to have been passed as self-evident. I dissent, even at the risk of being held incorrect or not sober. But I will not here enter into debate, nor attempt at length a defence of the mythical mode of imagination, and the disentanglement of the confusion between myth and folk-tale into which these judgements appear to have fallen. The myth has other forms than the (now discredited) mythical allegory of nature: the sun, the seasons, the sea, and such things. The term "folk-tale" is misleading; its very tone of depreciation begs the question. Folktales in being, as told—for the "typical folk-tale," of course, is merely an abstract conception of research nowhere existing—do often contain elements that are thin and cheap, with little even potential virtue; but they also contain much that is far more powerful, and that cannot be sharply separated from myth, being derived from it, or capable in poetic hands of turning into it: that is of becoming largely significant—as a whole, accepted unanalysed. The significance of a myth is not easily to be pinned on paper by analytical reasoning. It is at its best when it is presented by a poet who feels rather than makes explicit what his theme portends; who presents it incarnate in the world of history and geography, as our poet has done. Its defender is thus at a disadvantage: unless he is careful, and speaks in parables, he will kill what he is studying by vivisection, and he will be left with a formal or mechanical allegory, and, what is more, probably with one that will not work. For myth is alive at once and in all its parts, and dies before it can be dissected. It is possible, I think, to be moved by the power of myth and yet to misunderstand the sensation, to ascribe it wholly to something else that is also present: to metrical art, style, or verbal skill. Correct and sober taste may refuse to admit that there can be an interest for *us*—the proud *we* that includes all intelligent living people—in ogres and dragons; we then perceive its puzzlement in face of the odd fact that it has derived great pleasure from a poem that is actually about these unfashionable creatures. Even though it attributes "genius," as does Mr. Girvan, to the author, it cannot admit that the monsters are anything but a sad mistake.

It does not seem plain that ancient taste supports the modern as much as it has been represented to do. I have the author of *Beowulf*, at any rate, on my side: a greater man than most of us. And I cannot myself perceive a period in the North when one kind alone was esteemed: there was room for myth and heroic legend, and for blends of these. As for the dragon: as far as we know anything about these old poets, we know this: the prince of the heroes of the North, supremely memorable—*hans nafn mun uppi meðan veröldin stendr* [his name will live while the world lasts]—was a dragon-slayer. And his most renowned deed, from which in Norse he derived his title Fáfnisbani, was the slaying of the prince of legendary worms. Although there is plainly considerable difference between the later Norse and the ancient English form of the story alluded to in *Beowulf*, already there it had these two primary features: the dragon, and the slaying of him as the chief deed of the greatest of heroes—*he wæs wreccena wide mærost* [he was the most famous of exiles far and wide]. A dragon is no idle fancy. Whatever may be his origins, in fact or invention, the dragon in legend is a potent creation of men's imagination, richer in significance than his barrow is in gold. Even to-day (despite the critics) you may find men not ignorant of tragic legend and history, who have heard of heroes and indeed seen them, who yet have been caught by the fascination of the worm. More than one poem in recent years (since *Beowulf* escaped somewhat from the dominion of the students of origins to the students of poetry) has been inspired by the dragon of *Beowulf*, but none that I know of by Ingeld son of Froda. Indeed, I do not think Chambers very happy in his particular choice. He gives battle on dubious ground. In so far as we can now grasp its detail and atmosphere the story of Ingeld the thrice faithless and easily persuaded is chiefly interesting as an episode in a larger theme, as part of a tradition that had acquired legendary, and so dramatically personalized, form concerning moving events in history: the arising of Denmark, and wars in the islands of the North. In itself it is not a supremely potent story. But, of course, as with all tales of any sort, its literary power must have depended mainly upon how it was handled. A poet may have made a great thing of it. Upon this chance must be founded the popularity of Ingeld's legend in England, for which there is some evidence.[10] There is no inherent magical virtue about heroic-tragic stories as such, and apart from the merits of individual treatments. The same heroic plot can yield good and bad poems, and good and bad sagas. The recipe for the central situations of such stories, studied in the abstract, is after all as "simple" and as "typical" as that of folk-tales. There are in any case many heroes but very few good dragons.

Beowulf's dragon, if one wishes really to criticize, is not to be blamed for being a dragon, but rather for not being dragon enough, plain pure fairy-story dragon. There are in the poem some vivid touches of the right kind—as *Þa se wyrm onwoc, wroht wæs geniwad; stonc æfter stane* [when the dragon awoke, the strife was renewed; he crawled sniffing along the stone], 2285—in which this dragon is real worm, with a bestial life and thought of his own, but the conception, none the less, approaches *draconitas* rather than *draco:* a personification of malice, greed, destruction (the evil side of heroic life), and of the undiscriminating cruelty of fortune that distinguishes not good or bad (the evil aspect of all life). But for *Beowulf*, the poem, that is as it should be. In this poem the balance is nice, but it is preserved. The large symbolism is near the surface, but it does not break through, nor become allegory. Something more significant than a standard hero, a man faced with a foe more evil than any human enemy of house or realm, is before us, and yet incarnate in time, walking in heroic history, and treading the named lands of the North. And this, we are told, is the radical defect of *Beowulf*, that its author, coming in a time rich in the legends of heroic men, has used them afresh in an original fashion, giving us not just one more, but something akin yet different: a measure and interpretation of them all.

[10] Namely the use of it in *Beowulf*, both dramatically in depicting the sagacity of Beowulf the hero, and as an essential part of the traditions concerning the Scylding court, which is the legendary background against which the rise of the hero is set—as a later age would have chosen the court of Arthur. Also the probable allusion in Alcuin's letter to Speratus: see Chambers's *Widsith*, p. 78.

We do not deny the worth of the hero by accepting Grendel and the dragon. Let us by all means esteem the old heroes: men caught in the chains of circumstance or of their own character, torn between duties equally sacred, dying with their backs to the wall. But *Beowulf*, I fancy, plays a larger part than is recognized in helping us to esteem them. Heroic lays may have dealt in their own way—we have little enough to judge by—a way more brief and vigorous, perhaps, though perhaps also more harsh and noisy (and less thoughtful), with the actions of heroes caught in circumstances that conformed more or less to the varied but fundamentally simple recipe for an heroic situation. In these (if we had them) we could see the exaltation of undefeated will, which receives doctrinal expression in the words of Byrhtwold at the battle of Maldon.[11] But though with sympathy and patience we might gather, from a line here or a tone there, the background of imagination which gives to this indomitability, this paradox of defeat inevitable yet unacknowledged, its full significance, it is in *Beowulf* that a poet has devoted a whole poem to the theme, and has drawn the struggle in different proportions, so that we may see man at war with the hostile world, and his inevitable overthrow in Time.[12] The particular is on the outer edge, the essential in the centre.

Of course, I do not assert that the poet, if questioned, would have replied in the Anglo-Saxon equivalents of these terms. Had the matter been so explicit to him, his poem would certainly have been the worse. None the less we may still, against his great scene, hung with tapestries woven of ancient tales of ruin, see the *hæleð* [hero] walk. When we have read his poem, as a poem, rather than as a collection of episodes, we perceive that he who wrote *hæleð under*

---

[11] This expression may well have been actually used by the *eald geneat* [old retainer], but none the less (or perhaps rather precisely on that account) is probably to be regarded not as new-minted, but as an ancient and honoured *gnome* of long descent.

[12] For the words *hige sceal þe heardra, heorte þe cenre, mod sceal þe mare þe ure mægen lytlað* [spirit must be the harder, heart the keener, courage must be the greater, as our strength lessens] are not, of course, an exhortation to simple courage. They are not reminders that fortune favours the brave, or that victory may be snatched from defeat by the stubborn. (Such thoughts were familiar, but otherwise expressed: *wyrd oft nereð unfægne eorl, þonne his ellen deah* [fate often protects the unfated earl, while his courage prevails].) The words of Byrhtwold were made for a man's last and hopeless day.

heofenum may have meant in dictionary terms "heroes under heaven," or "mighty men upon earth," but he and his hearers were thinking of the *eormengrund*, the great earth, ringed with *garsecg*, the shoreless sea, beneath the sky's inaccessible roof; whereon, as in a little circle of light about their halls, men with courage as their stay went forward to that battle with the hostile world and the offspring of the dark which ends for all, even the kings and champions, in defeat. That even this "geography," once held as a material fact, could now be classed as a mere folk-tale affects its value very little. It transcends astronomy. Not that astronomy has done anything to make the island seem more secure or the outer seas less formidable.

Beowulf is not, then, the hero of an heroic lay, precisely. He has no enmeshed loyalties, nor hapless love. *He is a man, and that for him and many is sufficient tragedy*. It is not an irritating accident that the tone of the poem is so high and its theme so low. It is the theme in its deadly seriousness that begets the dignity of tone: *lif is læne: eal scæceð leoht and lif somod* [life is transitory: light and life together all hasten away]. So deadly and ineluctable is the underlying thought, that those who in the circle of light, within the besieged hall, are absorbed in work or talk and do not look to the battlements, either do not regard it or recoil. Death comes to the feast, and they say He gibbers: He has no sense of proportion.

I would suggest, then, that the monsters are not an inexplicable blunder of taste; they are essential, fundamentally allied to the underlying ideas of the poem, which give it its lofty tone and high seriousness. The key to the fusion-point of imagination that produced this poem lies, therefore, in those very references to Cain which have often been used as a stick to beat an ass—taken as an evident sign (were any needed) of the muddled heads of early Anglo-Saxons. They could not, it was said, keep Scandinavian bogies and the Scriptures separate in their puzzled brains. The New Testament was beyond their comprehension. I am not, as I have confessed, a man so diligent as duly to read all the books about *Beowulf*, but as far as I am aware the most suggestive approach to this point appears in the essay *Beowulf and the Heroic Age* to which I have already referred.[13] I will quote a small part of it.

[13] *Foreword* to Strong's translation, p. xxviii. See note 3.

In the epoch of *Beowulf* a Heroic Age more wild and primitive than that of Greece is brought into touch with Christendom, with the Sermon on the Mount, with Catholic theology and ideas of Heaven and Hell. We see the difference, if we compare the wilder things—the folk-tale element—in *Beowulf* with the wilder things of Homer. Take for example the tale of Odysseus and the Cyclops—the No-man trick. Odysseus is struggling with a monstrous and wicked foe, but he is not exactly thought of as struggling with the powers of darkness. Polyphemus, by devouring his guests, acts in a way which is hateful to Zeus and the other gods: yet the Cyclops is himself god-begotten and under divine protection, and the fact that Odysseus has maimed him is a wrong which Poseidon is slow to forgive. But the gigantic foes whom Beowulf has to meet are identified with the foes of God. Grendel and the dragon are constantly referred to in language which is meant to recall the powers of darkness with which Christian men felt themselves to be encompassed. They[14] are the "inmates of Hell," "adversaries of God," "offspring of Cain," "enemies of mankind." Consequently, the matter of the main story of *Beowulf*, monstrous as it is, is not so far removed from common mediaeval experience as it seems to us to be from our own. . . . Grendel hardly differs[15] from the fiends of the pit who were always in ambush to waylay a righteous man. And so Beowulf, for all that he moves in the world of the primitive Heroic Age of the Germans, nevertheless is almost a Christian knight.[16]

There are some hints here which are, I think, worth pursuing further. Most important is it to consider how and why the monsters become "adversaries of God," and so begin to symbolize (and ultimately to become identified with) the powers of evil, even while they remain, as they do still remain in *Beowulf*, mortal denizens of the material world, in it and of it. I accept without argument throughout the attribution of *Beowulf* to the "age of Bede"— one of the firmer conclusions of a department of research most clearly serviceable to criticism: inquiry into the probable date of the effective composition of the poem as we have it. So regarded *Beowulf* is, of course, an historical document of the first order for

---

[14] This is not strictly true. The dragon is not referred to in such terms, which are applied to Grendel and to the primeval giants.

[15] He differs in important points, referred to later.

[16] I should prefer to say that he moves in a northern heroic age imagined by a Christian, and therefore has a noble and gentle quality, though conceived to be a pagan.

the study of the mood and thought of the period and one perhaps too little used for the purpose by professed historians.[17] But it is the mood of the author, the essential cast of his imaginative apprehension of the world, that is my concern, not history for its own sake; I am interested in that time of fusion only as it may help us to understand the poem. And in the poem I think we may observe not confusion, a half-hearted or a muddled business, but a fusion that has occurred *at a given point* of contact between old and new, a product of thought and deep emotion.

One of the most potent elements in that fusion is the Northern courage: the theory of courage, which is the great contribution of early Northern literature. This is not a military judgement. I am not asserting that, if the Trojans could have employed a Northern king and his companions, they would have driven Agamemnon and Achilles into the sea, more decisively than the Greek hexameter routs the alliterative line—though it is not improbable. I refer rather to the central position the creed of unyielding will holds in the North. With due reserve we may turn to the tradition of pagan imagination as it survived in Icelandic. Of English pre-Christian mythology we know practically nothing. But the fundamentally similar heroic temper of ancient England and Scandinavia cannot have been founded on (or perhaps rather, cannot have generated) mythologies divergent on this essential point. "The Northern Gods," Ker said, "have an exultant extravagance in their warfare which makes them more like Titans than Olympians; *only they are on the right side, though it is not the side that wins. The winning side is Chaos and Unreason*"—mythologically, the monsters—"*but the gods, who are defeated, think that defeat no refutation.*"[18] And in their war men are their chosen allies, able when heroic to share in this "absolute resistance, perfect because without hope." At least in this vision of the final defeat of the humane (and of the divine made in its image), and in the essential hostility of the gods and heroes on the one hand and the monsters on the other, we may suppose that pagan English and Norse imagination agreed.

[17] It is, for instance, dismissed cursorily, and somewhat contemptuously in the recent (somewhat contemptuous) essay of Dr. Watson, *The Age of Bede* in *Bede, His Life, Times, and Writings*, ed. A. Hamilton Thompson, 1935.
[18] *The Dark Ages*, p. 57.

But in England this imagination was brought into touch with Christendom, and with the Scriptures. The process of "conversion" was a long one, but some of its effects were doubtless immediate: an alchemy of change (producing ultimately the mediaeval) was at once at work. One does not have to wait until all the native traditions of the older world have been replaced or forgotten; for the minds which still retain them are changed, and the memories viewed in a different perspective: *at once they become more ancient and remote, and in a sense darker*. It is through such a blending that there was available to a poet who set out to *write* a poem—and in the case of *Beowulf* we may probably use this very word—on a scale and plan unlike a minstrel's lay, both new faith and new learning (or education), and also a body of native tradition (itself requiring to be learned) for the changed mind to contemplate together.[19] The native "learning" cannot be denied in the case of *Beowulf*. Its display has grievously perturbed the critics, for the author draws upon tradition at will for his own purposes, as a poet of later times might draw upon history or the classics and expect his allusions to be understood (within a certain class of hearers). He was in fact, like Virgil, learned enough in the vernacular department to have an historical perspective, even an antiquarian curiosity. He cast his time into the long-ago, because already the long-ago had a special poetical attraction. He knew much about old days, and though his knowledge—of such things as sea-burial and the funeral pyre, for instance—was rich and poetical rather than accurate with the accuracy of modern archaeology (such as that is), one thing he knew clearly: those days were heathen—heathen, noble, and hopeless.

But if the specifically Christian was suppressed,[20] so also were the

---

[19] If we consider the period as a whole. It is not, of course, necessarily true of individuals. These doubtless from the beginning showed many degrees from deep instruction and understanding to disjointed superstition, or blank ignorance.

[20] Avoidance of obvious anachronisms (such as are found in *Judith*, for instance, where the heroine refers in her own speeches to Christ and the Trinity), and the absence of all definitely *Christian* names and terms, is natural and plainly intentional. It must be observed that there is a difference between the comments of the author and the things said in reported speech by his characters. The two chief of these, Hrothgar and Beowulf, are again differentiated. Thus the only definitely Scriptural references, to Abel (108) and to Cain (108, 1261), occur where the poet is speaking as commentator. The theory of Grendel's

old gods. Partly because they had not really existed, and had been always, in the Christian view, only delusions or lies fabricated by the evil one, the *gastbona* [soul-slayer], to whom the hopeless turned especially in times of need. Partly because their old names (certainly not forgotten) had been potent, and were connected in memory still, not only with mythology or such fairy-tale matter as we find, say, in *Gylfaginning,* but with active heathendom, religion and *wigweorpung* [idol-worship]. Most of all because they were not actually essential to the theme.

The monsters had been the foes of the gods, the captains of men, and within Time the monsters would win. In the heroic siege and last defeat men and gods alike had been imagined in the same host. Now the heroic figures, the men of old, *hæleð under heofenum* [heroes under the heavens], remained and still fought on until defeat. For the monsters do not depart, whether the gods go or come. A Christian was (and is) still like his forefathers a mortal hemmed in a hostile world. The monsters remained the enemies of mankind, the infantry of the old war, and became inevitably the enemies of the one God, *ece Dryhten* [Eternal Lord], the eternal Captain of the new. Even so the vision of the war changes. For it begins to dissolve, even as the contest on the fields of Time thus takes on its largest aspect. The tragedy of the great temporal defeat remains for a while poignant, but ceases to be finally important. It is no defeat, for the end of the world is part of the design of Metod, the Arbiter who is above the mortal world. Beyond there appears a possibility of eternal victory (or eternal defeat), and the real battle is between the soul and its adversaries. So the old monsters became images of the evil spirit or spirits, or rather the evil spirits entered into the monsters and took visible shape in the hideous bodies of the *pyrsas* [giants] and *sigelhearwan* [Ethiopians] of heathen imagination.

---

origin is not known to the actors: Hrothgar denies all knowledge of the ancestry of Grendel (1355). The giants (1688 ff.) are, it is true, represented pictorially, and in Scriptural terms. But this suggests rather that the author identified native and Scriptural accounts, and gave his picture Scriptural colour, since of the two accounts Scripture was the truer. And if so it would be closer to that told in remote antiquity when the sword was made, more especially since the *wundorsmiþas* [wondrous blacksmiths] who wrought it were actually giants (1558, 1562, 1679): they would know the true tale. See note 25.

But that shift is not complete in *Beowulf*—whatever may have been true of its period in general. Its author is still concerned primarily with *man on earth,* rehandling in a new perspective an ancient theme: that man, each man and all men, and all their works shall die. A theme no Christian need despise. Yet this theme plainly would not be so treated, but for the nearness of a pagan time. The shadow of its despair, if only as a mood, as an intense emotion of regret, is still there. The worth of defeated valour in this world is deeply felt. As the poet looks back into the past, surveying the history of kings and warriors in the old traditions, he sees that all glory (or as we might say "culture" or "civilization") ends in night. The solution of that tragedy is not treated—it does not arise out of the material. We get in fact a poem from a pregnant moment of poise, looking back into the pit, by a man learned in old tales who was struggling, as it were, to get a general view of them all, perceiving their common tragedy of inevitable ruin, and yet feeling this more *poetically* because he was himself removed from the direct pressure of its despair. He could view from without, but still feel immediately and from within, the old dogma: despair of the event, combined with faith in the value of doomed resistance. He was still dealing with the great temporal tragedy, and not yet writing an allegorical homily in verse. Grendel inhabits the visible world and eats the flesh and blood of men; he enters their houses by the doors. The dragon wields a physical fire, and covets gold not souls; he is slain with iron in his belly. Beowulf's *byrne* [chain-mail shirt] was made by Weland, and the iron shield he bore against the serpent by his own smiths: it was not yet the breastplate of righteousness, nor the shield of faith for the quenching of all the fiery darts of the wicked.

Almost we might say that this poem was (in one direction) inspired by the debate that had long been held and continued after, and that it was one of the chief contributions to the controversy: shall we or shall we not consign the heathen ancestors to perdition? What good will it do posterity to read the battles of Hector? *Quid Hinieldus cum Christo?* [What does Ingeld have to do with Christ?] The author of *Beowulf* showed forth the permanent value of that *pietas* which treasures the memory of man's struggles in the dark past, man fallen and not yet saved, disgraced but not dethroned. It would seem to have been part of the English temper in its strong sense of tradition, dependent doubtless on dynasties, noble houses, and their code of honour, and strengthened, it may be, by the more inquisitive and less severe Celtic learning, that it should, at least in some quarters and despite grave and Gallic voices, preserve much from the northern past to blend with southern learning, and new faith.

It has been thought that the influence of Latin epic, especially of the *Aeneid,* is perceptible in *Beowulf,* and a necessary explanation, if only in the exciting of emulation, of the development of the long and studied poem in early England. There is, of course, a likeness in places between these greater and lesser things, the *Aeneid* and *Beowulf,* if they are read in conjunction. But the smaller points in which imitation or reminiscence might be perceived are inconclusive, while the real likeness is deeper and due to certain qualities in the authors independent of the question whether the Anglo-Saxon had read Virgil or not. It is this deeper likeness which makes things, that are either the inevitabilities of human poetry or the accidental congruences of all tales, ring alike. We have the great pagan on the threshold of the change of the world; and the great (if lesser) Christian just over the threshold of the great change in his time and place: the backward view: *multa putans sortemque animo miseratus iniquam* [thinking of many things and deploring the unequal lot].[21]

But we will now return once more to the monsters, and consider especially the difference of their status in the northern and southern mythologies. Of Grendel it is said: *Godes yrre bær* [He bore God's ire]. But the Cyclops is god-begotten and his maiming is an offence against his begetter, the god Poseidon. This radical difference in mythological status is only brought out more sharply by the very closeness of the similarity in conception (in all save mere size) that is seen, if we compare *Beowulf,* 740 ff., with the description of the Cyclops devouring men in *Odyssey,* ix—or still more in *Aeneid,* iii. 622 ff. In Virgil, whatever may be true of the fairy-tale world of the

---

[21] In fact the real resemblance of the *Aeneid* and *Beowulf* lies in the constant presence of a sense of many-storied antiquity, together with its natural accompaniment, stern and noble melancholy. In this they are really akin and together differ from Homer's flatter, if more glittering, surface.

Odyssey, the Cyclops walks veritably in the historic world. He is seen by Aeneas in Sicily, *monstrum horrendum, informe, ingens* [a horrible monster, formless, huge], as much a perilous fact as Grendel was in Denmark, *earmsceapen on weres wæstmum . . . næfne he wæs mara þonne ænig man oðer* [a wretched one in man's shape . . . except that he was larger than any other man]; as real as Acestes or Hrothgar.[22]

At this point in particular we may regret that we do not know more about pre-Christian English mythology. Yet it is, as I have said, legitimate to suppose that in the matter of the position of the monsters in regard to men and gods the view was fundamentally the same as in later Icelandic. Thus, though all such generalizations are naturally imperfect in detail (since they deal with matter of various origins, constantly reworked, and never even at most more than partially systematized), we may with some truth contrast the "inhumanness" of the Greek gods, however anthropomorphic, with the "humanness" of the Northern, however titanic. In the southern myths there is also rumour of wars with giants and great powers not Olympian, the *Titania pubes fulmine deiecti* [youth thrown down by a Titanic bolt], rolling like Satan and his satellites in the nethermost Abyss. But this war is differently conceived. It lies in a chaotic past. The ruling gods are not besieged, not in ever-present peril or under future doom.[23] Their offspring on earth may be

[22] I use this illustration following Chambers, because of the close resemblance between Grendel and the Cyclops in kind. But other examples could be adduced: Cacus, for instance, the offspring of Vulcan. One might ponder the contrast between the legends of the torture of Prometheus and of Loki: the one for assisting men, the other for assisting the powers of darkness.

[23] There is actually no final principle in the legendary hostilities contained in classical mythology. For the present purpose that is all that matters: we are not here concerned with remoter mythological origins, in the North or South. The Gods, Cronian or Olympian, the Titans, and other great natural powers, and various monsters, even minor local horrors, are not clearly distinguished in origin or ancestry. There could be no permanent policy of war, led by Olympus, to which human courage might be dedicated, among mythological races so promiscuous. Of course, nowhere can absolute rigidity of distinction be expected, because in a sense the foe is always both within and without; the fortress must fall through treachery as well as by assault. Thus Grendel has a perverted human shape, and the giants or *jötnar* [giants], even when (like the Titans) they are of super-divine stature, are parodies of the human-divine form. Even in Norse, where the distinction is most rigid, Loki dwells in Asgarðr, though he is an evil and lying spirit, and fatal monsters come of him. For it is true of man, maker

heroes or fair women; it may also be the other creatures hostile to
men. The gods are not the allies of men in their war against these
or other monsters. The interest of the gods is in this or that man
as part of their individual schemes, not as part of a great strategy
that includes all good men, as the infantry of battle. In Norse, at
any rate, the gods are within Time, doomed with their allies to
death. Their battle is with the monsters and the outer darkness.
They gather heroes for the last defence. Already before euhemerism
saved them by embalming them, and they dwindled in antiquarian
fancy to the mighty ancestors of northern kings (English and
Scandinavian), they had become in their very being the enlarged
shadows of great men and warriors upon the walls of the world.
When Baldr is slain and goes to Hel he cannot escape thence any
more than mortal man.

This may make the southern gods more godlike—more lofty,
dread, and inscrutable. They are timeless and do not fear death.
Such a mythology may hold the promise of a profounder thought.
In any case it was a virtue of the southern mythology that it could
not stop where it was. It must go forward to philosophy or relapse
into anarchy. For in a sense it had shirked the problem precisely
by not having the monsters in the centre—as they are in *Beowulf*
to the astonishment of the critics. But such horrors cannot be left
permanently unexplained, lurking on the outer edges and under
suspicion of being connected with the Government. It is the strength
of the northern mythological imagination that it faced this problem,
put the monsters in the centre, gave them victory but no honour,
and found a potent but terrible solution in naked will and courage.
"As a working theory absolutely impregnable." So potent is it, that
while the older southern imagination has faded for ever into
literary ornament, the northern has power, as it were, to revive its
spirit even in our own times. It can work, even as it did work with
the *goðlauss* [godless] viking, without gods: martial heroism as its
own end. But we may remember that the poet of *Beowulf* saw
clearly: the wages of heroism is death.

For these reasons I think that the passages in *Beowulf* concerning

---

of myths, that Grendel and the Dragon, in their lust, greed, and malice, have
a part in him. But mythically conceived the gods do not recognize any bond with
Fenris úlfr [Fenris the wolf], any more than men with Grendel or the serpent.

the giants and their war with God, together with the two mentions
of Cain (as the ancestor of the giants in general and Grendel in
particular) are specially important.

They are directly connected with Scripture, yet they cannot be
dissociated from the creatures of northern myth, the ever-watchful
foes of the gods (and men). The undoubtedly scriptural Cain is
connected with _eotenas_ [giants] and _ylfe_ [elves], which are the
jötnar and *álfar* of Norse. But this is not due to mere confusion—
it is rather an indication of the precise point at which an imagination, pondering old and new, was kindled. At this point new Scripture and old tradition touched and ignited. It is for this reason that
these elements of Scripture alone appear in a poem dealing of
design with the noble pagan of old days. For they are precisely the
elements which bear upon this theme. Man alien in a hostile
world, engaged in a struggle which he cannot win while the world
lasts, is assured that his foes are the foes also of Dryhten, that his
courage noble in itself is also the highest loyalty: so said thyle and
clerk.

In *Beowulf* we have, then, an historical poem about the pagan
past, or an attempt at one—literal historical fidelity founded on
modern research was, of course, not attempted. It is a poem by a
learned man writing of old times, who looking back on the heroism
and sorrow feels in them something permanent and something symbolical. So far from being a confused semi-pagan—historically unlikely for a man of this sort in the period—he brought probably
first to his task a knowledge of Christian poetry, especially that of
the Cædmon school, and especially *Genesis*.[24] He makes his minstrel
sing in Heorot of the Creation of the earth and the lights of
Heaven. So excellent is this choice as the theme of the harp that
maddened Grendel lurking joyless in the dark without that it
matters little whether this is anachronistic or not.[25] *Secondly*, to his

[24] The *Genesis* which is preserved for us is a late copy of a damaged original,
but is still certainly in its older parts a poem whose composition must be
referred to the early period. That *Genesis A* is actually older than *Beowulf* is
generally recognized as the most probable reading of such evidence as there is.

[25] Actually the poet may have known, what we can guess, that such creation-
themes were also ancient in the North. *Völuspá* describes Chaos and the making
of the sun and moon, and very similar language occurs in the Old High German
fragment known as the *Wessobrunner Gebet*. The song of the minstrel Iopas,
who had his knowledge from Atlas, at the end of the first book of the *Aeneid*

task the poet brought a considerable learning in native lays and traditions: only by learning and training could such things be acquired; they were no more born naturally into an Englishman of the seventh or eighth centuries, by simple virtue of being an "Anglo-Saxon," than ready-made knowledge of poetry and history is inherited at birth by modern children.

It would seem that, in his attempt to depict ancient pre-Christian days, intending to emphasize their nobility, and the desire of the good for truth, he turned naturally when delineating the great King of Heorot to the Old Testament. In the *folces hyrde* [people's keeper: king] of the Danes we have much of the shepherd patriarchs and kings of Israel, servants of the one God, who attribute to His mercy all the good things that come to them in this life. We have in fact a Christian English conception of the noble chief before Christianity, who could lapse (as could Israel) in times of temptation into idolatry.[26] On the other hand, the traditional matter in English, not to mention the living survival of the heroic code and temper among the noble households of ancient England, enabled him to draw differently, and in some respects much closer to the actual heathen *hæleð* [hero], the character of Beowulf, especially as a young knight, who used his great gift of *mægen* [strength] to earn *dom* [glory] and *lof* [renown] among men and posterity.

Beowulf is not an actual picture of historic Denmark or Geatland or Sweden about A.D. 500. But it is (if with certain minor defects) on a general view a self-consistent picture, a construction bearing clearly the marks of design and thought. The whole must

---

is also in part a song of origins: *hic canit errantem lunam solisque labores, unde hominum genus et pecudes, unde imber et ignes* [he sang about the wandering of the moon and the labor of the sun, and the origin of mankind and cattle, and of rain and fire]. In any case the Anglo-Saxon poet's view throughout was plainly that true, or truer, knowledge was possessed in ancient days (when men were not deceived by the Devil); at least they knew of the one God and Creator, though not of heaven, for that was lost. See note 20.

[26] It is of Old Testament lapses rather than of any events in England (of which he is not speaking) that the poet is thinking in lines 175 ff., and this colours his manner of allusion to knowledge which he may have derived from native traditions concerning the Danes and the special heathen religious significance of the site of Heorot (*Hleiðrar, æt hærgtrafum*, the tabernacles)—it was possibly a matter that embittered the feud of Danes and Heathobards. If so, this is another point where old and new have blended. On the special importance and difficulty for criticism of the passage 175–88 see the Appendix.

have succeeded admirably in creating in the minds of the poet's contemporaries the illusion of surveying a past, pagan but noble and fraught with a deep significance—a past that itself had depth and reached backward into a dark antiquity of sorrow. This impression of depth is an effect and a justification of the use of episodes and allusions to old tales, mostly darker, more pagan, and desperate than the foreground.

To a similar antiquarian temper, and a similar use of vernacular learning, is probably due the similar effect of antiquity (and melancholy) in the *Aeneid*—especially felt as soon as Aeneas reaches Italy and the *Saturni gentem . . . sponte sua veterisque dei se more tenentem. Ic þa leode wat ge wið feond ge wið freond fæste worhte, æghwæs untæle ealde wisan* [I know the people firmly disposed toward friend and foe both, entirely faultless in the old way]. Alas for the lost lore, the annals and old poets that Virgil knew, and only used in the making of a new thing! The criticism that the important matters are put on the outer edges misses this point of artistry, and indeed fails to see why the old things have in *Beowulf* such an appeal: it is the poet himself who made antiquity so appealing. His poem has more value in consequence, and is a greater contribution to early mediaeval thought than the harsh and intolerant view that consigned all the heroes to the devil. We may be thankful that the product of so noble a temper has been preserved by chance (if such it be) from the dragon of destruction.

The general structure of the poem, so viewed, is not really difficult to perceive, if we look to the main points, the strategy, and neglect the many points of minor tactics. We must dismiss, of course, from mind the notion that *Beowulf* is a "narrative poem," that it tells a tale or intends to tell a tale sequentially. The poem "lacks steady advance": so Klaeber heads a critical section in his edition.[27] But the poem was not meant to advance, steadily or unsteadily. It is essentially a balance, an opposition of ends and beginnings. In its simplest terms it is a contrasted description of two moments in a great life, rising and setting; an elaboration of the ancient and intensely moving contrast between youth and age, first

---

[27] Though only explicitly referred to here and in disagreement, this edition is, of course, of great authority, and all who have used it have learned much from it.

achievement and final death. It is divided in consequence into two opposed portions, different in matter, manner, and length: A from 1 to 2199 (including an exordium of 52 lines); B from 2200 to 3182 (the end). There is no reason to cavil at this proportion; in any case, for the purpose and the production of the required effect, it proves in practice to be right.

This simple and *static* structure, solid and strong, is in each part much diversified, and capable of enduring this treatment. In the conduct of the presentation of Beowulf's rise to fame on the one hand, and of his kingship and death on the other, criticism can find things to question, especially if it is captious, but also much to praise, if it is attentive. But the only serious weakness, or apparent weakness, is the long recapitulation: the report of Beowulf to Hygelac. This recapitulation is well done. Without serious discrepancy[28] it retells rapidly the events in Heorot, and retouches the account; and it serves to illustrate, since he himself describes his own deeds, yet more vividly the character of a young man, singled out by destiny, as he steps suddenly forth in his full powers. Yet this is perhaps not quite sufficient to justify the repetition. The explanation, if not complete justification, is probably to be sought in different directions.

For one thing, the old tale was not first told or invented by this poet. So much is clear from investigation of the folk-tale analogues. Even the legendary association of the Scylding court with a marauding monster, and with the arrival from abroad of a champion and deliverer was probably already old. The plot was not the poet's; and though he has infused feeling and significance into its crude material, that plot was not a perfect vehicle of the theme or themes that came to hidden life in the poet's mind as he worked upon it. Not an unusual event in literature. For the contrast—youth and

---

[28] I am not concerned with minor discrepancies at any point in the poem. They are no proof of composite authorship, nor even of incompetent authorship. It is very difficult, even in a newly invented tale of any length, to avoid such defects; more so still in rehandling old and oft-told tales. The points that are seized in the study, with a copy that can be indexed and turned to and fro (even if never read straight through as it was meant to be), are usually such as may easily escape an author and still more easily his natural audience. Virgil certainly does not escape such faults, even within the limits of a single book. Modern printed tales, that have presumably had the advantage of proof-correction, can even be observed to hesitate in the heroine's Christian name.

death—it would probably have been better, if we had no journeying. If the single nation of the *Geatas* had been the scene, we should
have felt the stage not narrower, but symbolically wider. More
plainly should we have perceived in one people and their hero all
mankind and its heroes. This at any rate I have always myself felt
in reading *Beowulf*; but I have also felt that this defect is rectified
by the bringing of the tale of Grendel to Geatland. As Beowulf
stands in Hygelac's hall and tells his story, he sets his feet firm
again in the land of his own people, and is no longer in danger of
appearing a mere *wrecca*, an errant adventurer and slayer of bogies
that do not concern him.

There is in fact a double division in the poem: the fundamental
one already referred to, and a secondary but important division at
line 1887. After that the essentials of the previous part are taken
up and compacted, so that all the tragedy of Beowulf is contained
between 1888 and the end.[29] But, of course, without the first half we
should miss much incidental illustration; we should miss also the
dark background of the court of Heorot that loomed as large in
glory and doom in ancient northern imagination as the court of
Arthur: no vision of the past was complete without it. And (most
important) we should lose the direct contrast of youth and age in
the persons of Beowulf and Hrothgar which is one of the chief
purposes of this section: it ends with the pregnant words *oþ þæt
hine yldo benam mægenes wynnum, se þe oft manegum scod* [until
that he was deprived of the joys of strength by old age, which has
often harmed many].

In any case we must not view this poem as in intention an
exciting narrative or a romantic tale. The very nature of Old
English metre is often misjudged. In it there is no single rhythmic
pattern progressing from the beginning of a line to the end, and
repeated with variation in other lines. The lines do not go according to a tune. They are founded on a balance; an opposition
between two halves of roughly equivalent [30] phonetic weight, and
significant content, which are more often rhythmically contrasted

---

[29] The least satisfactory arrangement possible is thus to read only lines 1–1887
and not the remainder. This procedure has none the less been, from time to
time, directed or encouraged by more than one "English syllabus."

[30] Equivalent, but not necessarily *equal*, certainly not as such things may be
measured by machines.

than similar. They are more like masonry than music. In this fundamental fact of poetic expression I think there is a parallel to the total structure of *Beowulf*. *Beowulf* is indeed the most successful Old English poem because in it the elements, language, metre, theme, structure, are all most nearly in harmony. Judgement of the verse has often gone astray through listening for an accentual rhythm and pattern: and it seems to halt and stumble. Judgement of the theme goes astray through considering it as the narrative handling of a plot: and it seems to halt and stumble. Language and verse, of course, differ from stone or wood or paint, and can be only heard or read in a time-sequence; so that in any poem that deals at all with characters and events some narrative element must be present. We have none the less in *Beowulf* a method and structure that within the limits of the verse-kind approaches rather to sculpture or painting. It is a composition not a tune.

This is clear in the second half. In the struggle with Grendel one can as a reader dismiss the certainty of literary experience that the hero will not in fact perish, and allow oneself to share the hopes and fears of the Geats upon the shore. In the second part the author has no desire whatever that the issue should remain open, even according to literary convention. There is no need to hasten like the messenger, who rode to bear the lamentable news to the waiting people (2892 ff.). They may have hoped, but we are not supposed to. By now we are supposed to have grasped the plan. Disaster is foreboded. Defeat is the theme. Triumph over the foes of man's precarious fortress is over, and we approach slowly and reluctantly the inevitable victory of death.[31]

"In structure," it was said of *Beowulf*, "it is curiously weak, in a sense preposterous," though great merits of detail were allowed. In structure actually it is curiously strong, in a sense inevitable, though there are defects of detail. The general design of the poet is not only defensible, it is, I think, admirable. There may have previously existed stirring verse dealing in straightforward manner

[31] That the particular bearer of enmity, the Dragon, also dies is important chiefly to Beowulf himself. He was a great man. Not many even in dying can achieve the death of a single worm, or the temporary salvation of their kindred. Within the limits of human life Beowulf neither lived nor died in vain—brave men might say. But there is no hint, indeed there are many to the contrary, that it was a war to end war, or a dragon-fight to end dragons. It is the end of Beowulf, and of the hope of his people.

and even in natural sequence with the Beowulf's deeds, or with the fall of Hygelac; or again with the fluctuations of the feud between the houses of Hrethel the Geat and Ongentheow the Swede; or with the tragedy of the Heathobards, and the treason that destroyed the Scylding dynasty. Indeed this must be admitted to be practically certain: it was the existence of such connected legends— connected in the mind, not necessarily dealt with in chronicle fashion or in long semi-historical poems—that permitted the peculiar use of them in *Beowulf*. This poem cannot be criticized or comprehended, if its original audience is imagined in like case to ourselves, possessing only *Beowulf* in splendid isolation. For *Beowulf* was not designed to tell the tale of Hygelac's fall, or for that matter to give the whole biography of Beowulf, still less to write the history of the Geatish kingdom and its downfall. But it used knowledge of these things for its own purpose—to give that sense of perspective, of antiquity with a greater and yet darker antiquity behind. These things are mainly on the outer edges or in the background because they belong there, if they are to function in this way. But in the centre we have an heroic figure of enlarged proportions.

Beowulf is not an "epic," not even a magnified "lay." No terms borrowed from Greek or other literatures exactly fit: there is no reason why they should. Though if we must have a term, we should choose rather "elegy." It is an heroic-elegiac poem; and in a sense all its first 3136 lines are the prelude to a dirge: *him þa gegiredan Geata leode ad ofer eorðan unwaclicne* [Then the Geatish people made ready no mean pyre on the earth]: one of the most moving ever written. But for the universal significance which is given to the fortunes of its hero it is an enhancement and not a detraction, in fact it is necessary, that his final foe should be not some Swedish prince, or treacherous friend, but a dragon: a thing made by imagination for just such a purpose. Nowhere does a dragon come in so precisely where he should. But if the hero falls before a dragon, then certainly he should achieve his early glory by vanquishing a foe of similar order.

There is, I think, no criticism more beside the mark than that which some have made, complaining that it is monsters in both halves that is so disgusting; one they could have stomached more easily. That is nonsense. I can see the point of asking for *no* monsters. I can also see the point of the situation in *Beowulf*. But no point at all in mere reduction of numbers. It would really have been preposterous, if the poet had recounted Beowulf's rise to fame in a "typical" or "commonplace" war in Frisia, and then ended him with a dragon. Or if he had told of his cleansing of Heorot, and then brought him to defeat and death in a "wild" or "trivial" Swedish invasion! If the dragon is the right end for Beowulf, and I agree with the author that it is, then Grendel is an eminently suitable beginning. They are creatures, *feond mancynnes* [enemies of mankind], of a similar order and kindred significance. Triumph over the lesser and more nearly human is cancelled by defeat before the older and more elemental. And the conquest of the ogres comes at the right moment: not in earliest youth, though the nicors are referred to in Beowulf's *geogoðfeore* [period of youth] as a presage of the kind of hero we have to deal with; and not during the later period of recognized ability and prowess;[32] but in that first moment, which often comes in great lives, when men look up in surprise and see that a hero has unawares leaped forth. The placing of the dragon is inevitable: a man can but die upon his death-day.

I will conclude by drawing an imaginary contrast. Let us suppose that our poet had chosen a theme more consonant with "our modern judgement"; the life and death of St. Oswald. He might then have made a poem, and told first of Heavenfield, when Oswald as a young prince against all hope won a great victory with a remnant of brave men; and then have passed at once to the lamentable defeat of Oswestry, which seemed to destroy the hope of Christian Northumbria; while all the rest of Oswald's life, and the traditions of the royal house and its feud with that of Deira might be introduced allusively or omitted. To any one but an historian in search of facts and chronology this would have been a fine thing, an heroic-elegiac poem greater than history. It would be much better

---

[32] We do, however, learn incidentally much of this period: it is not strictly true, even of our poem as it is, to say that after the deeds in Heorot Beowulf "has something else to do." Great heroes, like great saints, should show themselves capable of dealing also with the ordinary things of life, even though they may do so with a strength more than ordinary. We may wish to be assured of this (and the poet has assured us), without demanding that he should put such things in the centre, when they are not the centre of his thought.

than a plain narrative, in verse or prose, however steadily advancing. This mere arrangement would at once give it more significance than a straightforward account of one king's life: the contrast of rising and setting, achievement and death. But even so it would fall far short of *Beowulf*. Poetically it would be greatly enhanced if the poet had taken violent liberties with history and much enlarged the reign of Oswald, making him old and full of years of care and glory when he went forth heavy with foreboding to face the heathen Penda: the contrast of youth and age would add enormously to the original theme, and give it a more universal meaning. But even so it would still fall short of *Beowulf*. To match his theme with the rise and fall of poor "folk-tale" Beowulf the poet would have been obliged to turn Cadwallon and Penda into giants and demons. It is just because the main foes in *Beowulf* are inhuman that the story is larger and more significant than this imaginary poem of a great king's fall. It glimpses the cosmic and moves with the thought of all men concerning the fate of human life and efforts; it stands amid but above the petty wars of princes, and surpasses the dates and limits of historical periods, however important. At the beginning, and during its process, and most of all at the end, we look down as if from a visionary height upon the house of man in the valley of the world. A light starts—*lixte se leoma ofer landa fela* [that light shined over many lands]—and there is a sound of music; but the outer darkness and its hostile offspring lie ever in wait for the torches to fail and the voices to cease. Grendel is maddened by the sound of harps.

And one last point, which those will feel who to-day preserve the ancient *pietas* towards the past: *Beowulf* is not a "primitive" poem; it is a late one, using the materials (then still plentiful) preserved from a day already changing and passing, a time that has now for ever vanished, swallowed in oblivion; using them for a new purpose, with a wider sweep of imagination, if with a less bitter and concentrated force. When new *Beowulf* was already antiquarian, in a good sense, and it now produces a singular effect. For it is now to us itself ancient; and yet its maker was telling of things already old and weighted with regret, and he expended his art in making keen that touch upon the heart which sorrows have that are both poignant and remote. If the funeral of Beowulf moved once like the echo of an ancient dirge, far-off and hopeless, it is to us as a memory brought over the hills, an echo of an echo. There is not much poetry in the world like this; and though *Beowulf* may not be among the very greatest poems of our western world and its tradition, it has its own individual character, and peculiar solemnity; it would still have power had it been written in some time or place unknown and without posterity, if it contained no name that could now be recognized or identified by research. Yet it is in fact written in a language that after many centuries has still essential kinship with our own, it was made in this land, and moves in our northern world beneath our northern sky, and for those who are native to that tongue and land, it must ever call with a profound appeal—until the dragon comes.

Appendix

(A) GRENDEL'S TITLES

The changes which produced (before A.D. 1066) the mediaeval devil are not complete in *Beowulf,* but in Grendel change and blending are, of course, already apparent. Such things do not admit of clear classifications and distinctions. Doubtless ancient pre-Christian imagination vaguely recognized differences of "materiality" between the solidly physical monsters, conceived as made of the earth and rock (to which the light of the sun might return them), and elves, and ghosts or bogies. Monsters of more or less human shape were naturally liable to development on contact with Christian ideas of sin and spirits of evil. Their parody of human form (*earmsceapen on weres wæstmum* [wretched in human form]) becomes symbolical, explicitly, of sin, or rather this mythical element, already present implicit and unresolved, is emphasized: this we see already in *Beowulf,* strengthened by the theory of descent from Cain (and so from Adam), and of the curse of God. So Grendel is not only under this inherited curse, but also himself sinful: *manscaða* [wicked-ravager], *synscaða* [malefactor], *synnum beswenced* [crime-afflicted]; he is *fyrena hyrde* [keeper of sins]. The same notion (combined with others) appears also when he is called (by the author, not by the characters in the poem) *hæþen* [heathen], 852, 986, and *helle hæfton* [hell-captive], *feond in helle* [fiend in hell]. As an image of man estranged from God he is called not only by all names applicable to ordinary men, as *wer, rinc, guma, maga,* but he is conceived as having a spirit, other than his body, that will be punished. Thus *alegde hæþene sawle: þær him hel onfeng* [he laid down his heathen soul: there hell received him], 852; while Beowulf himself says *ðær abidan sceal miclan domes, hu him scir Metod scrifan wille* [there he must abide a great judgment, how the glorious Lord will decree for him], 978.

   But this view is blended or confused with another. Because of his ceaseless hostility to men, and hatred of their joy, his super-human size and strength, and his love of the dark, he approaches to a *devil,* though he is not yet a true devil in purpose. Real devilish qualities (deception and destruction of the soul), other than those which are undeveloped symbols, such as his hideousness and habita-tion in dark forsaken places, are hardly present. But he and his mother are actually called *deofla* [devils], 1680; and Grendel is said when fleeing to hiding to make for *deofla gedræg* [company of devils]. It should be noted that *feond* cannot be used in this ques-tion: it still means "enemy" in *Beowulf,* and is for instance applic-able to Beowulf and Wiglaf in relation to the dragon. Even *feond on helle,* 101, is not so clear as it seems (see below); though we may add *wergan gastes* [accursed creature], 133, an expression for "devil" later extremely common, and actually applied in line 1747 to the Devil and tempter himself. Apart, however, from this expression little can be made of the use of *gast, gæst.* For one thing it is under grave suspicion in many places (both applied to Grendel and otherwise) of being a corruption of *gæst, gest* "stranger"; compare Grendel's title *cwealmcuma* [murderous visitor], 792 = *wælgæst* [slaughter demon], 1331, 1995. In any case it cannot be translated either by the modern *ghost* or *spirit. Creature* is probably the near-est we can now get. Where it is genuine it applies to Grendel probably in virtue of his relationship or similarity to bogies (*scin-num ond scuccum* [demons and devils]), physical enough in form and power, but vaguely felt as belonging to a different order of being, one allied to the malevolent "ghosts" of the dead. Fire is conceived as a *gæst* (1123).

This approximation of Grendel to a devil does not mean that there is any confusion as to his habitation. Grendel was a fleshly denizen of this world (until physically slain). *On helle* and *helle* (as in *helle gast* 1274) mean "hellish," and are actually equivalent to the first elements in the compounds *deaþscua* [death-shadow], *sceadugengea* [shadow-goer], *helruna* [hell-secret-one]. (Thus the original genitive *helle* developed into the Middle English adjective *helle, hellene* "hellish," applicable to ordinary men, such as usurers; and even *feond on helle* could be so used. Wyclif applies *fend on helle* to the friar walking in England as Grendel in Denmark.) But the symbolism of darkness is so fundamental that it is vain to look for any distinction between the *þystru* [darkness] outside Hrothgar's hall in which Grendel lurked, and the shadow of Death, or of hell after (or in) Death.

Thus in spite of shifting, actually in process (intricate, and as difficult as it is interesting and important to follow), Grendel remains primarily an ogre, a physical monster, whose main function is hostility to humanity (and its frail efforts at order and art upon earth). He is of the *fifelcyn* [race of monsters], a *þyrs* [giant] or *eoten* [giant]; in fact the *eoten,* for this ancient word is actually preserved in Old English only as applied to him. He is most frequently called simply a foe: *feond* [enemy], *lað* [hostile-one], *sceaða* [harmer], *feorhgeniðla* [life-enemy], *laðgeteona* [hostile-spoiler], all words applicable to enemies of any kind. And though he, as ogre, has kinship with devils, and is doomed when slain to be numbered among the evil spirits, he is not when wrestling with Beowulf a materialized apparition of soul-destroying evil. It is thus true to say that Grendel is not yet a real mediaeval devil—except in so far as mediaeval bogies themselves had failed (as was often the case) to become real devils. But the distinction between a devilish ogre, and a devil revealing himself in ogre-form—between a monster, devouring the body and bringing temporal death, that is inhabited by an accursed spirit, and a spirit of evil aiming ultimately at the soul and bringing eternal death (even though he takes a form of visible horror, that may bring and suffer physical pain)—is a real and important one, even if both kinds are to be found before and after 1066. In *Beowulf* the weight is on the physical side: Grendel does not vanish into the pit when grappled. He must be slain by plain prowess, and thus is a real counterpart to the dragon in Beowulf's history.

(Grendel's mother is naturally described, when separately treated, in precisely similar terms: she is *wif* [woman], *ides* [lady], *aglaec wif* [monster-woman]; and rising to the inhuman: *merewif* [sea-woman], *brimwylf* [sea-wolf], *grundwyrgen* [bottom-monstress]. Grendel's title *Godes andsaca* has been studied in the text. Some titles have been omitted: for instance those referring to his *outlawry*, which are applicable in themselves to him by nature, but are of course also fitting either to a descendant of Cain, or to a devil: thus *heorowearh* [savage-foe], *daedhata* [persecutor], *mearcstapa* [march-stepper], *angengea* [alone-goer].)

(B) "LOF" AND "DOM"; "HELL" AND "HEOFON"

Of pagan "belief" we have little or nothing left in English. But the spirit survived. Thus the author of *Beowulf* grasped fully the idea of *lof* or *dom*, the noble pagan's desire for the *merited praise* of the noble. For if this limited "immortality" of renown naturally exists as a strong motive together with actual heathen practice and belief, it can also long outlive them. It is the natural residuum when the gods are destroyed, whether unbelief comes from within or from without. The prominence of the motive of *lof* in *Beowulf*— long ago pointed out by Earle—may be interpreted, then, as a sign that a pagan time was not far away from the poet, and perhaps also that the end of English paganism (at least among the noble classes for whom and by whom such traditions were preserved) was marked by a twilight period, similar to that observable later in Scandinavia. The gods faded or receded, and man was left to carry on his war unaided. His trust was in his own power and will, and his reward was the praise of his peers during his life and after his death.

At the beginning of the poem, at the end of the first section of the exordium, the note is struck: *lofdædum sceal in mægþa gehwære man geþeon* [by famous deeds a man shall flourish in every tribe]. The last word of the poem is *lofgeornost* [most eager for fame], the summit of the praise of the dead hero: that was indeed *lastworda betst* [best memorial]. For Beowulf had lived according to his own philosophy, which he explicitly avowed: *ure æghwylc sceal ende*

✳

*gebidan worolde lifes; wyrce se ðe mote domes ær deaþe: þæt bið
dryhtguman æfter selest* [each of us must abide the end of life in
this world; whoever can should endeavor to win fame before death:
for that is best afterwards for the warrior], 1386 ff. The poet as
commentator recurs again to this: *swa sceal man don, þonne he æt
guðe gegan þenceð longsumne lof: no ymb his lif cearað* [so should
a man do, when he at battle hopes to gain enduring fame; never
care about his life], 1534 ff.

Lof is ultimately and etymologically *value, valuation,* and so
praise, as we say (itself derived from *pretium*). *Dom* is *judgement,
assessment,* and in one branch *just esteem, merited renown.* The
difference between these two is not in most passages important.
Thus at the end of *Widsith,* which refers to the minstrel's part in
achieving for the noble and their deeds the prolonged life of fame,
both are combined: it is said of the generous patron, *lof se gewyrceð,
hafað under heofonum heahfæstne dom* [he earns fame, has under
heavens permanent glory]. But the difference has an importance.
For the words were not actually synonymous, nor entirely commen-
surable. In the Christian period the one, *lof,* flowed rather into the
ideas of heaven and the heavenly choirs; the other, *dom,* into the
ideas of the judgement of God, the particular and general judgements of the dead.

The change that occurs can be plainly observed in *The Seafarer,*
especially if lines 66–80 of that poem are compared with Hrothgar's
giedd [song] or sermon in *Beowulf* from 1755 onwards. There is a
close resemblance between *Seafarer* 66–71 and Hrothgar's words,
1761–68, a part of his discourse that may certainly be ascribed to
the original author of *Beowulf,* whatever revision or expansion the
speech may otherwise have suffered. The Seafarer says:

> *ic gelyfe no
> þæt him eorðwelan ece stondað.
> Simle þreora sum þinga gehwylce
> ær his tid[d]ege to tweon weorþeð:
> adl oþþe yldo oþþe ecghete
> fægum fromweardum feorh oðþringeð.*

[I do not believe that earthly-wealth will remain eternally. Each of
three things is always uncertain before its appointed day: illness or old-
age or sword-edge-hate wrests life away from the man fading or fated].

Hrothgar says:

> oft sona bi∂
> *þæt þec adl o∂∂e ecg eafoþes getwæfe∂,*
> *o∂∂e fyres feng, o∂∂e flodes wylm,*
> *o∂∂e gripe meces, o∂∂e gares fliht,*
> *o∂∂e atol yldo; o∂∂e eagena bearhtm*
> *forsite∂ ond forsworce∂. Semninga bi∂*
> *þæt þec, dryhtguma, dea∂ oferswy∂e∂.*

[but soon it will be that illness or sword-edge shall cut you off from your power, or the grip of fire, or the ocean's wave, or sword's bite, or spear's flight, or terrible old-age; or the eyes' brightness diminishes and darkens. Straightway it will be, warrior, that death shall over-power you].

Hrothgar expands *þreora sum* [one of three] on lines found else-where, either in great elaboration as in the *Fates of Men,* or in brief allusion to this well-known theme as in *The Wanderer* 80 ff. But the Seafarer, after thus proclaiming that all men shall die, goes on: "Therefore it is for all noble men *lastworda betst* (the best memorial), and praise (*lof*) of the living who commemorate him after death, that ere he must go hence, he should merit and achieve on earth by heroic deeds against the malice of enemies (*feonda*), opposing the devil, that the children of men may praise him after-wards, and his *lof* may live with the angels for ever and ever, the glory of eternal life, rejoicing among the hosts."

This is a passage which from its syntax alone may with unusual certainty be held to have suffered revision and expansion. It could easily be simplified. But in any case it shows a modification of heathen *lof* in two directions: first in making the deeds which win *lof* resistance to spiritual foes—the sense of the ambiguous *feonda* is, in the poem as preserved, so defined by *deofle togeanes* [against the devil]; secondly, in enlarging *lof* to include the angels and the bliss of heaven. *lofsong, loftsong* are in Middle English especially used of the heavenly choirs.

But we do not find anything like this definite alteration in *Beowulf.* There *lof* remains pagan *lof,* the praise of one's peers, at best vaguely prolonged among their descendents *awa to ealdre* [for-ever]. (On *so∂fæstra dom* [truth-firm fame], 2820, see below). In *Beowulf* there is *hell*: justly the poet said of the people he depicted *helle gemundon on modsefan* [they thought of hell in their thoughts]. But there is practically no clear reference to *heaven* as its opposite, to heaven, that is, as a place or state of reward, of eternal bliss in the presence of God. Of course *heofon*, singular and plural, and its synonyms, such as *rodor*, are frequent; but they refer usually either to the particular landscape or to the sky under which all men dwell. Even when these words are used with the words for God, who is Lord of the heavens, such expressions are primarily parallels to others describing His general governance of nature (e.g. 1609 ff.), and His realm which includes land and sea and sky.

Of course it is not here maintained—very much the contrary—that the *poet* was ignorant of theological heaven, or of the Christian use of *heofon* as the equivalent of *caelum* in Scripture: only that this use was of intention (if not in practice quite rigidly) excluded from a poem dealing with the pagan past. There is one clear exception in lines 186 ff: <u>*wel bið þæm þe mot æfter deaðdæge Drihten secean, ond to Fæder fæþmum freoðo wilnian*</u> [Well will it be for <u>him who may after his death-day go to the Lord, and in the Father's</u> <u>embrace asks for protection</u>]. If this, and the passage in which it occurs, is genuine—descends, that is, without addition or alteration from the poet who wrote *Beowulf* as a whole—and is not, as, I believe, a later expansion, then the point is not destroyed. For the passage remains still definitely an aside, an exclamation of the Christian author, who knew about heaven, and expressly denied such knowledge to the Danes. The characters within the poem do not understand heaven, or have hope of it. They refer to *hell*—an originally pagan word.[33] Beowulf predicts it as the destiny of Unferth and Grendel. Even the noble monotheist Hrothgar—so he is drawn, quite apart from the question of the genuineness of the bulk of his sermon from 1724-60—refers to no heavenly bliss. The reward of virtue which he foretells for Beowulf is that his *dom* shall live *awa to ealdre* [forever], a fortune also bestowed upon Sigurd in

[33] Free as far as we know from definite physical location. Details of the original northern conception, equated and blended with the Scriptural, are possibly sometimes to be seen colouring the references to Christian hell. A celebrated example is the reference in *Judith* to the death of Holofernes, which recalls remarkably certain features in *Völuspá*. Cf. *Judith* 115: *wyrmum bewunden* [wound with worms], and 119: *of ðam wyrmsele* [from the worm-hall] with *Völ.* 36 *sá's undinn salr orma hryggjum*: which translated into O.E. would be *se is wunden sele wyrma hrycgum* [the hall is wound with worm backs].

Norse (that his name *æ mun uppi* [shall live forever]). This idea of lasting *dom* is, as we have seen, capable of being christianized; but in *Beowulf* it is not christianized, probably deliberately, when the characters are speaking in their proper persons, or their actual thoughts are reported.

The author, it is true, says of Beowulf that *him of hreðre gewat sawol secean soðfæstra dom* [his soul departed from his breast to seek truth-firm fate]. What precise theological view he held concerning the souls of the just heathen we need not here inquire. He does not tell us, saying simply that Beowulf's spirit departed to whatever judgement awaits such just men, though we may take it that this comment implies that it was not destined to the fiery hell of punishment, being reckoned among the good. There is in any case here no doubt of the transmutation of words originally pagan. *soðfæstra dom* could by itself have meant simply the "esteem of the true-judging," that *dom* which Beowulf as a young man had declared to be the prime motive of noble conduct; but here combined with *gewat secean* it must mean either the glory that belongs (in eternity) to the just, or the judgement of God upon the just. Yet Beowulf himself, expressing his own opinion, though troubled by dark doubts, and later declaring his conscience clear, thinks at the end only of his barrow and memorial among men, of his childlessness, and of Wiglaf the sole survivor of his kindred, to whom he bequeathes his arms. His funeral is not Christian, and his reward is the recognized virtue of his kingship and the hopeless sorrow of his people.

The relation of the Christian and heathen thought and diction in *Beowulf* has often been misconceived. So far from being a man so simple or so confused that he muddled Christianity with Germanic paganism, the author probably drew or attempted to draw distinctions, and to represent moods and attitudes of characters conceived dramatically as living in a noble but heathen past. Though there are one or two special problems concerning the tradition of the poem and the possibility that it has here and there suffered later unauthentic retouching,[34] we cannot speak in general either of con-

---

[34] Such as 168–69, probably a clumsily intruded couplet, of which the only certain thing that can be said is that it interrupts (even if its sense were plain) the natural connexion between 165–67 and 170; the question of the expansion

fusion (in one poet's mind or in the mind of a whole period), or of patch-work revision producing confusion. More sense can be made of the poem, if we start rather with the hypothesis, not in itself unlikely, that the poet tried to do something definite and difficult, which had some reason and thought behind it, though his execution may not have been entirely successful.

The strongest argument that the actual language of the poem is not in general the product either of stupidity or accident is to be found in the fact that we can observe *differentiation*. We can, that is, in this matter of philosophy and religious sentiment distinguish, for instance: (*a*) the poet as narrator and commentator; (*b*) Beowulf; and (*c*) Hrothgar. Such differentiation would not be achieved by a man himself confused in mind, and still less by later random editing. The kind of thing that accident contrives is illustrated by *drihten wereda*, "lord of hosts," a familiar Christian expression, which appears in line 2186, plainly as an alteration of *drihten Wedera* "lord of the Geats." This alteration is obviously due to some man, the actual scribe of the line or some predecessor, more familiar with *Dominus Deus Sabaoth* than with Hrethel and the Weder-Geatish house. But no one, I think, has ventured to ascribe this confusion to the author.

That such differentiation does occur, I do not attempt here to prove by analysis of all the relevant lines of the poem. I leave the matter to those who care to go through the text, only insisting that it is essential to pay closer attention than has usually been paid to the *circumstances* in which the references to religion, Fate, or mythological matters each appear, and to distinguish in particular those things which are said in *oratio recta* [direct discourse] by one of the characters, or are reported as being said or thought by them. It will then be seen that the narrating and commenting poet obviously stands apart. But the two characters who do most of the speaking, Beowulf and Hrothgar, are also quite distinct. Hrothgar is consistently portrayed as a wise and noble monotheist, modelled largely it has been suggested in the text on the Old Testament patriarchs and kings; he refers all things to the favour of God, and never omits explicit thanks for mercies. Beowulf refers sparingly to God,

---

(in this case at any rate skilful and not inapt) of Hrothgar's *giedd* [song], 1724-60; and most notably lines 175-88.

except as the arbiter of critical events, and then principally as
Metod [Ruler], in which the idea of God approaches nearest to the
old Fate. We have in Beowulf's language little differentiation of
God and Fate. For instance, he says *gæð a wyrd swa hio scel* [fate
does whatever it pleases] and immediately continues that *dryhten*
[lord] holds the balance in his combat (441); or again he definitely
equates *wyrd* and *metod* (2526 f.).[35] It is Beowulf who says *wyrd oft
nereð unfægne eorl, þonne his ellen deah* [fate often protects the
unfated earl, while his courage is strong] (immediately after calling
the sun *beacen Godes* [beacon of God]), which contrasts with the
poet's own comment on the man who escaped the dragon (2291):
*swa mæg unfæge eaðe gedigean wean ond wræcsið, se ðe Wealdendes
hyldo gehealdeþ* [so may an unfated earl easily survive woe and
exile-journeying, he who has the Lord's grace]. Beowulf only twice
explicitly thanks God or acknowledges His help: in lines 1658–61,
where he acknowledges God's protection and the favour of *ylda
Waldend* [Ruler of men] in his combat under the water; in his last
speech, where he thanks *Frean Wuldurcyninge . . . ecum Dryhtne*
[Lord Glory-King . . . eternal Lord] for all the treasure, and for
helping him to win it for his people. Usually he makes no such
references. He ascribes his conquest of the nicors to luck—*hwæþre
me gesælde* [anyway it befell me], 570 ff. (compare the similar words

[35] Of course the use of words more or less equivalent to "fate" continued
throughout the ages. The most Christian poets refer to *wyrd*, usually of unfortunate events; but sometimes of good, as in *Elene* 1047, where the conversion of
Judas is ascribed to *wyrd*. There remains always the main mass of the workings
of Providence (*Metod*) which are inscrutable, and for practical purposes dealt
with as "fate" or "luck." *Metod* is in Old English the word that is most nearly
allied to "fate," although employed as a synonym of *god*. That it could be so
employed is due probably to its having anciently in English an agental significance (as well as an abstract sense), as in Old Norse where *mjötuðr* has the
senses "dispenser, ruler" and "doom, fate, death." But in Old English *metodsceaft*
means "doom" or "death." Cf. 2814 f. where *wyrd* is more active than *metodsceaft*. In Old Saxon *metod* is similarly used, leaning also to the side of the
inscrutable (and even hostile) aspects of the world's working. Gabriel in the
Héliand says of John the Baptist that he will not touch wine: *so habed im
uurdgiscapu, metod gimarcod endi maht godes* [so had fate, the ruler, and God's
might decreed for him] (128); it is said of Anna when her husband died: *that
sie thiu mikila maht metodes todelda, uured uurdigiscapu* [that the great might
of the ruler dealt it] (511). In Old Saxon *metod(o)giscapu* and *metodigisceft*,
equal Fate, as O.E. *metodsceaft*.

used of Sigemund, 890). In his account to Hygelac his only explanation of his preservation in the water-den is *næs ic fæge þa gyt* [then
I was not yet fated] (2141). He does not allude to God at all in this
report.

Beowulf knows, of course, of hell and judgement: he speaks of it
to Unferth; he declares that Grendel shall abide *miclan domes*
[great judgment] and the judgement of *scir metod* [glorious Ruler];
and finally in his last examination of conscience he says that
Waldend fira [Ruler of men] cannot accuse him of *morðorbealo
maga* [murder of kin]. But the crimes which he claims to have
avoided are closely paralleled in the heathen *Völuspá*, where the
grim hall, *Náströndu á*, contains especially *menn meinsvara ok
morðvarga* (perjurers and murderers).

Other references he makes are casual and formal, such as *beorht
beacen Godes* [bright beacon of God], of the sun (571). An exceptional case is *Godes leoht geceas* [he chose God's light] 2469, describing the death of Hrethel, Beowulf's grandfather. This would appear
to refer to heaven. Both these expressions have, as it were, inadvertently escaped from Christian poetry. The first, *beacen Godes,* is
perhaps passable even for a heathen in this particular poem, in
which the theory throughout is that good pagans, when not tempted
or deluded by the devil, knew of the one God. But the second, especially since Beowulf himself is formally the speaker, is an item of
unsuitable diction—which cannot be dismissed as a later alteration.
A didactic reviser would hardly have added this detail to the description of the heathen king's death: he would rather have removed
the heathen, or else sent him to hell. The whole story alluded to is
pagan and hopeless, and turns on blood-feud and the motive that
when a son kills his brother the father's sorrow is intensified because
no vengeance can be exacted. The explanation of such occasional
faults is not to be sought in Christian revision, but in the fact that
before *Beowulf* was written Christian poetry was already established, and was known to the author. The language of *Beowulf* is
in fact partly "re-paganized" by the author with a special purpose,
rather than christianized (by him or later) without consistent purpose. Throughout the poem the language becomes more intelligible,
if we assume that the diction of poetry was already christianized and

familiar with Old and New Testament themes and motives. There is a gap, important and effective poetically whatever was its length in time, between Cædmon and the poet of *Beowulf*. We have thus in Old English not only the old heroic language often strained or misused in application to Christian legend (as in *Andreas* or *Elene*), but in *Beowulf* language of Christian tone occasionally (if actually seldom) put inadvertently in the mouth of a character conceived as heathen. All is not perfect to the last detail in *Beowulf*. But with regard to *Godes leoht geceas* the chief defect of this kind, it may be observed that in the very long speech of Beowulf from 2425–2515 the poet has hardly attempted to keep up the pretence of *oratio recta* throughout. Just before the end he reminds us and himself that Beowulf is supposed to be speaking by a renewed *Beowulf maðelode* [Beowulf spoke] (2510). From 2444 to 2489 we have not really a monologue in character at all, and the words *Godes leoht geceas* go rather with *gewat secean soðfæstra dom* [departed to seek truth-firm fate] as evidence of the author's own view of the destiny of the just pagan.

When we have made allowance for imperfections of execution, and even for some intentional modification of character in old age (when Beowulf becomes not unnaturally much more like Hrothgar), it is plain that the characters and sentiments of the two chief actors in the poem are differently conceived and drawn. Where Beowulf's thoughts are revealed by the poet we can observe that his real trust was in *his own might*. That the possession of this might was a "favour of God" is actually a comment of the poet's, similar to the comment of Scandinavian Christians upon their heathen heroes. Thus in line 665 we have *georne truwode modgan mægenes, metodes hyldo* [he trusted eagerly in his courageous strength, the Lord's grace]. No *and* is possible metrically in the original; none should appear in translation: the favour of God *was* the possession of *mægen* [strength]. Compare 1272–73: *gemunde mægenes strenge, gimfæste gife ðe him God sealde* [he remembered his greatness of strength, the ample gift which God gave him].[36] Whether they knew

---

[36] Compare, for instance, the intrusive commentary in *Fóstbrœðra saga* which observes in a description of a grim pagan character: *ekki var hjarta hans sem fóarn í fugli, ekki var þat blóð ult, svá at þat skylfi af hræðslu, heldr var þat*

it or not, *cuþon* (or *ne cuþon*) *heofena Helm herian* [they knew (or did not know) to praise the Protector of heavens], the supreme quality of the old heroes, their valour, was their special endowment by God, and as such could be admired and praised.

Concerning Beowulf the poet tells us finally that when the dragon's ruinous assault was reported, he was filled with doubt and dismay, and *wende se wisa þæt he Wealdende ofer ealde riht ecean Dryhtne bitre gebulge* [the wise one thought that he had sorely angered the Ruler, the eternal Lord, over some old law]. It has been said that *ofer ealde riht*, "contrary to ancient law," is here given Christian interpretation; but this hardly seems to be the case. This is a heathen and unchristian fear—of an inscrutable power, a *Metod* that can be offended inadvertently: indeed the sorrow of a man who, though he knew of God, and was eager for justice, was yet far estranged, and "had hell in his heart."

(c) LINES 175–88

These lines are important and present certain difficulties. We can with confidence accept as original and genuine these words as far as *helle gemundon on modsefan* [they thought of hell in their minds] —which is strikingly true, in a sense, of all the characters depicted or alluded to in the poem, even if it is here actually applied only to those deliberately turning from God to the Devil. The rest requires, and has often received, attention. If it is original, the poet must have intended a distinction between the wise Hrothgar, who certainly knew of and often thanked God, and a certain party of the pagan Danes—heathen priests, for instance, and those that had recourse to them under the temptation of calamity—specially de-

---

hert af enum hæsta höfuðsmið i öllum hvatleik [his heart was not like the crop of a bird, nor was it full of blood so that it quivered with fear, rather it was hardened by the highest creator in every kind of courage] (ch. 2); and again *Almáttigr er sá sem svá snart hjarta ok óhrætt lét i brjóst Þorgeiri; ok ekki var hans hugpryði af mönnum ger né honum i brjóst borin, heldr af enum hæsta höfuðsmið* [It was the Almighty who put such a hard-twisted and fearless heart in Þorgeir's breast; and his courage was not made or infused in his breast by human means, but by the highest creator] (ib.). Here the notion is explicitly (if unseasonably and absurdly) expressed.

luded by the *gastbona*, the destroyer of souls.[37] Of these, particularly
those permanently in the service of idols (*swylce wæs þeaw hyra*
[such was their custom]), which in Christian theory and in fact did
not include all the community, it is perhaps possible to say that
they did not know (*ne cuþon*), nor even know of (*ne wiston*), the
one God, nor know how to worship him. At any rate the hell (of
fire) is only predicted for those showing malice (*sliðne nið*), and it is
not plain that the *freoðo* [peace] of the Father is ultimately obtain-
able by none of these men of old. It is probable that the contrast
between 92–98 and 175–88 is intentional: the song of the minstrel
in the days of untroubled joy, before the assault of Grendel, telling
of the Almighty and His fair creation, and the loss of knowledge
and praise, and the fire awaiting such malice, in the time of temptation and despair.

But it is open to doubt whether lines 181–88 are original, or at
any rate unaltered. Not of course because of the apparent discrepancy—though it is a matter vital to the whole poem: we cannot
dismiss lines simply because they offer difficulty of such a kind. But
because, unless my ear and judgement are wholly at fault, they
have a ring and measure unlike their context, and indeed unlike
that of the poem as a whole. The place is one that offers at once
special temptation to enlargement or alteration and special facilities
for doing either without grave dislocation.[38] I suspect that the
second half of line 180 has been altered, while what follows has

---

[37] It is not strictly true to say, as is said, for instance, by Hoops that he is
"identified" with their heathen god. The Christian theory was that such gods
did not exist, and were inventions of the Devil, and that the power of idols was
due to the fact that he, or one of his emissaries, often actually inhabited them,
and could be seen in their real hideousness if the veil of illusion was removed.
Compare Aelfric's homilies on St. Bartholomew, and St. Matthew, where by the
power of an angel or saint the devil residing in idols was revealed as a black
silhearwa [Ethiopian].

[38] Similarly it is the very marked character already by the poet given to
Hrothgar which has induced and made possible without serious damage the
probable revision and expansion of his sermon. Well done as the passage in itself
is, the poem would be better with the excision of approximately lines 1740–60;
and these lines are on quite independent grounds under the strongest suspicion
of being due to later revision and addition. The actual joints have, nevertheless,
if that is so, been made with a technical competence as good as that which I
here assume for the earlier passage.

remodelled or replaced a probably shorter passage, making the comment (one would say, guided by the poem as a whole) that they *forsook* God under tribulation, and incurred the danger of hell-fire. This in itself would be a comment of the *Beowulf* poet, who was probably provided by his original material with a reference to *wig-weorþung* [honor to idols] in the sacred site of Heorot at this juncture in the story.

In any case the *unleugbare Inkonsequenz* [undeniable inconsistency] (Hoops) of this passage is felt chiefly by those who assume that by references to the Almighty the legendary Danes and the Scylding court are depicted as "Christian." If that is so, the mention of heathen *þeaw* [custom] is, of course, odd; but it offers only one (if a marked) example of a confusion of thought fundamental to the poem, and does not then merit long consideration. Of all the attempts to deal with this *Inkonsequenz* [inconsistency] perhaps the least satisfactory is the most recent: that of Hoops,[39] who supposes that the poet had to represent the Danish prayers as addressed to the Devil for the protection of the honour of the *Christengott* [Christian God], since the prayers were not answered. But this attributes to the poet a confusion (and insincerity) of thought that an "Anglo-Saxon" was hardly modern or advanced enough to achieve. It is difficult to believe that he could have been so singularly ill instructed in the nature of Christian prayer. And the pretence that *all* prayers to the *Christengott* are answered, and swiftly, would scarcely have deceived the stupidest member of his audience. Had he embarked on such bad theology, he would have had many other difficulties to face: the long time of woe before God relieved the distress of these Christian Danes by sending Scyld (13); and indeed His permission of the assaults of Grendel at all upon such a Christian people, who do not seem depicted as having perpetrated any crime punishable by calamity. But in fact God did provide a cure for Grendel—Beowulf, and this is recognized by the poet in the mouth of Hrothgar himself (381 ff.). We may acquit the maker of *Beowulf* of the suggested motive, whatever we may think of the *Inkonsequenz*. He could hardly have been less aware than we that in history (in England and in other lands), and in Scripture, people

[39] *Kommentar zum Beowulf*, p. 39.

could depart from the one God to other service in time of trial—
precisely because that God has never guaranteed to His servants
immunity from temporal calamity, before or after prayer. It is to
idols that men turned (and turn) for quick and literal answers.

The Style and Structure of *Beowulf*

by Joan Blomfield *

The unity of *Beowulf* has long been taken for granted, but the sure construction of the poem has only of late been wholeheartedly affirmed.[1] Discrepancies and weaknesses which have puzzled earlier critics now begin to fall into their rightful places in a scheme of poetic conception with its own values. I do not attempt to probe these underlying values, but rather to indicate how they emerge in the plan and method of the poem. It is unfortunate that *Beowulf* is in many ways unique. Since no other poem of sufficient scope on the full heroic plan has survived, only in *Beowulf* can we follow the crystallization of structural processes in style and observe the features that certain modes of thought produce in each.

The setting out of the material is not in *Beowulf* an evolution, following one main line or connecting thread. Instead, the subject is disposed as a circumscribed field in which the themes are drawn out by a centre of attraction—in this case, the character of the good warrior. Far-flung tales and allusions, apparently scattered material and disconnected events are grouped in a wide sweep around the hero's character. In fact, these *are* his character, and their significance in the poem consists in this particular relation; by comparisons we are shown Beowulf's nature, by searchlights into the past and future we are to sense the magnitude and true import of his

"The Style and Structure of *Beowulf*." From *Review of English Studies*, XIV (1938), pp. 396–403. Copyright © 1938 by *Review of English Studies*. Reprinted by permission of the publisher.

* Miss Blomfield is now Mrs. G. Turville-Petre.

[1] Most notably by Professor Tolkien (*Beowulf: the Monsters and the Critics*, British Academy, 1936). His remarks on structure (especially pp. 34–38) contain the substance of almost everything I would wish to say. But this aspect of the poem has in general received so little attention that there seems to be room still for detailed exposition.

achievements. From this periphery he draws his substance and reality. By these means he lives and his destiny impregnates the whole poem. The good warrior is displayed as a being consummated through all phases of his life and in all aspects of his character. The whole progress from adventurous youth to wisdom-weighted old age, many discreet elements—the bear-warrior strength, the knightly courtesy, vanity beside humility, and so on—are comprehended in this static unity. It has often been observed that there is no development of plot or character. The concluding state of affairs must be implicit in the beginning. With such a plan, a pre-ordained course of events, familiar topics, and stock situations are essential for the achievement of depth and scope. Not by transitions and transformations but by suggestion of the ever-present identity of seed in fruit and fruit in seed does the poet adjust the emotional tension. The reference to the burning of Heorot woven into the description of its first glories, and the forecast of family strife while yet all is well in Hroðgar's court are straightforward instances. More complex is the messenger's announcement of Beowulf's death:[2] at great length he recounts the rising to power of the Geats—now to fall a prey to peoples they had overcome; their downfall will be the direct consequence of Beowulf's death—who died in defending them; he *þe us beagas geaf* [he who gave us rings] has gained with his last breath yet more *beagas* [rings],[3] treasure which is thus his personal perquisite, which in perishing with him on the pyre, shall symbolize the joys now to pass for ever from the Geats.[4] This tendency to antithesis, frequently verging on paradox, and the constant play of irony are but stylistic manifestations of those movements of the poet's thought which shape the very stuff of the poem.

Stylistic detail might be expected to give reliable indications of the lines on which the theme is constructed; and it is fortunate that

---

[2] 2900–3075.
[3] 3011–14:

> þær is maðma hord
> gold unrime grimme gecea(po)d
> ond nu æt siðestan sylfes feore
> beagas (geboh)te.

[there is a horde of treasures, countless gold grimly purchased and now at last rings bought with his own life.]

[4] 3015–24.

the style of *Beowulf* has attracted a large share of the most discerning criticism. Analysis of style is in this case a justifiable approach to analysis of structure. The general impression that *Beowulf,* lacking clarity and speed, is remarkable rather for depth and vibrancy needs explanation in terms both of style and of structure. These effects are partly due to a method of evocation and cross-reference in which contrast is an important element. Notable examples of description by contrast are the allusions to Sigemund, Heremod, and Offa; and there are constant lesser instances of this method and its corollary, parallelism. As a structural principle, it may be traced in the antiphonal exordium. We hear first of the mighty destiny and wide fame of the Scyldings.[5] The crescendo of Scylding power rouses opposing forces of cunning evil ever lurking to reverse the prosperity of mankind; by Grendel's raids the fame of the Scyldings is blasted, the utmost human effort frustrated, the mightiest of rulers made impotent. Beowulf is then introduced in all-powerful enterprise of untried youth. Here the concentration of the double flow increases: for Beowulf is connected with Hroðgar both by grateful allegiance, because of the favour shown to his father, and by his undertaking the trial of valour where others have failed. Complementing the knowledge that Hroðgar his *hold wine* [trusty friend] is in need is Beowulf's desire to crown his exploits by the supreme enterprise of *ðing wið þyrse* [affair against the monster]. The duty of allegiance emerges in Hroðgar's recapitulation of Beowulf's *æþelu* [noble descent] (457–72), the demands of Beowulf's career in his own account of his setting forth[6] (405–41). Both are presaged in the greeting of Wulfgar (338–39), who recognizes in the bearing of Beowulf the *wlenco* [daring] and *higeþrymm* [greatness of heart] which have brought him to Heorot, as contrasted with *wræcsið* [exile-journey] (which brought his father). The allusion is oblique— Wulfgar is challenging Beowulf as a stranger—and its application by so much the more pointed. This same alternation is at work

---

[5] Contributory themes in the same manner are insinuated: Scyld's rich burial is contrasted with his destitute arrival, and the last state of Heorot with the first.
  [6] *Cf.*

> *hæbbe ic mærða fela*
> *ongunnen on geogoþe*

[I have undertaken many famous deeds in youth] and the emphasis on *ana* [alone] (425, 431).

throughout the poem. The suspension of the theme—the "balance" of which Professor Tolkien speaks—demands a constant confrontation of similar and dissimilar.

A fundamental element in this balance is the poet's distribution of his material within the orbit of a central idea. The descriptive method of recurrence-with-elaboration distributes epithets and qualifying phrases in this way. The simplest form is piling of varied repetition, of the type: *eorlscipe efnde, ealdre geneðde, mærðo fremede* [I did heroic deeds, risked my life, performed glorious feats] (2132–33).[7] More complicated is the type: *þonne heoru bunden, hamere geþruen, sweord swate fah swin ofer helme ecgum dyhtig andweard scireð* [when the bound blade, forged by the hammer, the sword adorned with blood, with strong edges cuts against the swine over the helmet] (1285–87), or *forðon he ær fela nearo neðende niða gedigde, hildehlemma, syððan he Hroðgares, sigoreadig secg, sele fælsode; ond æt guðe forgrap Grendeles mægum laðan cynnes* [since he before, braving many distresses, endured the battle, the crash of combat, after he, the victory-blessed warrior, cleansed Hrothgar's hall; and crushed in fighting Grendel's family, the hostile race] (2349–53).[8] Here the amplification of several interdependent ideas is carried through by turns, so that the parts of the sentence are interlocked by a spaced and cumulative reinforcement—a method which reaches its ultimate development in the poetry of the Norse skalds. And in the last analysis, the "synonyms" so characteristic of Old English poetic diction express in little the multiplicity, the resolution into separate aspects, shown in the presentation of the theme itself.

For the structure of the poem is not sequential, but complemental; at the outset certain parts of a situation are displayed, and these are given coherence and significance by progressive addition of its other parts. Already Klaeber has noticed a circumscribing movement, and in the most penetrating passages of his criticism he constantly recurs to this idea.[9] He recognizes "an organic relation be-

---

[7] See also 50–52; 1228–59; 1408–10; 2421–23; 2602–4.
[8] See also 194–98; 1368–72; 1417–20; 1448–54; 2356–59.
[9] "Irregular, circuitous movements," p. lxv; "circuitous route," p. lxiii; "The thought of this passage, though proceeding by a circuitous route, is not obscure," note on 86–114: Klaeber's *Beowulf*, 3rd edition, 1936.

tween the rhetorical characteristics and certain narrower linguistic facts as well as the broader stylistic features and peculiarities of the narrative" (p. lxv), citing in particular "retardation by means of variations and parenthetical utterances" and further elaborating the idea in his statement: "The preponderance of the nominal over the verbal element, one of the outstanding features of the ancient diction, runs parallel to the favourite practice of stating merely the result of an action and of dwelling on a state or situation." Yet having worked out this organic relation and as good as stated the pervading conception imposing form on the whole material out to its fringes of verbal detail, he can suggest no structural unity, but speaks instead of "looseness" and "matter more or less detached from the chief narrative" (pp. liii, lvii).

Klaeber has noted the outstanding instances of a circumambient structure, although the heading under which he groups them—Lack of Steady Advance—again shows that he does not allow the principle its fundamental importance. Most clearly in the fight with Grendel, but also to some extent in the slaying of Grendel's mother and the account of the dragon's hoard, we see the unfolding of an event into its separate aspects. Apparently, the sum of them all—synchronism and the momentary visual impression—is the one aspect not considered poetically significant. The course of the fight in the hall is several times reviewed,[10] each time in different terms and with varying emphasis. Grendel's movements and motives and his final sense of defeat are first described (745–57). The poet next reverts to Beowulf's grapple, considered as a fulfilment of his *æfenspræc* [night-speech]. In 764–65 the climax, the tearing off of Grendel's arm, is obscurely stated in a metaphor.[11] The fight is then represented from the point of view of the Danes (765–90) who hear the din raging within their hall; the climax is here marked by the shriek of defeat, which is elaborated at some length (782–88). Lastly, the sensations of the Geats when they see their lord at grips with the monster provide an opportunity for contrasting Grendel's magic

---

[10] *Cf.* Klaber, pp. lviii and note on 710 ff.

[11] In support of this interpretation, *cf.* other instances of the concrete defined in abstract terms: *fela laf* [leavings of the file]; *wæteregesa,* "the terrible waters"; *fugles wynn,* [joy of the bird], Riddle 27, line 7, and the probable double entendre in *feorhlastas* [life-tracks], 846.

immunity from bite of iron with his impotence against the decrees
of providence (801–15); these reflections are concluded with an
explicit account of the severing of the claw, darkly alluded to before.
The outcome for each of the three parties—Beowulf, Grendel, and
the Danes—is then summed up, and the severed claw again mentioned, this time as the proof and symbol of Grendel's final defeat.
A similar disregard for the synchronizing of the separate aspects of
an action is seen in the defeat of Grendel's mother. Throughout the
struggle the poet draws out the implications of each stage; he describes the virtues of the magic sword which Beowulf seizes in his
desperation (1557 ff.), occupies seven lines with the brandishing
and victorious thrust, and next proceeds to display in one of his rare
similes the flash of light which marks the defeat of the sorceress
(1570–72). The beheading of Grendel's corpse is also worthy of note.
Much space is given to the retribution implied in this act, and the
appearance of the huge headless body is touched upon: only in the
final phrase is it stated *ond hine þa heafde becearf* [and then he
chopped off his head].

We learn of the dragon and his hoard by the same method of dis-
tributing essential parts of a situation into distinct groups. The first
mention of the dragon

> *oð ðæt an ongan*
> *deorcum nihtum draca ricsian*

[until that on dark nights one, a dragon, began to hold sway] (2211)

is followed by the incursion of the thief, which leads on to a description of the hoard as the heritage of a vanished line. By means
of the last survivor's speech as he consigned them to the earth, the
treasures are shown as emblems of mortal joys stilled by death in
the dim past. We hear no more of the history of the hoard until the
fight is over, and the Geats have only to look upon the ruin and
perform the exequies of their lord. Then another feature is brought
into play: the hoard is the direct cause of the deaths of the dragon
and Beowulf by reason of the heavy curse laid upon it. Thus the
functions of the hoard, as provoker of strife and as bringer of the
inevitable *worulde gedal* [parting from the world], are elaborated
in the appropriate contexts: not to mention its subsidiary contributions by way of contrast and symbolism.

To illustrate yet wider distribution of elements cohering in one theme, we may take the knitting together of Danish and Geatish history and the relation between Beowulf's account of the fights at Heorot and the earlier description. In the central portion of the poem, which is dominated by domestic and dynastic affairs and courtly observances, one of the three essential elements in the warrior's character is displayed. He must have violence and strength as of a beast, most fully exemplified in youth when he must win his spurs by marvellous deeds. Wisdom and submission to the decrees of providence again are essential. But equally he must take his place as an aristocrat fit to move among kings. When communal court life first comes into the scene (491–661) it is little more than a scaffolding for Beowulf's adventure with the sea-monsters and his *beot* [boast]. Its next appearance (1008–1237) is much more substantiated. The affairs of both Danish and Geatish courts are included: allusions to the *facenstafas* [treachery] between Hroðgar and Hroþulf (1018, 1164), the tale of Hnæf Scyldinga who fell in Freswæle, and also the downfall of Hygelac (1202). Beowulf is very honourably taken into this milieu, and his sphere extending over both courts is delineated. The next episode *þær guman druncon* [where the men drank] (1647) is entirely occupied with the glorification of Beowulf; the part he is to play as king of the Geats (1707–9, 1845–53) and the function of kingship is defined, by contrast with Heremod and by comparison of the tried wisdom of the elder ruler with the sagacity already apparent in the younger (1842–43).

Beowulf returns to the Geatish court (1928). In accordance with the filling and deepening of the courtly scene in this part, a disquisition on the ideal type of high-born lady, shown by contrast with Þryðo just as the ideal king is contrasted with Heremod, is attached to the person of Hygd. In Beowulf's subsequent relation of his adventure, the stress on the affairs of the Danish court is accentuated by a full account of the Heaðobard attack merely hinted at in connection with the building of the hall (82 ff.). All this helps to fill out the picture of court life. This strain is concluded in 2199, where we hear that Beowulf is accorded a position among the Geatish nobility differing only in degree from that of Hygelac himself. The account of the fights at Heorot depicts the value of these episodes as an approach to an assured position in the knightly hierarchy. The struggles are much toned down. Savage and fantastic elements are attributes of the earlier, more primitive Beowulf: here is no mention of the _leoht unfæger_ [light un-fair] streaming from Grendel's eyes, nor of the fearful din and the cry, nor of the fens beyond; of the severed claw it is said merely _him sio swiðre swaðe weardade_ [his stronger (hand) stayed behind]. Flatter, less vivid terms are used: _wearð . . . to muðbonan_ [was . . . the devourer] instead of _synsnædum swealh_ [he swallowed the huge morsel]; _eatol æfengrom_ [horrid evening-angry-one] is a concise but not very picturesque description of Grendel; the phrases _wæs . . . hild onsæge_ [the fight was fatal] (2076), _wæs . . . feorh uðgenge_ [was parted from life] (2123), _unc hwile wæs handgemæne_ [we two were for a while hand-joined] (2137) could not well be more abstract. Room is found for prosaic and curious detail, such as the name of the warrior Grendel devours and the description of the _glof_ [glove or pouch], neither given elsewhere. Emphasis is laid on the advancement of Beowulf's career: the princely rewards given (2101–3, 2134, 2142–47), his rôle as emissary of the Geats (2095–96), and his reliance on his _heafodmaga_ [near-relative] Hygelac (2148–51). The theme is brought out still further by innuendos defining knightly conduct by contrast (2166–69, 2177–83), and is finally closed on the dominant of Beowulf by a description of his boorish beginnings (2183–88)—a fact we learn only when it is introduced to heighten Beowulf's eminence and substantiate the comment that a _tireadig mann_ [glory-blessed man] will always make good.

The poetry of this time (like the visual art) reaches a high degree of abstraction and formalism. As far as his medium, a sequence of words, will allow, the poet has detached his theme from the processes of time and space and disregarded the appearances which for practical purposes constitute reality. He is able to evaluate his "action" directly, by exhibiting the parts in their aesthetic and moral relations. Hence the "moralizing" passages should be regarded as an integral part of the subject and are in no sense digressions—indeed, they are inextricably blended with some of the finest poetry in _Beowulf_. Emphasis on the causal relation is not required. The structure is not a progression, and follows no direct line. The writer of _Beowulf_ is in fact a true poet; he has created a tragic unity, he sees with the poet's eye which splits and recombines the elements of everyday perceptions. The signs and symbols that he uses are now unfamiliar, representations which need to be interpreted; we should not be misled into thinking them accidents. The ritual of language and exploitation of its metaphysical aspects which are the most outstanding features of this style have repeatedly won the attention of critics,[12] and provide the best clues to the underlying structural unity.

[12] *Cf.* Klaeber, pp. lxiii–lxvi.

Beowulf

by Richard Wilbur

The land was overmuch like scenery,
The flowers attentive, the grass too garrulous green;
In the lake like a dropped kerchief could be seen
The lark's reflection after the lark was gone;
The Roman road lay paved too shiningly
For a road so many men had traveled on.

Also the people were strange, were strangely warm.
The king recalled the father of his guest,
The queen brought mead in a studded cup, the rest
Were kind, but in all was a vagueness and a strain,
Because they lived in a land of daily harm.
And they said the same things again and again.

It was a childish country; and a child,
Grown monstrous, so besieged them in the night
That all their daytimes were a dream of fright
That it would come and own them to the bone.
The hero, to his battle reconciled,
Promised to meet that monster all alone.

So then the people wandered to their sleep
And left him standing in the echoed hall.
They heard the rafters rattle fit to fall,
The child departing with a broken groan,
And found their champion in a rest so deep
His head lay harder sealed than any stone.

"Beowulf." From *Ceremony and Other Poems* (New York: Harcourt, Brace & World, Inc.; London: Faber & Faber Ltd.), pp. 36–37. Copyright © 1948, 1949, 1950 by Richard Wilbur. Reprinted by permission of the author, Harcourt, Brace & World, Inc., and Faber & Faber Ltd.

The land was overmuch like scenery,
The lake gave up the lark, but now its song
Fell to no ear, the flowers too were wrong,
The day was fresh and pale and swiftly old,
The night put out no smiles upon the sea;
And the people were strange, the people strangely cold.

They gave him horse and harness, helmet and mail,
A jeweled shield, an ancient battle-sword,
Such gifts as are the hero's hard reward
And bid him do again what he has done.
These things he stowed beneath his parting sail,
And wept that he could share them with no son.

He died in his own country a kinless king,
A name heavy with deeds, and mourned as one
Will mourn for the frozen year when it is done.
They buried him next the sea on a thrust of land:
Twelve men rode round his barrow all in a ring,
Singing of him what they could understand.

Beowulf and Christian Allegory:
An Interpretation of Unferth

by Morton W. Bloomfield

In the discussion of the Christian elements in *Beowulf,* it seems to have escaped the notice of scholars that the character of Unferth may provide an example of Christian allegory consciously employed by the poet. If the name Unferth means mar-peace or strife, an important clue to his significance in the poem is being ignored. I wish to suggest that the author of *Beowulf* is employing, or at least thinking of, Unferth as an abstract personification in the manner of Prudentius, Martianus Capella or Sedulius, and that the poem has even closer connections with the Christian tradition than has hitherto been perceived. If we can accept Unferth as, say, *Discordia* [Discord], we shall find how well this interpretation fits in with the suggestion Schücking made some years ago that the character of Beowulf has been molded, to some extent at least, by the Christian ideal of the perfect ruler, the *rex justus* [just ruler], as set forth by St. Augustine, Gregory the Great and others, and that the ethical ideal set up by the epic is that of *ordinata concordia* [ordered concord] or *mensura* [measure].[1]

First, however, the meaning of the word *Unferth* must be discussed. Can we accept the traditional etymology and assume that the

---

"*Beowulf* and Christian Allegory: An Interpretation of Unferth." From *Traditio,* VII (1949–51), 410–15. Copyright © 1951 by the Fordham University Press. Reprinted by permission of the author and the Fordham University Press.

[1] Das Königsideal im Beowulf," *Englische Studien* LXVII (1932–33), 1–14. See also E. Otto, *Typische Schilderungen von Lebewesen, Gegenständlichem u. Vorgängen im weltlichen Epos der Angelsachsen* (Inaugural-Dissertation, Berlin, 1901) and A. Pirkhofer, *Figurengestaltung im Beowulf-Epos* (Anglistische Forschungen LXXXVII; Heidelberg, 1940) for somewhat similar approaches to the poem.

word is a combination of *un* (not) plus *ferth* or *frith* (peace), forming not-peace? Although this meaning is almost universally accepted, it must at least be pointed out that there are several alternate possibilities.

The name appears in the MS four times and always as Hunferð. It has been emended to Unferth, following Rieger's suggestion,[2] because it consistently alliterates with other vowels. The fact that the name is always misspelled by the Cotton Vitellius scribe or his model testifies to its unusual nature. He or one of his forbears simply did not understand the name and changed it to a more familiar form.[3]

It has been assumed by most scholars that the first theme in the name, *un,* is the negative particle. There is a possibility, however, that it may be an intensive as in the OE. *unhar* (very old).[4] It may even be a form of the ON. *hunn* (bear).[5] Germanic names do not, at least in historic times, have to mean anything.[6]

About the second theme, *-ferth,* there can be little room for disagreement. It is obviously a metathesized form of *frith* (peace) which occurs in many Germanic names both as a first and second name element.

It must also be recorded that forms similar to Unferth turn up among Continental Germanic peoples. There are no Scandinavian parallels to the name,[7] but we do find a Lombard *Unifridus*[8] and

---

[2] See *Zeitschrift für deutsche Philologie* III (1871), 414. It should also be noted that the use of *h* before *i* and *u* is especially common among late Latin and Celtic scribes merely to indicate the vowel quality of these letters, for *i* and *u* could also be consonants (*j* and *v*). Anglo-Saxon palaeography is much indebted to Celtic scribal habits.

[3] Hunfrid, and variants, was a fairly common Anglo-Saxon and early Middle English name. See T. Forssner, *Continental-Germanic Personal Names in England, in Old and Middle English Times* (Uppsala, 1916), pp. 158–59.

[4] See Forssner, *op cit.* p. 236 and W. Bruckner, *Die Sprache der Langobarden* (Quellen und Forschungen xxv; Strassburg, 1895), p. 84.

[5] See Forssner, *op. cit.* pp. 158–59 and Bruckner, *op. cit.* p. 314.

[6] See H. B. Woolf, *The Old Germanic Principles of Name-Giving* (Dissertation submitted to . . . The Johns Hopkins University . . . , Baltimore, 1939), pp. 263–64.

[7] Its ON. form would be * Ufriðr. See E. Björkmann, *Studien über die Eigennamen im Beowulf* (Studien zur Englischen Philologie, ed. L. Morsbach LVIII; Halle a. S. 1920), pp. 112–13.

[8] See Bruckner, *op. cit.* p. 269. The ending *-us* here is, of course, from the Latin documentary source.

various German forms—Unfrid, Unfrit, Umfrid.[9] Because of the various possible etymologies, however, these Continental parallels may not be true cognates.

Professor Kemp Malone has suggested another possibility for the etymology of Unferth.[10] But even he has to fall back in the last analysis upon the influence of "marpeace." In an endeavor to equate Unferth etymologically with the name of the villain Ívarr in the Hrethric story as told in the Icelandic *Sögubrot*, Professor Malone assumes, as a cognate form of Ívarr, an OE. *Infere which the *Beowulf*-poet touched up to Unferth, "trouble-maker," in the interests of poetry. Whether this rather unconvincing argument is acceptable or not, Professor Malone at least recognizes the influence of the accepted meaning of the name in shaping its final form.

The strongest argument, however, for the traditional view that Unferth means "mar-peace" is the role Unferth plays in the epic, at least in the beginning. The fact, too, that this name is an onomastic *hapax legomenon* [unique occurrence] in English or Scandinavian documents must also argue for its special and invented character. It occurs nowhere else in Old English or Old Norse records. Taking everything known so far into consideration, we may say that the name in *Beowulf* has an unusual character and must have the special significance suggested by its accepted meaning.

Unferth's part in the epic may be summarized as follows. After Beowulf has been welcomed at the Court of Hrothgar and speeches have been exchanged between the hero and the king, Unferth, a courtier, pricked on, the poet tells us, by jealousy, accuses Beowulf of foolhardy conduct in a swimming match with Breca years before and points out that he had been worsted by his opponent. It is obvious, Unferth says, that Beowulf will not be able to defeat Grendel. In his answer, Beowulf accuses his antagonist of having drunk too much beer and corrects his false story. He tells Unferth and the whole court that the swimming contest was the result of a youthful

---

[9] See E. Förstemann, *Altdeutsches Namenbuch*, I, *Personennamen* (Nordhausen etc., 1856), 1214. The later edition of Förstemann is not available to me, but we find sufficient examples here to show that the name was known. Förstemann suggests another possible etymology for *un:* from OHG, *unnan*, to give (see *ibid.* I, 1212). Hunfrid is very common in German records. Unfrid occurs, however, only eight times in those which Förstemann examined.

[10] *PMLA*, XLII (1927), 300 ff.

boast and that both he and Breca covered themselves with honor. Further, he taunts Unferth with having failed to destroy Grendel himself and of having killed his own brother. Unferth, son of Ecglaf, is thereupon silenced.

Later, after the victory over Grendel, there is rejoicing in the hall, and a scop relates the Finn episode. After the lay has been recited, Unferth, now called a *thyle* [court speaker], is again mentioned. Wealtheow, Hrothgar's queen, approaches the throne where Unferth is sitting at the feet of Hrothgar. Both she and the king, the poet tells us, trust him and his courage, even though he did kill his kinsman. Then the queen addresses Hrothgar and, after praising Beowulf, speaks of her worries about her young children. She lauds Hrothulf, the king's nephew. This speech has been rightly interpreted as referring to Hrothulf's ambition to seize the throne (which, as Scandinavian sources indicate, he actually did upon Hrothgar's death) and as an appeal to Beowulf for aid in that eventuality. From this allusion, it has been assumed that Unferth played an important role in the later dynastic quarrel and that he is really unessential in the Beowulf story and only a necessary "figure in the origin of the Scylding feud." [11] Olrik believes he instigated the quarrel between Hrothulf and Hrothgar's sons, supporting the latter.[12] The evidence for this is highly conjectural.

Unferth makes his final appearance in the poem just before Beowulf plunges into the fearsome mere for his struggle with Grendel's mother. He presents the hero with his own special sword, Hrunting, as a sign of reconciliation and submission. He had apparently, the poet says, forgotten his scornful words when drunk.

This, then, is the story of Unferth's activities. He first pours scorn upon Beowulf to discredit him and then finally is brought to recognize a superior being. A brief allusion before the reconciliation

---

[11] See A. Olrik, *The Heroic Legends of Denmark,* trans. Lee M. Hollander (Scandinavian Monographs IV; New York, 1919), p. 58. Olrik seems to be somewhat confused in his discussion of Unferth. He appears to be saying that he was and was not invented by the *Beowulf*-poet. It is possible that he is making a distinction between Unferth's name and role. It is clear, however, that Olrik believes that he belongs originally to the Scylding rather than the Beowulf episodes. "Therefore the figure of Unferth cannot have been created for the purposes of a Beowulf epic but is a necessity in the economy of the Scylding story"; *ibid.* p. 58.

[12] *Ibid.* p. 60.

scene may hint at Unferth's participation in the dynastic quarrels of the Scyldings. He held the office of *thyle* [court speaker] and had earlier slain a brother.

Various explanations of Unferth have been put forth, most of them concerned with the origin of the figure, but my purpose is not really to refute any theory except perhaps that which Olrik has urged, that he is not essential to the Beowulf story. My concern here is not with the genesis of the figure. Unferth may have originally been an essential element of the Bear Son's folktale.[13] He may have had an historical role in the Scylding dynastic quarrels.[14] He may even have been influenced by the character of Bricriu in the Irish *Fled Bricrend*.[15] These suggestions are all really concerned with the question of the *genesis* of the figure, but I am concerned with what the *Beowulf*-poet did with Unferth, no matter where he came from—from folklore, history, Irish or Scandinavian sagas, or from the poet's own subconscious. To the author, Unferth had a function in his epic. What did he conceive of his character, wherever he may have come from? And if Unferth did come from some source other than the imagination of the poet, he, as we have seen, was given a new name, probably to indicate his role in the work.

✗ It is my contention that the author of *Beowulf* consciously patterned the figure of Unferth after the personified abstractions currently used in the Christian Latin poetry with which he was familiar. I am not concerned with any particular identification, but I do suggest that he did think of Unferth as *Discordia*, as his name indicates. Perhaps the most famous figure of that name which could have been known to him occurs in Prudentius' *Psychomachia* where *Discordia* (heresy) is the antagonist of *Concordia*. The *Beowulf*-poet may have used Unferth as *Discordia*, however, without especially modeling him on the Prudentian character. I do urge, however, that he was consciously using the allegorical method in shaping Unferth

[13] See F. Panzer, *Studien zur Germanischen Sagengeschichte*, I: *Beowulf* (Munich, 1910), 279 ff.

[14] As Olrik, *op. cit.* suggests. See also H. Munro Chadwick, *The Heroic Age* (Cambridge, 1912), pp. 159–60.

[15] See M. Deutschbein, "Die sagenhistorischen und literarischen Grundlagen des Beowulfepos," *Germanisch-Romanische Monatsschrift* I (1909), 114–15. Deutschbein has been effectively answered by O. L. Olson, "*Beowulf and The Feast of Bricriu*," *Modern Philology* XI (1913–14), 418 ff.

and that this method is a legacy of the Christian tradition brought to England after 597.

Beowulf was written, as most commentators agree, around 700 in England, possibly in Northumbria. It is also agreed, as is quite obvious, that *Beowulf* contains Christian elements or "coloring" in spite of its pagan story. The Christianity of the poem is so deeply embedded in the texture of the epic that it could not have been interpolated. The poet was a Christian and, as such, was indebted to the Christian tradition as it manifested itself in England at the end of the seventh or beginning of the eighth century. His point of view, his references to Biblical story, his ethical standards, even if we do not accept Schücking's *mensura* [measure], and his eschatology are all Christian. If we grant these elements—and we must—why cannot we accept allegory, which was introduced into England as part of Christian culture? The lives of Aldhelm and Bede were at least partially contemporary with that of our poet. Prudentius was referred to and drawn upon by both.[16] Sedulius and Paulinus of Nola, both of whom employed allegory, were known to Aldhelm at least.[17] Nor were pagan Latin allegorists, such as Claudian, unknown in England. Aldhelm used the allegorical method extensively in his own poetry and prose.

In contradiction to Girvan's statement that "it [the personification of a sentiment] is a recognized method of Germanic poetry," [18] we may say that personification is a recognized method of Christian Latin poetry. When allegory is used in Germanic poetry,[19] it is a Christian element. In fact, it is a sign of Christian influence.

I do not wish to over-emphasize the role of allegory in *Beowulf*. The poet was telling a concrete story about historical or semi-historical people. It is primarily a narrative poem, not a *Romance of the Rose*. Yet if we recognize allegory in the work as an element in the whole, we can only enrich and deepen our appreciation of it. The *Beowulf*-poet is struggling with various types of material and

---

[16] See J. D. A. Ogilvy, *Books Known to Anglo-Latin Writers from Aldhelm to Alcuin (670–804)* (The Mediaeval Academy of America, Studies and Documents II; Cambridge, Mass., 1936), pp. 76–77.

[17] *Ibid.* pp. 79–80 and 70.

[18] *Beowulf and the Seventh Century, Language and Content* (London, 1935), pp. 67–68.

[19] Girvan's examples of "Germanic" allegory are simply not to the point.

endeavoring to work them into a whole. He is relating a story, moralizing upon that story, endeavoring to weld together the concepts of pagan *wyrd* [fate] and Christian grace, and employing pagan folklore. Together with all these elements, he introduces in the figure of Unferth, Christian allegory. If he conceived of Beowulf as the *rex justus* [just ruler] or ideal king, the defeat of discord in the person of Unferth is demanded. If the ethic of the poem is based on *ordinata concordia* [ordered concord], *discordia* [discord] must be overthrown. Prudentius tells the story of how Discord wounds Concord and is killed by Faith. Beowulf, however, defeats his antagonist, not by force, but by example, and Unferth hands over his sword, the symbol of his might. Without trying to reduce the relation of Beowulf to Unferth to the purely allegorical level of Faith or Concord versus Discord, I do urge that such concepts were in the poet's mind as he dealt with what was perhaps a well-known story and that by giving the enemy the name of Unferth he wished to suggest this overhanging meaning (not necessarily as in Prudentius) to his readers. The story was colored by the allegorical pattern.

Several other possible abstractions appear in the poem. Wonred, father of Wulf and Eofor,[20] it has already been pointed out by Weyhe,[21] may well be "void of advice" or "void of power"; terms which could well indicate the fate the Geats were to undergo. Hygd, Hygelac's queen, is "thought." Unferth is not unique in the epic. In the contemporary *Widsith,* Unwen may be "hopelessness," "despair," rather than "the unexpected one." [22] True allegory is the personification of an abstract quality. On the other hand, a descriptive name such as Widsith (the far-traveller) is not allegorical. Widsith is rather a nickname. This distinction between quality and descriptive names must be maintained.

One further point. Unferth is called a *thyle,* a word which is usually translated as "orator" or "spokesman," on the basis of later Latin glosses. This office has been assumed to be an official court position.[23] It has been suggested, however, that a *thyle* (cognate

---

[20] Line 2971.

[21] See "König Ongentheows Fall," *Englische Studien* XXXIX (1908), 36.

[22] Line 114. See K. Malone, *Widsith* (London, 1936), p. 193.

[23] Recently it has been suggested that Unferth is the "Urbild des Hofnarren" [prototype of court jesters]; see R. Stumpfl, *Kultspiele der Germanen als Ursprung des mittelalterlichen Dramas* (Berlin, 1936), p. 397.

with ON. *þulr*) may have been a pagan priest.[24] If such is the case, would it not be appropriate for the Christian *rex justus* to bring about the submission of paganism in the person of Unferth, discord-heresy? [25] Not all the pagan priests would be as obliging as Coifi, who, seventy-five years before *Beowulf* was written, profaned his own heathen altars after hearing Paulinus preach.[26] The obscurity of the word *thyle*, however, prevents us from pushing this interpretation too far.

Nineteenth-century romantic and nationalistic scholarship, often German, to which we owe much of both good and evil, over-emphasized the pagan aspects of the oldest known Germanic epic. It has been difficult to shed this point of view and to see the essential Christianity of *Beowulf*.[27] It belongs to the Christian tradition, not only in mood and ideals, and in occasional Biblical references, but, at least partially and tentatively, in literary technique. An old Scandinavian tale has been changed into a Christian poem. Viewing Unferth as colored by the allegorical figure *Discordia*, enables us to join *Beowulf* with the Christian Middle Ages in a way not hitherto possible. It is the work of a poet who was close to the new religion which was transforming Britain in his time, as it had earlier transformed the Roman Empire, and was later, by the help of his fellow-countrymen and others, to be carried beyond its borders into Germany and Eastern Europe. The character of Unferth is an integral part of *Beowulf*. He is the opponent and the foil of the hero; he enhances his might; he is proof of his moderation, faith and glory.

[24] See B. S. Phillpotts, *The Elder Edda and Ancient Scandinavian Drama* (Cambridge, 1920), 181 ff. and H. Munro & N. Kershaw Chadwick, *The Growth of Literature*, I: *The Ancient Literatures of Europe* (Cambridge, 1932), 618 ff. The murder of Unferth's brother may have had a ritual significance. See also Professor Kemp Malone's review of W. H. Vogt's *Stilgeschichte der eddischen Wissensdichtung* in *Modern Language Notes* XLIV (1929), 129-30.

[25] The word "heresy" was used in a loose sense in the early Middle Ages. Any enemy of the Holy Catholic faith could be termed heretical.

[26] Bede, *Historia ecclesiastica gentis Anglorum* pp. 2, 13.

[27] "For the essential Christianity of *Beowulf* impresses me more and more with each re-reading of the poem" (from a private letter to me from Professor Henry Bosley Woolf dated January 7, 1948). See Professor Woolf's recent article, "Unferth," *Modern Language Quarterly* X (1949), 45-52, published since this paper was written, for an acute analysis of the role of Unferth in the structure of *Beowulf*, which supplements and reinforces my arguments.

The Dramatic Audience in *Beowulf*

by R. M. Lumiansky

Since it is usually assumed that the events in the main plot of *Beowulf*—that is, the fights against the monsters—were well known to the poet's contemporaries, and since the poet makes frequent use of anticipatory comment concerning the outcome of these fights, the conclusion seems to be held generally that "disregard of the element of suspense was not considered a defect in story telling." [1] A recent critic, however, opposes this view, and maintains that for the *Beowulf* poet's contemporaries suspense lay in their desire to know just "how the [foreshadowed] end will be reached" in the poem.[2] While I agree that the poet did not disregard the element of suspense, there is, I think, a more tangible reason for this suspense which is inherent in the events of the primary narrative of *Beowulf* even though the poet has regularly foreshadowed the outcome. That reason lies in the poet's employing a device which may be called *the dramatic audience,* an audience made up of functional onlookers for the narrative event. For Beowulf's encounter in Heorot with Grendel, the terror-stricken Danes and the bewildered Geats serve as dramatic audience; for his underwater struggle against Grendel's dam, the Danes and Geats who wait at the water's edge fill this role; for his fight against the dragon, Wiglaf and the cowardly thanes are the functional onlookers. In each instance, I shall maintain, the reader's

"The Dramatic Audience in *Beowulf*." From *Journal of English and Germanic Philology,* LI (1952), 545-50. Copyright © 1952 by *Journal of English and Germanic Philology.* Reprinted by permission of the publisher.

[1] F. Klaeber, *Beowulf* (3d edition with two supplements, 1950), p. lvii. See also W. W. Lawrence, *Beowulf and Epic Tradition* (1928), p. 23; Adrien Bonjour, "The Use of Anticipation in *Beowulf*," *RES*, XVI (1940), 290-99; J. R. R. Tolkien, "Beowulf: The Monsters and the Critics," *Proceedings of the British Academy,* XXII (1936), 250, 272-75.

[2] J. R. Hulbert, "*Beowulf* and the Classical Epic," MP, XLIV (1946), 71.

interest in the event is heightened because he experiences Beowulf's action in large part through the dramatic audience, whose very safety depends upon the outcome, of which they have no previous knowledge. In other words, by means of this device, the poet establishes suspense in spite of anticipatory comment. Let us now examine the operation of the dramatic audience for each of the three fights.

When Beowulf, with his fourteen Geatish companions and an unstated number of Danes, takes up his station in Heorot to await Grendel, there is no least doubt that the monster will appear that night. The hall is quiet; all the warriors are asleep except Beowulf; Grendel breaks down the door, eats Handscio, and reaches for Beowulf. The latter grasps Grendel's arm; realizing that he has met a greater fighter, Grendel at once tries to flee. At this point, the poet shifts to the dramatic audience, the Danish warriors. They were presumably awakened when Grendel burst through the door, and since the hall is dark, illumined only by the horrible light flashing from Grendel's eyes, these Danes know nothing of the progress of the fight except what they hear. For twenty-four lines (ll. 767–90) the poet follows the fight through the reactions of the waiting Danes, whose thoughts are concentrated on Heorot, the symbol for them of tribal security and prosperity. First, convinced from the commotion that all is lost, they feel sharp regret that their hall is doomed. Next, they experience wonder, a kind of disbelief, that the hall can withstand the heavy buffeting which is resulting from the fight. Finally, they are gripped by stark terror when they hear Grendel's awful cry. The poet has skilfully arranged these three reactions climactically,[8] and though by expository comment he earlier indicated clearly Grendel's defeat in the encounter, his centering of attention here upon the waiting Danes establishes suspense, for they have no way of knowing what is happening until Grendel has fled. Further, the poet also uses the thirteen remaining Geats for a similar purpose. They, unlike the Danes, are not terrified by the noise of the fight; rather, they draw their swords in order to help their leader, but, so far as we can tell, they succeed only in floundering about confusedly in the darkness. It goes without saying that both Danes and Geats await the outcome with the keenest concern. Thus, through use of

[8] For a more detailed analysis of this passage, see *JEGP*, XLVIII (1949), 116–26.

the two groups, the poet has led the reader to view this fight, the result of which he already knows, with heightened interest.

We move now to Beowulf's fight with Grendel's dam. When the hero goes into the mere to seek the monster, the Danes and Geats sit on the shore to await his return. The poet then rapidly relates the three phases of Beowulf's struggle with Grendel's dam: first, his sword fails to harm her; second, they grapple and she would have killed him except that his corselet turns away the point of her *seax* [knife]; third, he kills her with the wondrous sword, "ealdsweord eotenisc" [gigantic old-sword], cutting through her neck bones. Then he chops off the head of Grendel. For the outcome of this encounter the poet used only one anticipatory comment, which comes just after Beowulf's corselet has saved his life:

> Hæfde ðā forsīðod   sunu Ecgþēowes
> under gynne grund,   Gēata cempa,
> nemne him heaðobyrne   helpe gefremede,
> herenet hearde,—   and hālig God
> gewēold wīgsigor;   wītig Drihten,
> rodera Rǣdend   hit on ryht gescēd
> ȳðelīce, syþðan hē eft āstōd.   [Ll. 1550–56.]

[Then he would have perished, the son of Ecgtheow, under the wide ground, the champion of the Geats, had not his battle-mailshirt rendered him aid, his hard war-net,—and holy God brought about battle-victory; the wise Lord, Ruler of the heavens decided it rightly with ease, after he stood up again.]

But, having completed the rapid account of the fight, the poet shifts (ll. 1591–1605) to the warriors who wait with Hroðgar on the shore; though we now know the outcome and the details of the fight, these warriors whose security depends upon the result are completely without this knowledge. And once again the reader experiences an event through the reactions of a dramatic audience. The Danes and Geats soon notice that the waves are stained with blood. The elders of the Scylding tribe conclude that Grendel's dam has killed Beowulf; Hroðgar and his warriors, having waited until the ninth hour, depart homeward. The Geats remain, staring at the water, hoping almost without hope that Beowulf will reappear. By means of this fourteen-line passage the poet has effectively presented, first, the nervous anxiety, second, the deep despair, and third, the almost hopeless uncertainty of the watchers by the shore.

There is one further point which calls for discussion in connection with this passage. Here, as in the previous fight-scene, the author has treated the reactions of the two national groups—Danes and Geats—separately and somewhat differently. When Beowulf fought Grendel in the darkness of Heorot, the Danes, as we saw, were terror stricken, while the Geats were steadfast though bewildered. Now, at the water's edge, both groups, assuming that the blood which mingles with the waves is Beowulf's, seem convinced that the hero is dead. First, the poet remarks of the Danish group: "Blondenfeaxe, / gomele ymb gōdne ongeador spræcon, / þæt hig þaes æðelinges eft ne wēndon, / þæt hē sighreðig sēcean cōme / mǣrne pēoden. . . ." [The grey-haired old men spoke together about the brave one, that they did not expect the noble again, that he victory-rejoicing would come to seek their famous prince.] Shortly thereafter, with reference to the Geats, the poet says: "Gistas sētan / mōdes sēoce ond on mere staredon; / wīston ond ne wēndon, þæt hīe heora winedrihten / selfne gesāwon." [The visitors sat down, sick in spirit, and stared upon the pool; they hoped but did not expect that they would see their friendly-lord himself again.] But the Danes leave the scene, while the Geats remain. Most commentators upon and translators of the poem appear to feel that this departure of the Danes is to be blamed, that they "forsook" Beowulf. Klaeber, following P. F. Jones, suggests that the Danes' leaving at this point is a vestige of the Bear's Son Tale, in that they represent the faithless companions of the tale.[4] To my mind, the passage permits of an entirely different interpretation. The crucial line reads, "Næs ofgēafon hwate Scyldingas," which means literally, "The valiant Scyldings left the bluff." The verb-form *ofgēafon* does not usually imply *desertion,* and the adjective *hwate* can mean only *valiant, brave, spirited,* or the equivalent. I think that a more easily understandable explanation of the Danes' departure is that Hroðgar and his warriors, like the Geats, convinced that Beowulf is dead, courteously withdraw to allow the Geats to mourn their supposedly lost leader in private. Surely, if the poet meant to show the Danes in a despicable, faithless role he would not have pointed out that

⁴ Klaeber, *op. cit.,* p. xiv, n. 2; P. F. Jones, *MLN,* XLV (1930), 300 f.

they waited at the shore until the ninth hour; and, especially, he would not have called them *valiant* just when they are in the act of leaving the bluff.

In either case, we have seen that the poet's shift for fourteen lines to the reactions of the watchers by the water's edge has served to invest Beowulf's fight against Grendel's dam with an atmosphere of heightened suspense. Let us look now at the last encounter, in which Beowulf kills and is killed by the dragon. Almost from the very moment that the dragon discovers the theft of the cup from his hoard, the reader is aware that this fight will end in Beowulf's death. The poet says: "Wæs se fruma egeslīc/lēodum on lande, swā hyt lungre wearð/on hyra sincgifan sāre geendod" [The beginning was fearful to the people of the land, as it was forthwith for their treasure-giver sorely ended.] (ll. 2309–11). Time after time this anticipatory note of doom is sounded in the poet's expository comment, and Beowulf himself feels that his end is near: "brēost innan wēoll/þēostrum geþoncum, swā him geþȳwe ne wæs" [His breast welled within with dark thoughts, which was not customary with him.] (ll. 2331–32). But Beowulf resolutely prepares to meet the dragon, and selects eleven warriors to accompany him. The unwilling thief guides the group to the vicinity of the dragon's mound. Beowulf instructs his companions to await on a nearby hill the outcome of the fight, and advances to meet the monster. In the first phase of the battle, Beowulf's sword fails to cut through the dragon's scales, and the hero is scorched by the monster's fiery breath.

At this point (ll. 2592–2601) the poet shifts to the dramatic audience, the companions who are watching the fight. He says that as Beowulf and the dragon came together for the second time Beowulf, surrounded by fire, suffered greatly; then his companions, rather than coming to help him, flee to the wood to save their lives. This terrified reaction of the dramatic audience, differing so sharply from the primary virtues of courage and loyalty expected of a Germanic warrior, certainly broadens the reader's interest in the fight; and throughout the reader is kept aware of this cowardly group by Wiglaf's recriminatory speeches to them and by his contrasting bravery in aiding his leader.

We need here to examine briefly the character and actions of young Wiglaf. The view is apparently widely held that when the cowardly companions flee to the wood Wiglaf bravely stands his ground and then advances to aid Beowulf. Klaeber, for example, says, "[Beowulf's] terrified companions flee to the wood, all save Wiglaf, who, mindful of the obligations of loyalty and gratitude, hastens to the assistance of his kinsman." [5] But, as I understand the text, Wiglaf first flees with the others. As we saw, the passage in which the flight is stated points out that the companions—presumably all eleven of them—instead of helping Beowulf, flee to the wood. Then the immediately following lines read: "Hiora in ānum wēoll / sefa wið sorgum; sibb æfre ne mæg / wiht onwendan þām ðe wēl þenceð" [The heart of one of them welled with sorrows; not ever may he put aside kinship who thinks rightly.] (ll. 2599–2601). The crucial word here is *sorgum,* literally *sorrows;* but the best translation for the word in this context is, I think, *remorse;* Wiglaf feels remorse because he fled; unless he had fled with the group he could hardly have attempted to rally them with words, as he does. Surely, we are not meant to understand that he delivers this twenty-seven-line speech (ll. 2633–60) from the hill to the thanes who have fled to the wood, presumably some distance away. The point is that the poet presents important dramatic development in young Wiglaf, the untried kinsman of Beowulf, who in the moment of excitement flees with the group, but who quickly realizes his mistake and acts accordingly.

The remainder of the fight is rapidly recorded. Beowulf smites the dragon with his sword, but Nægling breaks; the dragon injures Beowulf in the neck; Wiglaf wounds the dragon in his soft underbelly; then Beowulf delivers the death blow with his dagger. But Beowulf's own death, so frequently predicted in the anticipatory comment, follows quickly after Wiglaf has shown him some of the treasures from the mound. Then the cowardly thanes, who have remained in the wood since Wiglaf left them, come forward shame-facedly and receive their punishment. By contrast, this cowardly group serves to emphasize one of the chief themes of the whole poem, as Wiglaf's concluding words to them indicate: "Dēað bið sēlla / eorla gehwylcum þonne edwītlīf!" [Death is better for every noble than a life of disgrace!] (ll. 2890–91). But the poet's inclusion

[5] *Op. cit.,* p. xii.

of these deserters in his account of the fight has also played a vital part in sustaining and deepening the reader's interest in the narrative.

We have seen, then, that the question of plot originality for the poet's contemporaries is more or less irrelevant in connection with the presence of lack of sustained suspense in the accounts of Beowulf's three great fights; for the poet has carefully foreshadowed the outcome of each. However, suspense does arise from the poet's skilful inclusion in each instance of a dramatic audience, whose security depends upon the result of the fight, and from whose point of view the reader is led to regard the fight. And we should not fail to note that the effectiveness of this device comes in part from the variety with which it is employed. In no two of the three cases are the situation and the reaction of the dramatic audience exactly similar. We hear the first fight through the ears of the frightened Danes and of the steadfast though confused Geats, who are right on the scene with Beowulf and Grendel in dark Heorot. In the second instance, we know that Beowulf has conquered Grendel's dam, but then we experience the deep despair of the watchers on the shore, who, having seen only the blood on the waters, conclude that Beowulf is dead. In the final encounter, we see the terrified flight of the thanes, and the dramatic recollection of his duty by Wiglaf, which results in a member of the dramatic audience himself becoming an important and unexpected participant in the action. That the *Beowulf* poet did not include these three dramatic audiences with the conscious purpose of heightening suspense and sustaining interest, I find hard to believe.

Oral-Formulaic Character of Anglo-Saxon
Narrative Poetry[1]

by Francis P. Magoun, Jr.

In the course of the last quarter-century much has been discovered about the techniques employed by unlettered singers in their composition of narrative verse. Whereas a lettered poet of any time or place, composing (as he does and must) with the aid of writing materials and with deliberation, creates his own language as he proceeds, the unlettered singer, ordinarily composing rapidly and extempore before a live audience, must and does call upon ready-made language, upon a vast reservoir of formulas filling just measures of verse. These formulas develop over a long period of time; they are the creation of countless generations of singers and can express all the ideas a singer will need in order to tell his story, itself usually traditional. This progress is primarily due to the work of two men, the late Milman Parry[2] and his former pupil and successor

[1] This paper is, with revisions, essentially the second ("The Formulaic Character of Anglo-Saxon Narrative Poetry") of three Special University Lectures (series-title "Oral-Formulaic Tradition in Anglo-Saxon Poetry"), delivered at the invitation of the University of London in the Senate House on January 10, 17, and 24, 1952, and was written in March 1952. The first two pages or so present the sense of the first lecture ("The Art and Craft of Oral Poetry"), while the last few pages similarly digest the third ("Some Problems of the Future"). Charts I and II are revisions of mimeographed counterparts distributed at the second lecture.

[2] For a complete bibliography of the writings of Milman Parry, see A. B. Lord, "Homer, Parry, and Huso," *American Journal of Archaeology*, LII (1948), 43–44. Two of Parry's papers may be specially noted as representing the full development of his thought: "Studies in the Epic Technique of Oral Verse-Making, I: Homer and Homeric Style," *Harvard Studies in Classical Philology*, XLI (1930),

in this field, Professor Albert Bates Lord of Harvard University.[3] First in connection with Homeric language, later as a result of fieldwork in Yugoslavia, chiefly among unlettered Muslim singers, Parry, aided by Lord, demonstrated that the characteristic feature of all orally composed poetry is its totally formulaic character. From this a second point emerged, namely, that the recurrence in a given poem of an appreciable number of formulas or formulaic phrases brands the latter as oral, just as a lack of such repetitions marks a poem as composed in a lettered tradition. Oral poetry, it may be safely said, is composed entirely of formulas, large and small, while lettered poetry is never formulaic, though lettered poets occasionally consciously repeat themselves or quote verbatim from other poets in order to produce a specific rhetorical or literary effect. Finally, it is clear that an oral poem until written down has not and cannot have a fixed text, a concept difficult for lettered persons; its text, like the text of an orally circulating anecdote, will vary in greater or lesser degree with each telling. The oral singer does not memorize either the songs of singers from whom he learns nor later does he memorize in our sense of the word songs of his own making. His apprenticeship involves the learning of thematic material, plots, proper names, and formulas with which he will gradually become able to compose in

---

73–147, esp. pp. 118–21 for charts exposing the formulaic character of ll. 1–25 of the *Iliad* and the *Odyssey* respectively; and "II: The Homeric Language as the Language of Oral Poetry," *ibid.*, XLIII (1932), 1–50, esp. pp. 12–17 ("The Art of Oral Poetry"). These papers are cited here as Parry I and II and by page.

[3] Parry in the summer of 1933, and Parry and Lord in the years 1934–35, studied the production of the oral epic style in Yugoslavia and collected some 12,500 texts, "The Parry Collection of South-Slavic Texts," now deposited in the Harvard College Library. Following Parry's lead and working with this opulent material Lord submitted in 1949 a Ph.D. thesis (Harvard, unpublished), "The Singer of Tales: A Study in the Process of Yugoslav, Greek, and Germanic Oral Poetry." Lord revisited Yugoslavia in 1950 and 1951; for his report on the collecting trip of 1950 see "Yugoslav Epic Folk Poetry," *Journal of the International Folk Music Council*, III (1951), 57–61. His thesis, revised and expanded, will be published by the Harvard University Press as *The Singer of Tales* in the series "Harvard Studies in Comparative Literature."

P.S. The work of Parry and Lord and the rich material preserved at Harvard were very familiar to Sir Cecil Maurice Bowra and utilized by him in his *Heroic Poetry* (London: Macmillan, 1952). This distinguished work appeared too late for me to use in preparing my London lectures or in preparing this paper, though I am happy to be able to add a specific reference or two in the footnotes below. For an excellent review of Sir Maurice's book see *The Times Literary Supplement*, Friday, December 12, 1952, p. 824.

regular verse songs of his own. A good singer is one able to make better use of the common fund of formulas than the indifferent or poor singer, though all will be drawing upon essentially the same body of material. The length of a song or, better, the length of a given performance (since there is no fixed text) will largely depend upon the audience-factor, on how much time an audience has to give to the singer on any given occasion. A good singer can go on as long as an audience will listen to him, be it persons assembled in a Bosnian coffee-house, or in the presence of a tape-recorder or a stenographer. The analogies with musical improvisation will be evident.

The present paper is essentially an extension into the realm of Anglo-Saxon narrative poetry of the work of Parry and Lord, to whom it is indebted at every turn and in more ways than can easily be expressed. Indeed, without the stimulation of Parry's published works and the works and spoken words of Albert Lord, the present paper or, indeed, anything like it could not have been written.

When one first reads of the existence of Anglo-Saxon poetry in the seventh century in Bede's account of Cædman (*H.E.*, IV, 22 [24]), there is every reason to believe that already behind this lay a long tradition, running back to the Continental home-land and into a distant common Germanic heritage, a tradition of at least seven centuries and probably more. Toward the end of the first century A.D. Cornelius Tacitus comments on the art of poetry among the Germanic peoples of his day, and from that time on there are allusions by authors from late antiquity to the singing of songs among various Germanic tribes. Since these ancient Germanic singers were unlettered, their poetry must have been oral, and its diction, accordingly, must have been formulaic and traditional. The birth of this diction must have taken place in a very distant past and, like the birth of any diction, is beyond observation. As Parry observes of Homeric language:

> A single man or even a whole group of men who set out in the most careful way could not make even a beginning at such an oral diction. It must be the work of many poets over many generations. When one singer . . . has hit upon a phrase which is pleasing and easily used, other singers will hear it, and then, when faced at the same (metrical) point in the line with the need of expressing the same idea, they will

recall it and use it. If the phrase is so good poetically and so useful metrically that it becomes in time the one best way to express a certain idea in a given length of verse, and as such is passed on from one generation of poets to another, it has won a place for itself in the oral diction as a formula. But if it does not suit in every way, or if a better way of fitting the idea into the verse and sentence is found, it is straightway forgotten or lives only for a short time, since with each new poet and with each new generation of poets it must undergo the twofold test of being found pleasing and useful. In time the needed number of such phrases is made up: each idea to be expressed in the poetry has its formula for each metrical need, and the poet, who would not think of trying to express ideas outside the traditional field of thought of poetry, can make his verses easily by means of a diction which time has proved to be the best.[4]

At this late date speculation about origins is rather idle, but one may perhaps imagine that in its earliest beginnings isochronous utterances in Old Germanic, almost surely based on the rhythmic beat of some instrument, involved short sequences of verse at first almost accidentally arrived at and consisting, say, of a maxim of a few verses or a protective charm or encomiastic song of similarly modest dimensions. By the time of Tacitus it would seem that more ambitious compositions were possible and the order of the day. In his *Germania* (ch. 2) he says of the Germanic peoples:

> In ancient songs (*carminibus antiquis*), which is the sole kind of record (*memoria*) or history (*annales*) among them, they celebrate the god Twisto, begotten of the earth, and his son Mannus, as the beginning and founder of their people. To Mannus they ascribe three sons from whose names those tribes nearest the Ocean are called Ingvaeones [North Sea Germans], the Central Erminones [Elbe Germans?], and the rest Istvaeones [Western Rhine Germans?].

This suggests possibly rather elaborate narrative and there seems to be little reason to assume that the apparently more or less mythological or cult songs of the North Sea and Inland Germans were merely mnemonic verses on the order of the *þular* [minstrels] in *Widsith* or in the Old-Norse *Hervarar saga* (ch. 12, Stanza 69).[5] In the *Annales* (Book II, §88, *ad fin.*) Tacitus further reports that songs

[4] Parry II, 7–8.
[5] E.g., Rudolf Much, *Die Germania des Tacitus* (Heidelberg, 1937), pp. 21–22.

about Arminius, who had died nearly a century earlier, were still being sung by Germans of his day. These familiar statements are adduced only to emphasize the presumably high antiquity of Old-Germanic poetry and the length of tradition behind it. Furthermore, in order to suggest the antiquity not merely of the art of Germanic poetry in general but specifically the antiquity of the metrical-rhythmical forms of Anglo-Saxon poetry as we know it, one may point to the fact that Anglo-Saxon verse is cast in a form to all intents and purposes identical with all Old-Germanic poetry—Old-Norse, Old-Saxon, Old-High-German—in a word, identical with everything except the later skaldic *vísur* [strophes] of Norway and Iceland. Since any theory of independent origins for the five basic metrical-rhythmical patterns, the "Sievers Five Types," is so exceedingly unlikely, one is forced to assume that something very close to the later preserved forms and patterns had been established and was in good running order before the Anglo-Saxons began to colonize Britain.

In the nature of the case we do not have and cannot have any record of Anglo-Saxon poetry before the introduction of the art of reading and writing by Christian missionaries from Rome and from Iona in the Hebrides; indeed, we have no poetical text which can in exactly the form preserved be thought of as having been put together very early at all. Consequently, it has been natural to think of the preserved poems as composed as we compose poetry, i.e., by lettered persons making use of writing materials, and until the time of Parry and Lord there was no available technique permitting one to decide on the basis of internal evidence alone to which tradition a given text might belong—to the oral or to the lettered. The recurrence of verses and verse-pairs in Anglo-Saxon poetry, the "Parallelstellen" of German scholars, has been much noted and commented upon, and cross-references accumulated and often cited by editors of individual poems, with the main conclusion drawn from this phenomenon being that those parallels might constitute evidence of the direct influence of one poem upon another (see p. 104, below). But with the discovery of the dominant rôle of the formula in the composition of oral poetry and of the non-existence of metrical formulas in the poetry of lettered authors, we have suddenly acquired a touchstone with which it is now possible to determine to which of the two great categories of poetry a recorded text belongs—to the oral or to the lettered tradition.

As a first test I have analyzed the first twenty-five lines or, better, the first fifty verses or twenty-five typographical lines of *Béowulf*, chosen because they deal with highly specialized thematic material not represented elsewhere in the poetry, for the presentation of which in verse one might suppose that a poet would need to create his own language if he would ever have to do so. The formulaic character of the verse is demonstrated by Chart I (pp. 108 ff, below).[6] A word-group of any size or importance which appears elsewhere in *Béowulf* or other Anglo-Saxon poems unchanged or virtually unchanged is marked with solid underlining and is a formula according to Parry's definition that a formula is "a group of words which is regularly employed under the same metrical conditions to express a given essential idea." [7] A word-group marked with solid and broken underlining, or with broken underlining only, may be called a formulaic phrase or system; such groups are of the same type and conform to the same verbal and grammatical pattern as the various other verses associated with them and cited in the supporting evidence. For verses which are unmarked I have found no supporting evidence. Following the marked text on the chart comes the supporting evidence assembled under numbers answering to the *a* and *b* parts of the respective typographical lines.

Looking at Chart I one notes first that of the fifty verses only some thirteen, or twenty-six per cent, are not matched wholly or in part elsewhere in Anglo-Saxon poetry. In a word, despite the relatively limited corpus of some 30,000 lines—about the same as the two Homeric poems—in which to find corresponding phrases, some seventy per cent of the text of this passage does occur elsewhere. Were the surviving corpus, say, twice as big and if, above all, we had other songs of any extent dealing with anything like the same thematic

---

[6] Quotations and line-references from *Béowulf* are based on Fr. Klaeber's third edition with First and Second Supplements (Boston, 1950), those from *Judith* on the edition of Benno J. Timmer (London: Methuen, 1952); all others on *The Anglo-Saxon Poetic Records* (New York: Columbia University Press, 1931–42). Spellings are normalized on the basis of early W.S. as set forth in *Les Langues modernes*, XLV (1951), 63–69. Title-abbreviations, coded in three letters, are based on the titles used in *The Anglo-Saxon Poetic Records*.
[7] Parry I, 80.

material, there well might be almost nothing in the language here used that could not be demonstrated as traditional.

Though usefulness rather than mere repetition, is what makes a formula, it is instructive to look at the repeated formulas first, since it is easier to recognize a formula as such when it occurs a second or third time,[8] and from this regular use in various songs one readily sees how it helps this and that singer to compose his verses. Verses 1b, 3a, 3b, 4b, 5a, 5b, 8a, 10b, 11b, 13a, 14a, 15a, 16a, 17a, 23a, and 25a are of this sort. They occur exactly the same elsewhere or with only some insignificant change in inflection about which a singer would scarcely have to devote conscious thought in order to fit them into some different context or slightly different grammatical situation. The very fact of their recurrence in and/or outside of this passage bears witness to their usefulness not only to the singer of *Béowulf* but to singers of many other songs dealing with quite different themes.

A number of these formulas are something more than mere repeats and form part of larger formulaic systems used to express the same, or almost the same, idea or used to fit some larger rhythmical-grammatical pattern. As Parry observes of such formulas in Homer, "any group of two or more such like formulas makes up a system, and the system may be defined in turn as a group of phrases which have the same metrical value and which are enough alike in thought and words to leave no doubt that the poet who used them knew them not only as a single formula, but also as formulas of a certain type."[9] Here belong verses 1b, 6b, 11b, 16a, and 19a.

1b. *on géar-dagum* [in days of old] is one phase of a system *on* x-*dagum* used to express the idea "long ago" and occurs twice elsewhere in *Béowulf* and in other poems as well. Either alone or with one or two preceding unstressed words it forms a complete C-verse. With the substitution for *géar,* with the sense "of yore," of *ær, eald,* or *fyrn* [earlier, old, or ancient], the formula remains unchanged in meaning and meter, though the variant first elements of the compound are patently more than useful in meeting the exigencies of alliteration, a restrictive and technical problem with which neither Homeric nor Yugoslav verse, for instance, have to contend. The de-

[8] Parry I, 122.
[9] Parry I, 85 and ff.

gree of thrift that marks the use of formulas in Homeric verse[10] is
scarcely conceivable in the construction of the much more restrictive
alliterative Germanic verse.

6b. *siþþan ǽrest wearþ* [after at first he was] shows us three words
repeated as a formula in *Béowulf* where it serves to express the general idea "after something or other has happened"; it must have
often been used by singers to express this same idea in a complete
D-verse. But *siþþan ærest* (or *furðum* [first]) can be followed by any
monosyllabic verb-form in the past tense and in the recorded instance with *wéox* [grew] expresses a closely related idea.

11b. *þæt wæs gód cyning!* [that was a good king!] is a formula that
may well have come into being in connection with encomiastic verse,
of which we hear so much and have so little. Stylistically this and related formulas stop the narrative for a moment and thus serve as a
kind of emphatic punctuation. It is used twice in *Beowulf,* and elsewhere with unfavorable adjectives it serves as a parallel phrase of
disapprobation. The system is *þæt wæs* (is) x *cyning.* There are
other more distantly related formulas noted in the supporting evidence, all referring to persons.

16a. *lange hwíle* is part of a large system expressing the idea "for
a long time" and is closely related to a similar system with *þráge*
[time], equally popular with the *Béowulf* singer. This formula or
formulaic system occurs with *ealle, góde,* and *mićele* [all, good, and
much] substituting for *lange* [long], alternates which affect neither
sense nor meter; here alliteration must dictate the singer's choice.
Whether he uses *hwíle* or *þráge* is surely a matter of accident or indifference, since both words fill the same measure of verse and here
will not enter into the alliteration.

19a. *Scieldes eafora* [son of Scild] is not repeated elsewhere in the
poetic corpus, for nowhere else does the need exist to use this particular patronymic. The value of this system, whereby an A-verse can
be constructed with the genitive of any monosyllabic personal name,
is obvious from the supporting evidence. For patronymics involving
the numerous dithematic names it may be observed that *sunu* [son]
is the favorite keyword and automatically forms a D- or E-verse, as
do the somewhat less common *maga* and *magu* [son and kinsman].

The present passage includes three nominal compounds which I

[10] Parry I, 86.

have underlined as formulas not merely because they are repeated elsewhere to make up whole verses but because their second elements constitute the core of many small systems of formulas. These are *þéod-cyninges* [king of the people] (2a), *ymbsittendra* [around-sitters', neighbors'] (9b), and *willgesíðas* [dear-companions] (23a).[11] If these words did not make up entire verses, one might perhaps be inclined to view them merely as repeated words, and just as formulas need not be mere repetitions, so mere repetitions need not constitute a formula.

þéod-cyninga [people-kings'] (2a) is one of a large number of compounds with inflected forms of *cyning,* usually in the genitive singular, which express the idea "king" within the limits of a D3-verse. In most cases the first element merely emphasizes in one way or another the importance of the king or kings in question, as here where the Danish *þéod-cyningas* are tacitly opposed, as it were, to *smákonungar* [kinglets] "roitelets" of ancient Scandinavia. Occasionally the first element will be more functional and will define or locate a king. In the on-verse position *Béowulf* 2795 has *Wuldorcyninge* [King of Glory] and in the off-verse position *eorþ-* [earth-], *héah-* [high-], *þéod-cyninges* [people-king's], also *Fris-cyninge* [Frisian-king] and *sæ-cyninga* [sea-kings']; of the same general order is *weorold-cyninga* [world-kings']. Except for *Fris-,* used to place geographically Dæghræfn's overlord, the first elements add little to the thought and were presumably chosen for alliterative convenience.[12]

ymbsittendra [around-sitters', neighbors'] (9b), a compound present part. forming a D1-verse, presents a somewhat similar situation; it handily expresses the idea of "persons residing round about." Very close is *ymbstandendra* [around-standers']. In a broader way *ymbsittendra* is to be associated with a large number of verses consisting of a compound present participle, of which there are many in *Béowulf,* which tend in turn to break down into various semantic systems such as the idea of "sea-farer" expressed by *brim-* [water-]

---

[11] For further instances of words of similar structure, and thus with similar rhythmical patterns, in *Béowulf* see John Collins Pope, *The Rhythm of Béowulf* (New Haven, Conn., 1942), pp. 300, 358 (type D1, No. 1) and 248 (type A1, No. 2a). Examples from other poems and with other first elements can be found in Christian W. M. Grein—Ferd. Holthausen—J. J. Köhler, *Sprachschatz der angelsächsischen Dichter* (Heidelberg, 1912).

[12] See further *ibid.,* p. 106, *col.* 1, under *cyning.*

and *sæ-liðende* [sea-farers] in *Béowulf,* and in other songs with the substitution of *éa-, mere-,* and *wæg-* [water-, pool-, and wave-] as the first element but with no change in thought.

will-gesiðas [dear-companions] (23a) is but one of a largish formulaic system centering on *gesíþ* to express in a complete A-verse the idea of "follower(s)" "retainer(s)," the large variety of available first elements being highly useful to the singers in connection with alliteration. Thus are found compounds with *dryht-, eald-, folc-, wéa-,* and *wynn-* [lord-, old-, folk-, woe-, and joy-].[13]

Within the first fifty verses of *Béowulf* occur three so-called kennings, two Christian: *Lif-fréa* [Life-Lord] (16b), varied by *wuldres Wealdend* [Glory-Ruler] (17a), and one non-Christian: *hran-ráde* [whale-road] (10a). Reserving the Christian formulas for later discussion in connection with the special diction of the Christian songs (pp. 97 ff below), we may examine here the formulaic character of the C-verse *ofer hran-ráde* [over the whale-road] and some closely related expressions by the aid of which the singers were able to place people on the sea or to get them over it. Much has been written about Anglo-Saxon kennings by themselves and as part of Old-Germanic poetical technique, but there is one particular aspect of this problem which can probably support further thought and investigation, namely, the formulaic character of the kenning. Like the rest of the language of oral poetry kennings must have developed over a long period of time and must be traditional and formulaic. An examination of the phrase *ofer hran-ráde* will tend to bear out this view. The feminine accusative singular *hran-ráde,* combined with the prepositions *geond, ofer,* and *on* [through, over, and on], forms a complete C-verse, whose repeated use marks it as formulaic. Yet it is more than that, in that it is also one phrase of a formulaic system *on (ofer, geond)* x-*ráde,* where for *x* one can substitute any appropriate monosyllabic first element. With the substitution of *swan* [swan] one finds *ofer swan-ráde* [over the swan-road] in *Béowulf* and *Elene, on swan-ráde* [on the swan-road] in *Juliana,* while *on segl-ráde* [on the sail-road] appears in *Béowulf* with little or no real difference in meaning, and none in meter, from the other combinations. The singers are presumably concerned not primarily with some refinement of

<hr/>

[13] *Ibid.,* p. 608, under *gesíþ.*

imagery produced by varying the first elements *hran, segl,* and *swan* —something for which an oral singer could scarcely have time—but with recalling a formula expressing the fundamental idea in question with availability for different alliterative situations. It is hard to believe that they had much concern with possible connotative effects produced by passing mention of sails, swans, or whales.

There is another aspect of this general problem that semantically at least is related to the *ofer hran-ráde* verse in *Béowulf.* Now this particular formula and related formulaic systems were obviously useful to Anglo-Saxon singers and provided them with a C-verse with the aid of which they could get their characters onto or across the sea. Nevertheless, this system imposed certain limitations, including the fact that a verse based on this formula cannot well contain a verb; yet the need for composing such verses was felt and was met in more than one way. A fair example centers on a parallel to *rád* [road], f., namely, *weg* [way], m. In the accusative singular of *weg* there will be no ending; hence any compound of *weg* in this grammatical case, where ending a verse, must be fitted into a metrical pattern other than C, one in which there will be place for a verb or some other important alliterating word at the beginning. The pertinent compounds of *weg* are *bæþ-, flód-, flot-,* and *hwæl-* [bath-, flood-, ship-, and whale-], of which *bæþ-weg* is the most frequent combination. *Ofer bæþ-weg* [Over bath-way] occurs three times, always with some form of *brecan* [to push] in the sense "pressing on across the sea": thus, *brecan ofer bæþ-weg (And 223, Ele 244)* and *brecaþ ofer bæþ-weg (And 513),* where the phrase *ofer bæþ-weg* combines with the alliterating verb to make a formula. The two *f*-compounds *flód-* and *flot-weg* [flood- and ship-way], serve their purpose in combination with *faran* [to journey]. *Flód-weg* appears in an instrumental construction *fóron flód-wege (Exo 106)* "[the sailors] journeyed on or over the sea"; while in the accusative plural there is *Fór flód-wegas (Rid 36, 9)* "[it, probably a ship] traversed the seas." With *on* the combination *flot-weg* appears in *faran on flot-weg (HbM 42)* "[was fated] to journey on the sea." Finally comes *hwæl-weg* [whale-way], in meaning identical with *hran-rád* [whale-road] of *Bwf* 10a and occurring in *hweteþ on hwæl-weg (Sea 63a)* "impels on [to?] the whale's route." Beside offering various alliterative alternates this cluster of *weg*-formulas permits the inclusion of a verb in a single D-verse, an opportunity of which the singers were obviously glad to avail themselves.

I shall conclude this discussion of the formulaic character of the first 50 verses of *Béowulf* with a brief word on the first five verses (1a–3a) of the poem, where the singer appears to have adjusted, combined, and recombined a number of formulas. He begins with a formula much used to start songs or to introduce an important new section of a song, a formula built around the weakly exclamatory *hwæt* [behold] plus a personal pronoun. This is in effect a sort of filler-in, something to let the singer get going; the phrase, ordinarily metrically unstressed, opens the way to a B- or C-verse. The total system, embracing all personal pronouns in the nom. and a few in oblique cases, is vast and cannot be presented here, but looking at all instances of the subvariety *Hwæt, wé* [Behold, we] (1a), collected on Chart I, one is struck by two points: (1) that in each case the singer includes his audience in assuming familiarity with the thematic material of his song,[14] and (2), more important, the fact that he is saying "we have all heard or learned about something or other," at times adding that the events took place long ago. *Hieran* [to hear] is the verb favored in preserved song, with *frignan* [learn by inquiring] of *Béowulf* running (perhaps by chance), a poor second. It will be noticed that the singers ordinarily work in the important verbal idea "hearing about," "learning about" in the course of the first two verses, but the *Béowulf* singer introduced mention of the Spear-Danes (*Gár-Dena*) before proceeding farther. This apparently spoiled his chance of getting in a verb in what appears to be the favored or ordinary position in the first verse. Comparable to Cynewulf in *Ele* 397b, he might in some fashion have worked in a suitable verb in 1b, had there been such a one capable of *g*-alliteration, but at all events he next called upon one of the several available formulas expressing the idea "long ago," already discussed (p. 89, above) under *on géar-dagum* [in days of old] (1b). Thus *gefrugnon* [we have learned] is put off to the fourth verse (2b), while the *hú* [how] of the total phrase *wé gefrugnon hú* [we have learned how] has to wait for

---

[14] See Dorothy Whitelock, *The Audience of Beowulf* (Oxford University Press, 1950), pp. 34–44 and ff. *passim* on audience-familiarity in gross and detail with the *Béowulf* stories and substories introduced for purposes of embellishment; the latter are not in any ordinary sense "digressions."

the fifth (3a). The basic formula is all there and the singer has used every scrap of it, though not in what would appear to be the usual way. One might interpret this exceptional treatment as an example of a first-rate singer coping quickly and deftly with an almost awkward situation into which he had got himself, even though the resulting order of words is perhaps not quite natural. To suggest that this order of words is [in] any sense "literary" is virtually to deny oral technique in the composition of the poem, a technique demonstrated in the preceding analysis of the first fifty verses of the poem. The traditional character of the recorded text is further borne out by the fact that at least fifteen per cent of the verses of the poem are to all intents and purposes repeated within the poem,[15] a phenomenon unthinkable in lettered tradition.

In the opening lines of *Béowulf* are two formulas which must be called Christian: *Líf-fréa* [Life-Lord] (16b) and *wuldres Wealdend* [Glory-Ruler] (17a). Neither of these so-called kennings could well refer to anything but the Deity and hence could not have formed part of the traditional language of pre-Christian poetry. They must be relatively young and their presence in *Béowulf* raises the general question of the relation of the language of Christian narrative poetry —by far the largest genre in the corpus—to the older traditional poetic language. There are no means of knowing when first a singer or singers started making songs based on such novel thematic material as that found in the Old Testament, Apocrypha, saints' lives, and homilies, but it cannot well have been before the arrival of Augustine in Kent in 597 and of Paulinus in York in 625, an influence fortified by the settlement of Aidan on Lindisfarne (Holy Island) off the Northumberland coast in 635. Yet somewhere in the neighborhood of 675, St. Aldhelm was quite possibly singing religious verse, interspersed among diverting secular songs, in public at Malmesbury in Wiltshire in order to get the local populace to stay on after mass for the sermon,[16] and sometime between 658 and 680,

---

[15] Communicated orally by Mr. Robert P. Creed of Smith College, who is presently studying the oral style in *Béowulf*.

[16] Reported by William of Malmesbury (d. 1125) in his *De Gestis Pontificum Anglorum* (ed. N. E. S. A. Hamilton, Rolls Ser., No. 52, London, 1870), Bk. V, Pt. 1 ("Life of Aldhelm"), p. 336, based on Alfred the Great's lost *Handbóc* (William's *Manuale*, ed. cit., pp. 332-33):
  Litteris itaque ad plenum instructus nativae quoque linguae non negligebat carmina, adeo ut, teste libro Elfredi de quo superius dixi, nulla umquam

the years during which Hild ruled as abbess of Whitby in the North Riding, the unlettered Cædman, farm-hand on the monastic estate, is said on first-rate authority[17] to have been successfully composing all sorts of songs based on Christian story. There is no way of learning more about Aidan's compositions but, as I hope to show elsewhere, Cædman was probably the father of nothing but his own songs and composed these against the background of a developed tradition.

In talking or thinking about the chronology, real or relative, of Anglo-Saxon poems one is notoriously treading on very swampy ground, but if one adopts the conservative view that a *Béowulf* song in form fairly close to the preserved performance had come into being not far from, say, 730 or even somewhat later, it is clear that

---

aetate par ei fuerit quisquam. Poesim Anglicam posse facere, cantum componere, eadem apposite vel canere vel dicere. Denique commemorat Elfredus carmen triviale adhuc vulgo cantitatur Aldelmum fecisse . . . Populum eo tempore semibarbarum, parum divinis sermonibus intentum, statim cantatis missis domos cursitare solitum. Ideo sanctum. Ideo sanctum virum super pontem qui rura et urbem continuat abeuntibus se opposuisse obicem quasi artem cantandi professum. Eo plus quam semel favorem et concursum emeritum. Hoc commento, sensim inter ludicra verbis Scripturarum insertis, cives ad sanitatem reduxisse.

And thus fully instructed in [Latin] literature he also did not neglect the songs of his native tongue, so that, according to Alfred's book of which I spoke above, at no time was anybody ever his equal. He was able to make English poetry, compose a melody, and properly sing or recite the same. Finally, Alfred remarks that Aldhelm composed a light song which was still [i.e., in Alfred's day] being commonly sung . . . The people, at that time [about 675] semibarbarous and too little intent on divine discourses, were in the habit of hurrying to their homes after masses had been sung. Therefore, the holy man stationed himself on a bridge [over the Avon] which connects the town [of Malmesbury] and the countryside as an obstacle to those going away, as though professing the art of song. After he had done this several times [lit. "more than once"] he gained the good-will and the attendance of the common people. By this device, gradually working in words of the Scriptures among entertaining words, he led the people back to right reason.

It may be remarked that the Scriptural words introduced in the course of the recitation of secular poems need not have been in verse, though this is a reasonable inference. It should also be noted that nothing is said about writing despite the rendering *"write* a poem" (*Poesim . . . facere*) of George F. Browne, *St. Aldhelm: His Life and Times* (London, 1903), p. 79.

[17] I refer not merely to Bede himself but to the tradition of the Whitby community on which Bede drew, surely completely reliable in this local matter, unless one assumes a monstrous conspiracy of falsification.

by that time Christian poetry was a commonplace and that its recitation was a familiar form of entertainment not only in monasteries but in lay circles. Were this not the case, the recitation in Heorot of a song about the Creation (*Bwf* 90–98) would, as Dr. Whitelock has recently pointed out, "surely have been incongruous, or even ludicrous, if minstrels never sang on such themes to lay audiences." [18] As it is, the Creation song seems to enjoy a status no different from that of songs sung about Sigemund and Fitela or the tragedy of Finn's stronghold in the same hall on another occasion. Indeed, apart from this, the entire fabric of *Béowulf* is shot through with the language and thought of Christianity and must be viewed as a Christian poem though of an unusual sort.[19]

Now, as Parry emphasizes, the traditional language of unlettered singers develops very, very slowly and over a long period of time and is created to deal only with traditional themes with which singers and audiences are in the main familiar. On his visits to Yugoslavia in 1950 and 1951 Professor Lord noted that the traditional singers were proving unable to cope with such radically new themes of a social-political nature as Marxism and related matters, for the simple reason that they lacked formulas necessary to express these new ideas in just measures of verse. Except for rather obvious substitutions of key-words in an old formula (e.g. *engla Dryhten* [Lord of angels] for *eorla dryhten* [lord of earls]), no one singer ever creates many new formulas and most of them never create any at all. Thus, standing on the threshold, so to speak, of the year 600, one might well have wondered whether and how Anglo-Saxon singers would be able to meet the challenge of adapting their traditional verses to the needs of singing about themes so different as Christian material would seem to be. In actual fact they did rise to this occasion and often magnificently.

A glance of Chart II (pp. 111 ff) analyzing ll. 512–35 of *Christ and Satan*, a poem of appreciably later date than *Béowulf* and mainly telling a story of Christ's harrowing of hell, exhibits plainly the formulaic character of the language. If not as many verses are underlined as in Chart I, this can, in the case of the unmarked

---

[18] Whitelock, *op. cit.*, p. 9; on pp. 9–11 Whitelock is on the verge of suggesting what I suggest here.

[19] *Idem*, pp. 3–4; Klaeber, *ed. cit.*, p. xlix, *ad fin.*

verses, only mean that the surviving corpus of Anglo-Saxon poetry does not happen to contain verses which furnish supporting evidence, that is, either exactly similar verses or, equally significant, verses constructed on closely similar formulaic patterns.

It will be unnecessary to take up the text of this chart in detail, for the supporting evidence will now be telling its own story. There are, however, two matters, quite different from one another, which the present passage brings to one's attention. The first concerns the "Christianity" of the language of this and perhaps any other Christian poem, while the second concerns the possibility of occasionally making use of an understanding of the nature and function of the formula in textual criticism.

The prime point of interest in the sample of verse analyzed on Chart II lies in the fact that it is from a Christian poem. It is a passage treating a most central event in Christian belief, the Ascension of Jesus Christ, and in that sense at least could scarcely be more Christian as opposed to the opening verses of *Béowulf*. What, as far as the language is concerned, is Christian about it? Very largely references to God, specifically Jesus Christ. This passage of forty-six verses includes thirteen such references, more than one for every four verses: *wuldres Weard* [Guardian of glory] (512a), *Meotod mann-cynnes* [God of mankind] (513a), *Dryhten God* [Lord God] (514a), *engla Dryhten* [Lord of angels] (518b), *God* (522b), *Godes Sunu* [Son of God] (526b), *Sunu Meotodes* [Son of God] (527b), *se Éca* [the Eternal One] (530b), *Þéodne* [Lord] (532a), *Scieppend engla* [Creator of angels] (533b), and *Dryhten* [Lord] (535a). These are all in one way or another different from one another. In addition there are ten other "Christian" words, that is, words which would normally only appear in a Christian context: Galilee is mentioned twice (522a, 529a), Simon called Peter twice (521b, 536b); there is one reference to the Holy Spirit (525b), two to the disciples (520b, 529b), and three to angels (518b, 520a, 533b), of which two occur as parts of kennings designating the Deity. In all these forty-six verses include twenty-three Christian words, or words used in a Christian way; thus there is one Christian word for every other verse or one for each typographical line. It might be hard to find a more "Christian" passage, and for these words and formulas used in a Christian way only *giengran* [disciples] lacks supporting evidence. This is no doubt due to the limits of the surviving corpus and, had the singer happened to have preferred formulas with the much more frequent equivalent of "disciple," namely *þegn* [retainer], it would probably be possible to collect no little supporting evidence.

In this so very Christian passage there may be a hint and more as to how Anglo-Saxon singers were able, apparently from early on, to sing in a slightly adjusted traditional language songs based on these novel and untraditional themes. In the first place and stated in most general terms, the Christian themes that the singers apparently liked best to sing about are in the main stories involving extraordinary and exciting adventures and events, such as the stories on which center *Andreas, Azarias, Daniel, Elene, Exodus, Judith,* and *Juliana.* To the ear of Anglo-Saxons not yet fully initiated in this new development most immediately striking and strange were no doubt the presence of non-Germanic proper nouns, names of persons such as Simon Peter and places such as Galilee. These could be and were, however, readily fitted into older formulas created to embody Germanic proper names, and since these strange new names were all but invariably accented on the first syllable, regardless of the stress in the original tongues, they offered few, if any, metrical problems to the singer. Some of them must have been awkwardly long and more than queer sounding, such as *Nabochodonossar,* used five times in *Daniel* (48, 411, 497, 618, 663) and once in *Azarias* (183) to form a complete A-type on-verse, yet the singers made do with them. Aside from the pre-Christian word *God* and elsewhere *Crist,* to be viewed as ordinary personal names, the singers had available from pre-Christian tradition, already evidently rich in words and kennings to express the idea of "ruler," a large number of expressions ready to take off the rack, available as substitutory epithets for the Deity. As a result of new formations on the analogy of the old, e.g., the weaving into compounds of such characteristically Christian word-elements as *heofon* [heaven] and *wuldor* [glory], the number of epithets for the Deity was increased to a point where this is by all odds the largest single group of kennings in the poetical corpus.[20]

---

[20] See Hendrik van der Merwe Scholtz, *The Kenning in Anglo-Saxon and Old-Norse Poetry* (Utrecht-Nijmegen, 1929), pp. 92–98, and Hertha Marquardt, *Die altenglischen Kenningar,* etc. (Schriften der Königsberger gelehrten Gesellschaft, XIV, 3, Halle, 1938), pp. 269–92, and cp. *ibid.,* pp. 266 ff. *passim* (§D "Christliche Begriffe").

The frequency and hence importance of this group can scarcely be overestimated. The concept "angel" is new as is the loan-word *engel* [angel], an idea also capable of being expressed by the old word *gást* [spirit]. The Latin titles *Sanctus* and *Beatus* were easily handled by the old words *hálig* [holy] (originally "inviolate") and *éadig* ("favored by fortune," "prosperous"). Expression of general conceptions of theology, dogma, and Christian doctrine is notably rare in the Christian songs,[21] as it is in *Béowulf,* where action predominates, and even in that most beautiful song of meditation or devotion, *The Dream of the Rood.* This lack is surely due neither to mere accident nor to ignorance or indifference, but to a lack of formulas capable of adaptation to such ideas. The lyrically keyed poem on the Advent (*Christ I*) and the song on the Ascension (*Christ II*), based on the latter part of Pope Gregory the Great's Ascension homily, are both traditional in diction and adhere pretty strictly to narrative.[22]

It would be wrong to suggest that the adaptation of the traditional language of the ancient poetry to this new and different thematic material did not take doing on the part of the singers or to withhold from them full credit for the successful exercise of what at the outset particularly must have called for skill and ingenuity. It is, however, fair to point out, in view of the obviously traditional language of the Christian poems—a matter that in essence has long since been noticed and stressed—that the singers did not make things unnecessarily hard for themselves by attempting to sing about matters for the expression of which the old diction would have been inadequate. As it was singers and audience probably felt little difference between the general style and narrative technique of, say, *Béowulf* and *Christ and Satan,* to mention two poems of very different thematic backgrounds. This marked uniformness or unity of style is largely to be

---

[21] Cp. Klaeber, *ed. cit.,* p. xlix, *ad init.*

[22] P. S. Robert E. Diamond, presently engaged in the study of "The Diction of the Signed Poems of Cynewulf" (Harvard thesis in preparation), tells me (April 30, 1953) that 20 per cent of the 5194 verses (i.e., 2598 numbered typographic lines of the editions) in the signed poems of Cynewulf are repeated in the signed poems themselves. A series of samples, amounting to 581 verses (including the entire *Fates of the Apostles,* the runic passages in the other three poems, and several 15–20 line samples chosen at random from the other three poems), checked against the entire Anglo-Saxon poetical corpus, shows 30.8 per cent of repeated verses, and 61.1 per cent of verses, of which parts, by virtue of recurrence elsewhere, demonstrate themselves to be formulaic.

accounted for by the continuity of the traditional formulaic language of the Anglo-Saxon singers, a continuity that seems to live until the Norman Conquest.

Many factors, political and social as well as linguistic, probably contributed to the death of the traditional poetry after the Conquest, and one must also reckon with the difficulties, probably insuperable, which the relatively swift introduction of ideas and activities incidental to the advent of the feudal age brought in their train, ideas which could not easily be sidestepped by singers trying to sing in the old tradition and for which they had no formulas.

Quite by chance the present passage from *Christ and Satan* offers an opportunity to consider the general possibility of the use of an understanding of the role of the formula in occasional matters of textual criticism. Verse 513b, with the manuscript reading *ǽr on morgen* (A), "early in the morning," technically violates a basic principle of alliteration in that the first down-beat or ictus in the off-verse does not here alliterate with the preceding on-verse where the alliteration is *m*. Acting on a suggestion of Professor Holthausen, Professor M.D. Clubb emended this verse in his edition of 1925 to read *on morgen ǽr*, thus producing which he rightly described as a normal (B) verse. Nevertheless, in the light of the supporting evidence which demonstrates the existence of a formula *ǽr on morgen*, taken together with the phrase *on ǽr-morgen*, with which may also be compared *mid ǽr-dæge* [about dawn] of similar meaning, one may wonder whether the singer did not himself violate the usual procedures of alliteration in order to make use of a formula that he needed, a formula or system in which *ǽr* preceded the word it modified. Consequently, one might do well, not only here but in other similar situations, to test such alliteratively defective verses for their formulaic character before embarking on a course of emendation, however much better emendation may make, or may seem to make, matters. If given time to think his verse over, in a word to compose at a more leisurely pace, a singer might well agree with what a modern editor was proposing to do; on the other hand, such an emendation might produce a sequence of words which would strike him as stranger than the technical defect in versification.

If this discussion of manuscript *ǽr on morgen* suggests that it should be left regardless of the technical imperfection that its use and retention produces, the case of manuscript *on þǽm fæstenne* (519a) would seem to speak in favor of emendation to *of þǽm fæstenne,* "from, out of the tomb," an emendation adopted by certain earlier editors, though not by Clubb or Krapp, last to edit the poem. The supporting evidence on Chart II exhibits two expressions, one with *fram* or *of,* meaning "from or out of the prison, stronghold or tomb," the other with *on,* always except here with the obvious meaning "in the prison, stronghold or tomb." Now it is true that Old-English uses expressions with *on* which are convenient to render by "from," generally in connection with removing something from a surface on which the object in question is lying or reposing (see B. T. *s.v.* "on," III, 2). From the Anglo-Saxon point of view *on* is in these cases entirely appropriate, though the approach to the act is different from ours. It is as if one said "he took the pencil *on* the table," that is, "he took the pencil which was lying on the table," in the sense that he took it *from* the table. When Grendel assails Béowulf, it is said that the troll *nam . . . rinc on ræste* (ll. 746–47), "took the warrior from his resting place." This is, however, far from saying that OE *on* means "from"; it is simply to say that the image of the action is different. In the verse in *Christ and Satan* such an image would in the nature of things be highly unlikely if not out of the question altogether. The singer must be trying to say that Our Lord went out of the tomb and thus it is all but certain that the manuscript *on* does not go back to the words of the singer or to anybody who was giving attention to the thought but to a miscopying by a scribe somewhere along the line of written transmission. If this is so, then in the small verbal matter of the preposition, manuscript *on,* the supporting evidence involving *on*'s does not support the manuscript reading, but rejects it rather.

The future is full of many problems involving a reappraisal of certain aspects of Anglo-Saxon poetical style and compositional technique and what these are, or at present seem likely to be, can here be merely adumbrated. First of all let it be said that, if further study of the formulaic character of the poetry is to be conducted in a thoroughgoing way, the first and most crying need is the construction of a concordance of the entire poetical corpus; without this the collecting of supporting evidence to test the formulaic character of a given-verse or group of verses will prove to be incredibly laborious and often uncertain.[23]

More sample analyses of narrative verse are certainly desirable, though it seems doubtful that any narrative poem will be found to be non-traditional in language. Particularly interesting will be a study from this point of view of the diction of the rather small body of lyrical-elegiac poetry. One might suspect that lyrical composition would call for formulas not elsewhere used and that for many of the verses there would be little or no supporting evidence of their formulaic character, due to the limited size of the body of lyric-elegiac verse. The same may be said of the literary *Riddles* of the *Exeter Book,* a genre new to the Anglo-Saxons and a direct imitation of Latin enigmas, specifically those 685–705? of Aldhelm, of which two are translated into Old English. At least some of the language of the *Riddles* is traditional, since verses from these appear in the support-evidence in the charts above, but it may turn out that many riddles, often very short compositions, were composed word by word. And what of the verses that embody runes other than isolated logograms (e.g., *éðel* [homeland] and *mann* [man]), notably Cynewulf's signature passages? [24]

Mention of Cynewulf raises a question concerning the relation between lettered persons and orally composed poetry. Not all Anglo-Saxon Christian poetry needs to have been composed by lettered singers—witness the story of Cædman. Any good unlettered singer

[23] For any comparative study of Old-Germanic formulaic diction concordances are equally needed for the Old-Norse Edda-type verse ((*Eddukvæði* of Mod. Icel. parlance) and for the Old-Saxon corpus (see n. 27, below).

Efficient techniques for concordance-making have been worked out by Professor Emeritus Lane Cooper of Cornell University and are set forth in considerable detail in "The Making and the Use of a Verbal Concordance," *Sewanee Review,* XXVII (1919), 188–206, esp. pp. 191–95, reprinted in his *Evolution and Repentance* (Ithaca, N. Y., 1935), esp. pp. 24–33. See also his "Instructions for preparing the Slips," three pages, inserted in *A Concordance to the Works of Horace* (Washington, D. C., 1916). No concordance should ever be attempted without consulting these writings.

[24] P. S. Mr. Diamond further informs me that the four verse paragraphs which include the runic signatures (72 typographic lines in all), checked against the entire Anglo-Saxon poetical corpus, show 25.6 per cent of repeated verses and 52.7 per cent of verses, of which parts, by virtue of recurrence elsewhere, show themselves to be formulaic.

who had translated for, or expounded to, him the *Apocryphal Gospel of St. Matthew and St. Andrew* could easily have composed *Andreas*. But Cynewulf was surely a lettered person, also how could he have conceived a plan to assure mention of his name in prayers by means of runic signatures which depend on a knowledge of spelling and reading for their efficacy?[25] If, however, the narrative parts of his poems prove on testing to be formulaic, one must assume that those parts at least he composed in the traditional way. That he subsequently got them written down, whether dictating to himself, as it were, or to another person—possibly a more convenient procedure— is beside the point. In any event there would be no conflict with, or contradiction to, tradition.[26]

A different view will, I think, have to be taken of the significance or lack of significance of phrasal similarities between this and that poem and poems than has prevailed up to now.[27] Certain verbal similarities among poems may in a sense represent borrowing from one poem to another, for traditional singers per force learn from other singers. But one verbal similarity or even a number of verbal similarities in themselves prove nothing beyond suggesting that given singers have found the same formulas useful to express a certain idea in a similar measure of verse. To quote Parry, "Plagiarism is not possible in traditional literature. One oral poet is better

---

[25] From *Juliana* 718b–22 it is clear that the poem was intended for recitation (*þe þis giedd wrece* [who this story told]) and that a prayer was hoped for from a singer rather than some indefinite reading public. Does this suggest that Anglo-Saxon poems got put on written record primarily for memorization by a class of later, memorizing entertainers, answering somewhat to the Greek rhapsodes of post-oral times? One thinks here of Asser's familiar ch. 23 (ed. W. H. Stevenson, p. 20, notes on p. 221) where we are told that Alfred learned by heart native poems read aloud to him by his mother.

[26] On oral-formulaic verse making by lettered persons see Parry II, 29, and Bowra, *op. cit.*, esp. pp. 370–72.

[27] E.g., Klaeber, *ed. cit.*, pp. cx–cxiii. For a competent survey of thought on "the testimony of the parallels" see Claes Schaar, *Critical Studies in the Cynewulf Group* (Lund Studies in English, XVII, Lund, 1949), pp. 235ff. Over sixty years ago J. Kail, "Über die Parallelstellen in der angelsächsischen Poesie," *Anglia*, XII (1889–90), 21–40, was clearly nearer right than he lived to know. In the case of Old-Saxon poetry a start was made by Eduard Sievers in his ed. of the *Hêliand* (Halle, 1878) through his very comprehensive though inconveniently arranged "Formelverzeichnis," pp. 391–463, a reference for which I am most grateful to Professor Fernand Mossé of the Collège de France.

than another not because he has by himself found a more striking way of expressing his thought, but because he has been better able to make use of the tradition." [28] When by the aid of a concordance we gradually get to know what the Anglo-Saxon formulas are and what, indeed, constitute their dimensions[29] and the like, it will perhaps be possible to begin to detect individual styles. Apart from general over-all organization of material, the broad architectonics of a given poem, a singer's individuality will, as in other traditional poetry, presumably emerge in rather small matters,[30] verbal and stylistic, and will not be revealed by the large and rather obvious components known to all or almost all singers.

Lack of truly early material will preclude our ever knowing much about the relative age of the formulas encountered in the preserved poems, but perhaps something can be done with verses containing words which in earlier times had suffered contraction, either from the simple contraction of two vowels (as *dón<dó-an*) or as a secondary result of the loss of intervocalic *h* (as *héan<héahan*).[31] The poetry

---

[28] Parry II, 13.

[29] Parry I, 84–85, n. 3, would for Homeric verse regard as a formula or a possible formula nothing less than four words or five syllables, a restriction that could not be applied to Anglo-Saxon verse.

[30] I am thinking of such small points as the *þe* of the formular *þe hit riht ne wæs* [as it was not right] (*Mal* 190) contrasted to the *swá's* of the parallel formula in *Gen* 901, *Vainglory* 61, with *gerisne* [proper] (*Gen* 1564), *gedéfe* [fitting] (*PPs* 105, 22; *Met* 26, 90), *geþiewe* [customary] (*Bwf* 2331), references for which I am grateful to Dr. Randolph Quirk of University College, London. Without the negative cp. *Bwf* 561, 1670 (with *gedéfe*).

[31] For a somewhat analogous phenomenon see Parry II, 10, 30–31, and *idem*, "Traces of the Digamma in Ionic and Lesbian Greek," *Language*, X (1934), 130–44, esp. p. 131 and n. 6, for reference to *Béowulf*. See also Whitelock, *op. cit.*, p. 27 and n. 1, for general observations on intervocalic *h* and for references. Since the formulas in which contracted forms occur are, like the rest of the diction, traditional, their occurrence can tell us little about the age of a text in which they appear.

P.S. In his splendid and welcome edition *Béowulf with the Finnesburg Fragment* (Boston: Heath, 1953) Professor C. L. Wrenn has taken the revolutionary step of decontracting the various contracted forms over which previous editors have placed a circumflex (see pp. 31–32), e.g., *fré[ge]a* (16b) for manuscript *fréa, dó[a]n* (1116b) for manuscript *dón*. Were there any evidence that such words (discussed in Luick, §§242–49, pp. 218–26) were pronounced as if uncontracted at the time when the text was first committed to writing, one would welcome such a procedure, however daring, as restoring the meter of otherwise metrically

abounds in such verses as *héan landes* [high land's] (*Gen* 2854b)
which, if pronounced as they almost surely were pronounced in later
times, were metrically deficient though at the time created they
formed metrically regular verses: *héahan landes* (A). The becoming
unmetrical of such a verse would have been a gradual process and
singers would naturally have hung on to it as long as possible, down,
in fact, to the time when the contraction-process had long since been
completed. This would suggest that later-day singers and their audiences became habituated to such metrical irregularities and accepted
these "deficient" verses as traditional.[32] This matter might profit-
ably be further explored.

Just as the half-hexameter is the basis of most Homeric formulas,
so is the single verse that of Old-Germanic poetry. But in the Homeric poems there are also whole-line formulas[33] answering in a
sense apparently to such Anglo-Saxon verse-pair formulas as *on
þǽm dǽges þisses lífes* [in the days of this life] (*Bwf* 197, 790, 806),
þæs oferéode: þisses swá mǽg [that passed away: so may this] (*Déo*
7, 13, 17, 20, 42), and *siþþan of líć-haman lǽded wǽre* [afterwards
out of the body were led] (Vercelli *SlB* 21) with which cp. *Bwf* 3177,
where *of líć-hamen lǽded weorðan* [from the body were led] is almost
surely the right reading (cp. *Jul* 670a).

Oral singers are often faced with situations where enjambement
is required,[34] and the Anglo-Saxon singers appear to be no exception.
Béowulf offers at least one interesting example where enjambement
is accomplished with the aid of a two-verse formula: *ende gebíden /
weorolde lífes* [await the end of this worldly life] (*Bwf* 1386b–87a,
2342b–43a); Dr. Whitelock has already pointed out how the formula

---

deficient verses (for literature see Luick §242, nn. 2–3, p. 219). But the
phenomenon of contraction had almost surely quite run its course by, say, 650.
(See Luick, §249, pp. 225–26: after the working of *i*-umlaut; for a few exceptional
survivals of sorts see Sievers-Brunner, 2d ed., §218, 3, p. 197; Northumbrian *dóan*'s
and the like are late and are analogical restorations comparable to Mod. Icel.
smáum for *smám* of the old language and do not help here.)

[32] See Parry II, 22–23, n. 1, for instances in Homeric verse where the retention
of a formula leads to a violation of meter.

[33] Parry, "Whole Formulaic Verses in Greek and Southslavic Heroic Song,"
Transactions of the American Philological Association, LXIV (1933), 179–97.

[34] See Lord, "Homer and Huso III: Enjambement in Greek and Southslavic
Song," *ibid.,* LXXXIX (1948), 113–24.

God éaðe mæg [God easily may] (*Bwf* 478b, *And* 425b, *Chr* 173b) operates in this situation.[35]

There is perhaps much that will never be known about the origin and special function, if any, of the expanded or hypermetric verses, but a casual survey suggests that, whereas the second measure of each such verse seems to be formulaic and out of its context would form a complete verse, the organization of the first measure would appear to be somewhat different, perhaps somewhat less rigid in structure, thus perhaps allowing the singer certain freedoms not available in a normal verse. Here, too, a concordance will be necessary for further study of the character of these first measures.[36]

At the end of these rather miscellaneous remarks on possible problems of the future, problems which will require the thought of many persons to test and solve, I should like to comment on the possible relation of one aspect of the physical preservation of our Anglo-Saxon poems that may reflect their oral background, namely, the fact of their all being written out as prose. It is a not uncommon view that this method was employed as a measure of economy, that the vernacular poetry was perhaps felt not quite worth, or worthy of, as much parchment as writing the poetry out as we today print it would require. I find it hard to believe this to be the case and suspect it was written as prose merely because neither scribes nor singers understood in a formal sense the metrics of the verse, even when they may have had an understanding of Latin verse studied in monastic schools. That tenth-eleventh century scribes at times separate verses (not our typographical lines) by dots may merely reflect a feeling for the basic rhythm, the onset of a down-beat, comparable to a musically unschooled person's tapping time with foot or finger though knowing nothing of the writing of music or of musical composition.

[35] *Op. cit.*, p. 10. This formula is a phase of the system *x éaðe mæg* [x easily may]; cp. *B* 2764 *sinc éaðe mæg* [treasure easily may]. There are other systems with forms of *magan* [to be able to] to express the idea of the possibility of something happening or being done.

[36] An impetus to a revaluation of the expanded verses has recently been given by Benno J. Timmer, "Expanded Lines in Old-English Poetry," *Neophilologus*, XXXV (1951), 226–30.

Chart I

(Béowulf, ll. 1–25)

Hwæt, wé Gár-Dena   on géar-dagum
þéod-cyninga   þrymm gefrugnon,
hú þá æðelingas   ellen fremedon.
Oft Scield Scéafing   sceaðena þréatum,
5   manigum mægðum   medu-setla oftéah,
egesode Eorle,   siþþan ǽrest wearþ
féasceaft funden;   hé þæs frófre gebád,
wéox under wolcnum,   weorþ-myndum þáh
oþ-þæt him ǽghwelć   ymbsittendra
10   ofer hran-ráde   híeran scolde,
gamban gieldan;   þæt wæs gód cyning!
þǽm eafora wæs   æfter cenned
geong on geardum,   þone God sende
folce to frófre;   firen-þearfe ongeat
15   þe híe ǽr drugon   ealdorléase
lange hwíle;   him þæs Líf-fréa,
wuldres Wealdend   weorold-áre forgeaf
Béow wæs bréme   —blǽd wíde sprang—
Scieldes eafora   Sceden-landum on.
20   Swá sceal geong guma   góde gewyrćan
framum feoh-giftum   on fæder bearme
þæt hine on ielde   eft gewunien
will-gesíðas   þanne wíg cume,
léode gelǽsten;   lof-dǽdum sceal
25   on mǽgða gehwǽm   man geþéon.

SUPPORTING EVIDENCE

1a–2b Hwæt, wé feorr and néah / gefrigen habbaþ (*Exo* 1); Hwæt,
wé gefrugnon / on fyrn dagum (*And* 1); Hwæt, wé þæt gehíerdon /
þurh hálge béć (*FAp* 63, *Ele* 364, 852); Hwæt, wé éac gehíerdon / be

Ióhanne (*FAp* 23); Hwæt, wé nú gehíerdon / hú þæt Hǽlubearn (*Chr* 586, *with whose* gehíerdon *cp.* *Bwf* 2b–3a gefrugnon hú); Hwæt, wé híerdon oft / þæt se hálige wer (*Glc* 108); Hwæt, wé þæt gehíerdon / hæleþ eahtian (*Jul* 1); Hwæt, wé Ebréisce ǽ leornodon / þá on fyrn-dagum fæderas cúðon (*Ele* 397–98). 1b *XSt* 367, *Wan* 44. Cp. *Chr* 251 þe on géar-dagum; *Bwf* 1354 þone on géar-dagum, 2233 swá híe on géar-dagum. *Note also instrum. use without on:* *And* 1519 giefum géar-dagum; *Ele* 290 þæt gé géar-dagum, 834 swá hie géar-dagum (*also Bwf* 2233). *Note closely related formulas:* on fyrn-dagum, on ǽr-dagum, *and* on eald-dagum (*Chr* 303, *SFt* 1). 2a *Nom. pl.* Gen 1965 þéod-cyningas / þrymme miċele; *gen. sg.* *Bwf* 2694 þá iċ æt þearfe gefrægn / þéod-cyninges; *FAp* 18 Ne þréodode hé fore þrymme / þéod-cyninges; *Edw* 34 þæs-þe þearf wæs / þæs þéod-cyninges. 2b *See 1–2 above for combination of formulas to express the idea of "having heard or learned long ago."* 3a *FAp* 3 hú þá æðelingas / ellen cýðdon, 85 þus þá æðelingas; *Rid* 49, 7 þá æðelingas. *Cp. without def. art. but with a preceding word, usually of light stress* Gen 1059 þára-þe æðelingas, 1647 þá nú æðelingas, 1868 ellor æðelingas; *Dan* 689, *And* 805 þáer æðelingas, 857 Him þá æðelingas. 3b *And* 1208 Scealt þú, Andréas,/ellen fremman. 4b *Jul* 672 sceaðena þréate; *cp. Glc* 902 féonda þréatum.

5a *Bwf* 75 manigre mǽgðe, 1771 manigum mǽgða. 6b *Bwf* 1947; cp. 1775 siþþan Grendel wearþ; *Ele* 913 siþþan furðum wéox. *Note the more general metrical scheme involving* siþþan *plus a two- or three-syllable word plus verb:* And 1223 siþþan ge-ypped wæs; *Ele* 18 siþþan wǽpen ahóf, 841 siþþan béacen geseah; *Bwf* 1077, 2124 siþþan morgen (mergen) cóm, 1233 siþþan ǽfen cóm, 1689 siþþan flód ofslóg. 7a Cp. *And* 181 onfindaþ féasceaftne. 8a *Gen* 1702 wéox þá under wolcnum; cp. *Bwf* 714 Wód under wolcnum; *Phx* 27 wrídaþ under wolcnum; *Gen* 1438 wǽre under wolcnum; *Phx* 247 awierde under wolcnum. 8b *Exo* 258 weorþ-myndum spræc. 9a *Ele* 865 oþ-þæt him gecýðde, 885 oþ-þæt him uppan. 9b *Bwf* 2734, *Ele* 33. *Cp. other in-flections: dat. pl.* ymbsittendum *PPs* 78, 4; 88, 35; *fem. acc. pl. Met* 35, 14 ymbsittenda. *Cp. closely related* Gen 2490 ymbstandendra; *PPs* 140, 4 ymbstandende.

10a *Gen* 205 geond hran-ráde; *And* 266, 821 on hran-ráde. *Cp. Bwf* 200, *Ele* 996 ofer swan-ráde; *Jul* 675 on swan-ráde; *Bwf* 1429 on

segl-ráde. 10b *Dan* 135; *Ele* 367; *Met* 9, 45; *Met* 1, 31 híeran scoldon.
11a *Gen* 1977b–78a níede scoldon, / gamban gieldan. 11b *Bwf* 863,
2390. *Cp. Bwf* 1885 þæt wæs án cyning; *Jul* 224 þæt is sóþ cyning;
Déo 23 þæt wæs grimm cyning; *Wid* 67 Næs þæt sǽne cyning, *and
further Bwf* 1075 þæt wæs geómru ides, 1812 þæt wæs módig secg;
Met 26, 35 (?) þæt wæs geó cyning, *etc.* 12a *Gen* 1188 Se eafora
wæs / Énoc háten. *Note and cp. Bwf* 12a–b eafora . . . cenned *with
Gen* 1159 þá wearþ on éðle / eafora féded, 2394 of idese biþ / eafora
wæcned. 12b *Cp. Cæd* 8 æfter téode; *Rid* 40, 44 and ić giestran geong
cenned. 13a *Phx* 355, 647; *Chr* 201 geongre on geardum. *Cp. Jul* 35
geong on gáste; *Bwf* 2446 geong on gealgan. 13b *Dan* 525 þe þider
God sende; *cp. Gen* 1371 Dryhten sende. 14a *Exo* 88; *And* 606; *Ele*
1142; *Men* 228 folcum to frófre; *Ele* 502 folca to frófre; *Rid* 39, 19
manigum to frófrę; *Men* 57, *Ps* 50 148 mannum to frófre.

15a *Bwf* 831, 1875; *Chr* 615 þe wé ǽr drugon; *Jud* 158 þe gé lange
drugon. 15b *Cp. Bwf* 2935; *And* 405 hláfordléase. *Ealdorléas* is ordinarily used in the sense "lifeless." 16a *Bwf* 2159, 2780; *Dan* 660;
DrR 24; *Jul* 674; *Rid* 28, 9; *Met* 4, 46. For *numerous formulas to
express a "long" or "short time" cp. DrR* 70 góde hwíle, *also* mićele,
lýtle, sume hwíle, *and with* þráge: *ealle, lýtle, lange, sume, also*
ǽnige stunde. 16b *Cp. Exo* 271 and éow Líf-fréa; *Chr* 27 hwanne ís
Líf-fréa. 17a *Bwf* 183, 1752; *Dan* 14; *And* 193, 539. 18a *Sol* 182 Salo-
man wæs brémra; *Dan* 104 þá wæs bréme; *Sol* 238 béć sind bréme.
18b *FAp* 6 Lof wíde sprang; *cp. Bwf* 1588 hráw wíde sprang; *Jul*
Léad wíde sprang; *also Max I* 194 wíde gesprungen. 19a *Bwf* 897
Wælses eafora; 1847 Hréðles eaforan; *Gen* 1133 Séthes eafora, 2054
þáres eafora; *Met* 26, 36 Ióbes ("*Jove's*") eafora; *Men* 136 Zebedes
eafora. *Cp. also Gen* 1578 eafora Nóes, 2834 eafora þáres. 19b *Bwf*
2357 Frís-landum on; *Gen* 1052 éast-landum on. *Cp. Jul* 83 wín-
(wynn?) burgum on.

20a *Bwf* 1172, 1534 Swá sceal man dôn; *cp.* 2066 Swá sceal mǽg
dôn, 2590 swá sceal ǽghwelć mann. 21b *Cp. Bwf* 35, *Exo* 375 on
bearm scipes, 896 bær on bearm scipes, 214 on bearm nacan. *Note
related formula with* fæðm: *Bwf* 188 and to Fæder fæðmum; *Max II*
661 on Fæder fæðm; *And* 616 on banan fæðme; *Ele* 765 on dracan
fæðme. 22a–b *Cp. FoM* 60 and on ielde eft / éadig weorðan. 22b
See 22a–b, *also Phx* 481 lang gewunien. 23a *Gen* 2003. 25a *Pre* 74
þá-þe hér on mǽgðe gehwǽm.

Chart II

(Christ and Satan, ll. 512–35)

Swá wuldres Weard   wordum sægde,

Meotod mann-cynnes,   ǽr on morgen,

þæs-þe Dryhten God   of déaðe arás.

515   Næs nán þæs strangliċe   stán gefæstnod,

þéah hé wǽre mid írne   eall ymbfangen

þæt meahte þǽm miċelan   mægene wiþhabban,

ac Hé út éode,   enġla Dryhten

on þǽm fæstenne.   And gefetian hét

enġlas eall-beorhte   endleofan giengran,

and húru secgan hét   Símon Pétre

þæt hé móste on Galiléam God sċéawian,

éċne and trumne,   swá hé ǽr dyde.

Þá iċ gangan gefrægn   giengran ætsamne

525   ealle to Galiléam;   hǽfdon Gástes blǽd,

(ongéaton) háligne   Godes Sunu

swá híe gesáwon,   hwǽr Sunu Meotodes

þá on upp (a-?) stód,   éċe Dryhten,

God on Galiléam.   To þæs giengran þider

530   ealle urnon,   þǽr se Éċa wæs.

Féollon on foldan,   to fótum hnigon;

þancodon Þéodne   þæt hit þus gelamp

þæt híe sċéawodon   Sċieppend enġla.

Þá sóna spræc   Símon Pétrus:

"Eart þú þis, Dryhten,   dómes geweorðod?"

SUPPORTING EVIDENCE

512a *XSt* 659. *Cp. Gen* 941 Híe þá wuldres Weard; *And* 596 hú
ús wuldres Weard; *Ele* 84 (beseoh) on wuldres Weard; *Chr* 527 þá
wæs wuldres Weard. 512b *Gen* 707, 2053, 2704, *Glc* 451. *Cp. Exo*
377, *Phx* 425 wordum secgaþ; *And* 624 wordum gesecgan; *Chr* 64
wordum sægdon; *Bwf* wordum secge. 513a *Sat* 457, *Gen* 459, *And*

172, 357, 446. 513b *Frag. Ps* 5, 3; *also cp. PPs* 107, 2, 118, 148 on
ǽrmergen, *PPs* 62, 7 and on ǽrmergen; *Met* 28, 37; *PPs* 56, 10 and
ić on ǽrmergene. 514a *XSt* 313 mid Dryhtne Gode; *And* 1281 Geseoh
nú Dryhten God, 1462 Þá cóm Dryhten God; *Pan* 55 Swá is Dryhten
God; *Bwf* 181 ne wisson híe Dryhten God; *Jud* 300 him féng Dryhten
God; *LPr* 3 18 Críst, Dryhten God. *Cp.* God Dryhten *in And* 897
Nú ić God Dryhten, *Ele* 759 Þæs Þú, God Dryhten; *also* Dryhten
Críst *in Glc* 592 gief éow Dryhten Críst; *Sol* 337 Dryhtne Críste. 514b
Ele 187; *FAp* 56 Þæt hé of déaðe arás; *Chr* 467 fram déaðe arás.

515a *Cp. Chr* 241 for-þon n'is ǽnig Þæs horsc; *GfM* 8 Ne biÞ ǽnig
Þæs / earfoÞ-sǽlig; *Sea* 39 For-þon n'is Þæs mód-wlanc. 515b *Cp.
Jul* 499 folde (*subj.*) gefæstnod. 516b *XSt* 143b (*cp.* 145a selfe mid
sange); *cp. Bwf* 2691 heals eallne ymbeféng. 518b *Exo* 559; *XSt* 395;
Sol 462. 519a *Wha* 71; *And* 1034 fram Þǽm fæstenne, 1177 of fæstenne;
cp. Gen 2536, *And* 1068 to Þǽm fæstenne; *Sol.* 320 on fæstenne; *Met*
1, 79 né on Þǽm fæstenne. 519b *Gen* 525 and mećhér standan hét;
XSt 521 and húru secgan hét; *And* 330 and ús féran hét, 587 and
wendan hét; *Bwf* 3095 and éowić grétan hét. *Cp. with subordination:
Gen* 1865 oÞ-Þæt hé lǽdan hét; *And* 823 Þá gelǽdan hét, 931 swá
ić Þećféran hét; *Ele* 863 ǽr hé asettan het, *also* 129 arǽran het. *With
finite verb first: Gen* 2667 hét him fetian tó; *Ele* 1160, *Jul* 60 hét
Þá gefetian; *Bwf* 2190a–b hét . . . inn fetian.

520a *Chr* 880; *Aza* 52 engel ealle-beorhta; *Dan* 336 engel eall-
beorht. *For this formula used to connect a verse-pair of consecutive
off- and on-verses see Chr* 506 Gesáwon híe eall-beorhte / englas
twégen, 548 Þæt him eall-beorhte / englas togéanes, 521a *see* 519b,
above. 521b *XSt* 534b Símon Pétrus. 522a–b *Cp.* 529a. 522b *For*
scéawian *with preceding object entering into the alliteration: see
Gen* 979 (tíber), 1679 (weorc), 1780, 1920 (land), 2595 (wić), *Chr*
1136 (weorod), 1206 (dolg), *Rid* 59, 2 (menn); *Bwf* 840, 3032 (wun-
dor), 1391 (gang), 1413 (wang), 2402 (dracan), 2744 (hord). 523a *Cp.
Chr* 1071 éće and edgeong. 523b *Gen* 1840; *XSt* 116, 278. *Cp. Chr*
1233 swá híe geworhton ǽr, 161 Þá Þú geworhtest ǽr. 524a *Gen* 2060
Þá ićnéðan gefrægn; *And* 1706 Þá ić lǽdan gefrægn; cp. *Sol* 179
Hwæt, ić flítan gefrægn.

525b *Cp. Phx* 549 Þurh gástes blǽd; *XSt* 644 gemunan Gástes
blǽd; 526b *Gen* 1163 Enoses sunu; *XSt* 118 Wealdendes Sunu; *Bwf*
1009 Healf-Denes sunu; 2602, 2862, 3076 Wéoh-stánes sunu; *Wal*

I, 11 Ælf-heres sunu. *For the closely parallel and more common patronymic formula* sunu X's *see* 527b. 527b *XSt* 142 þær Sunu Meotodes, 172 Sunu Meotodes; *And* 881 Swelće wé gesáwon / for Sunu Meotodes; *Ele* 1318 and to Suna Meotodes, 461, 564 sóþ Sunu Meotodes, 474 hú híe Sunu Meotodes, 686 þurh Sunu Meotodes. *Cp. XSt* Sunu Wealdendes. *With the substitution of various personal names cp.: Gen* 1064 (Enoses), 1081, 1086 (Lámeches), 1240 (Nóes), 2465 (Arones); *Bwf* 524 (Béan-stánes), 590 (Ecg-láfes), 645, 1040 (Healf-Denes), *etc. For a patronymic formula centering on* eafora *see Chart I,* 19b. 528a *Cp. And* 443 Hwílum upp astód, *and note other combinations of* upp *and* astandan *in Grein-Holthausen-Köhler, suggesting the XSt* 530a *Ms.* stód *should, perhaps be emended to* astód *vs.* gestód *of the editors.* 528b *Frag. Ps.* 5, 1, 3; *PPs* 53, 4; 70, 18, 20; 71, 19; 73, 17; 78, 1, *etc.; Cæd* 4; *and in inflected cases as follows: gen. sg. Bru* 16 *Men* 12 éćes Dryhtnes; *Gen* 7, 1885; *Chr* 396, 711; *Phx* 600; *PPs* 67, 3, 9; 68, 29 éćan Dryhtnes; *dat. sg. Bwf* 2796 éćum Dryhtne, 1779, 2330 éćan Dryhtne; *acc. sg. PPs* 55, 9; 65, 1, 3, 7 éćne Dryhten; *Bwf* 1692 éćan Dryhten.

530a *Cp. PPs* 61, 4 wíde urnon. 531a *XSt* 544 féolon to foldan, *And* 918 Féoll þá to foldan; *Bwf* 2975 féoll on foldan. *Cp. Phx* 74 Ne feallaþ þær on foldan; *Sol* 298 afielleþ hine on foldan. 531b *Cp. Gen* 2441 þá to fótum [féoll / on foldan] Loth; *Mal* 119 þæt him æt fótum féoll. 532a *Glc* 778, *and cp. with object (usually God) first: Dan* 86, *And* 1011, *Ele* 1138, *Bwf* 1397 Gode þancode; *Bwf* 227, 1626 Gode þancodon. *Note the combined formulas of Ele* 961–62, *Bwf* 625–26 Gode þancode . . . þæs(-þe) hire se willa gelamp (*see* 532b, *below*). 532b *XSt* 568 þá hit þus gelamp, *and cp. Ele* 961–62 *and Bwf* 625–26 *under* 532a, *above.* 533b *And* 434; *And* 119, *XSt* 562 enĝla Scieppend. 534a *Cp. Gen* 862 þá sóna ongann, 1589 and þá sóna ongeat; *Chr* 233 And þá sóna gelamp; *Bwf* 1280 þá þær sóna wearþ; *Fin* 46 þá hine sóna frægn. 534b *XSt* 522 Símon Pétre. 535a *Bwf* 506 Eart þú sé Béo-wulf.

Beowulf and Archaeology

by *Rosemary Cramp*

In the Anglo-Saxon period, where both the written and the archaeological evidence have so many gaps and difficulties of inter-pretation, the picture of Anglo-Saxon society given in *Beowulf* must be fully considered by archaeologists while on the other hand no critic of the poem can afford to neglect the new material evi-dence that is constantly being produced. *Beowulf* is the only poem that gives a full picture of secular life in this period and as such it has constantly been used to articulate the archaeologist's dumb evidence: Bateman[1] in 1848 ended his account of the boar-crested helmet discovered at Benty Grange by quotations from the poem, and when the rich burial from Sutton Hoo was published[2] it seemed equally appropriate to quote from the account of the burial of Scyld in *Beowulf*. The poem in fact provides a picture of a royal and aristocratic milieu, which until quite recent years has been largely unrepresented by archaeological evidence. Nevertheless the archaeologist wishes to know how far this poetic evidence can be trusted: the rich gold treasure from Sutton Hoo brought the im-mediate recognition that descriptions of lavish burials and gold-adorned armour in *Beowulf* could no longer be dismissed as poetic exaggeration or folk memories of an age of gold before the Anglo-Saxons came to England, just as the luxury items in the grave culled from all over Europe have left the uneasy impression that the poet was not just speaking in clichés when he talks of "many treasures

---

"*Beowulf* and Archaeology." From *Medieval Archaeology*, I (1957), 57–77. Copyright © 1957 by Miss Rosemary Cramp. Reprinted by permission of the author. Due to technical difficulties, the illustrations have been omitted.

[1] J. Bateman, *Ten Years Diggings in Celtic and Saxon Grave Hills* (London, 1861), p. 33.
[2] *The Sutton Hoo Ship Burial: a provisional guide* (British Museum, 1947).

and ornaments from distant lands," [3] among Scyld's burial equipment.

On the other hand the form of burial at Sutton Hoo revived the old controversy about Beowulf's funeral [4]—whether the cremation of treasure with the body followed by the inhumation of the dragon's hoard in the hero's mound was not "too much of a good thing" [5] and a mingling of one or more funeral descriptions handed down from antiquity which the poet did not wholly understand. When it is a question of pagan customs as described by a Christian poet, however, it is obvious that archaeological propriety must be a secondary matter, and specifically pagan practices will be left out. As for the dragon's treasure, such heathen gold may be an embarrassment, but tales of fabulous treasure have always stirred men's imaginations, especially when it is said to be still lying somewhere intact. Moreover, the archaeologists have been answered by Miss Whitelock's common-sense defence of the poet: [6]

> If the procedure he describes is irregular, the circumstances are unusual also. A poet might feel that he could afford to do unorthodox, extravagant things with an enormous treasure which he had just won from a dragon; it is not safe to accuse him of ignorance of what was done at more normal funerals.

There are in fact several points in the description of the hero's funeral that might support this defence. It is perhaps unsafe to place too much reliance on the late account of a Viking funeral by Ibn Fadlan, [7] but his description of the old woman who was in charge of the funeral ceremony may explain what the Beowulf poet means by the *geatisc meowle* [Geatish woman] (l. 3150), who sang the hero's lament. Likewise the property of the Viking dead was divided into three, one part only going to his heirs, the other two parts being used for funeral expenses and burial with the dead. In *Beowulf* (ll. 3010–12) it is decreed that "not one part only shall

---

[3] ll. 36–37.

[4] ll. 3157–77.

[5] K. Stjerna, *Essays on questions connected with the Old English poem of Beowulf* (Viking Club publications, extra ser. III, 1912), pp. 198–204; S. Lindqvist, "Sutton Hoo and Beowulf," *Antiquity*, XXII (1948), 139.

[6] *The Audience of Beowulf* (Oxford, 1951), pp. 82–83.

[7] The fullest translation of this text in English is by A. Cook, in *Journal of English and Germanic Philology*, XXII (1923), pp. 54 ff.

burn with the brave warrior" because the heirs of Beowulf, his people, have not deserved their share of the dragon's hoard and it shall all go with the dead.[8] These may be chance parallels: nevertheless, without mentioning any specifically heathen ritual or sacrifice, the poet has given us a coherent account [9] and leaves the impression that he does know what was the norm and where he was departing from it.

Yet because *Beowulf* is an isolated literary type one can never be sure how much editing of heathen conditions to allow to its poet and how much had already been done for him. If archaeology could help to find a date for the poem this might be easier to decide, but in fact this is not easy to do, and a circle of arguments can develop, for the archaeologist has to understand the literary and linguistic problems of the poem before he can give an opinion as to whether the poet has mingled together objects and conditions that could never have existed simultaneously. The issue is, however, less complicated in dealing with material objects than with social conditions.

Since Stjerna's work, although specific points have been treated, there has not been any detailed attempt to consider the poem as a whole in the light of archaeological evidence. Yet the archaeological picture of Anglo-Saxon England has changed completely since 1912, and nothing less than another book could draw together all the material satisfactorily: in a shorter space one can only state the problems involved and provide selective illustrations. As a preliminary, however, there is one of Stjerna's contentions that can be dismissed: the rich burial at Sutton Hoo and the impressive buildings at Yeavering have shown that there is no longer any need to seek a foreign milieu for the elaborate armour and buildings

---

[8] This does not explain why the gold is then buried and not burnt, but it is artistically satisfying that the treasure should still lie "useless and unprofitable as it was before."

[9] Lindqvist's contention that in ll. 3156–62 the poet is erroneously using some older account of the construction not of a mound but of a pyre, "a hollow construction of logs reminiscent of a beacon," seems to rest on a misunderstanding of the word *becn* (l. 3160), which has the meaning "sign," "distinguishing mark," and which, like *tacn* [token] or *mearc* [mark], which have a comparable semantic spread, could perfectly well be applied to a grave-mound. The poet explicitly states (ll. 2802–2808) that Beowulf wished the mound to be raised as a distinctive memorial.

mentioned by the English poet. Such finds are invaluable as illustrations and even explanations of difficult passages in the poem, but today one would hesitate even more than Stjerna did to rely on archaeological evidence for dating *Beowulf*; gaps in the material evidence after the cessation of heathen burials are still too immense.

Moreover the poet describes most often rare or expensive things for which archaeology provides limited examples, and there can be a danger of overworking these in an attempt to make them fit too many contexts. It is also impossible with only a few examples to form a datable chronology. For instance Stjerna[10] recognized that boar-figures on helmets were part of a pagan tradition which could not have had a very long life in Christian times, when Christian symbols of protection[11] would take their place. He also saw that the Celts, like the Germanic peoples, used the boar-image on their helmets, shields and standards, a usage in which they may have influenced the Germans. Only two helmets have so far been found in England—those from Benty Grange and Sutton Hoo: both are probably sixth-century and both might be called "boar-helmets" since the former has a full-scale figure of a boar on its top and the latter a stylized boar's head over the cheek-guards, but they derive from different traditions (pp. 119 ff.) and their dating makes nonsense of the sort of chronology Stjerna attempted, whereby he takes the Celtic boar-helmet from the Gundestrup vessel of about the second century B.C. calling it "before 500 A.D." and then attempts to show the animal gradually subsiding into the helmet after Benty Grange through the stage of losing its legs in the Öland plates until by the early seventh century it had become the terminal of a comb, such as one finds on the Vendel helmets, and at the close of the century had been lost altogether.

As well as such difficulties of chronology, there are the related problems of heirlooms and conventional epithets. Unlike obsolete social conditions obsolete weapons could be preserved and seen many years after they were superseded. Prince Aethelstan in the early eleventh century bequeathed to his brother the "sword that

---

[10] Stjerna, *op. cit.* in note 5, pp. 16–18.

[11] The protective value of boar images is stressed by the poet in ll. 303–306, but even as early as the date of the Benty Grange helmet a cross has been attached to the nose-piece as additional protection.

belonged to King Offa," which would then have been over 200 years old. It does not seem, then, to be foisting too sophisticated an antiquarianism on to the poet to assume that, when he says that items like the sword in ll. 1558 ff. and the helmet in 1445 ff. are of ancient manufacture, his audience would expect something different from what they knew to be modern. On the other hand when a weapon is said to have been made in former days, how far away are we to suppose this time to be? It could be two hundred years or a mere fifty.

As for conventional epithets, Girvan says:[12]

> It is well to distinguish here between conventional epithets or phrases inherited by tradition and real description which proves knowledge.

This is a very difficult thing to do. Old English religious poetry shows us that terms from the heroic tradition had become appropriate in descriptions of personages from the past, as when Cynewulf in *Elene* tells us that Constantine's Roman soldiers wore the Germanic boar-sign, *ænlic eofor cumbul* [unique boar standard], on their armour, and that Constantine, before he saw the image of Christ's cross, was asleep, *eofor cumble beþæht*,[13] "overshadowed or covered by the boar-sign." These references to the boar-sign, however, show no more than that Cynewulf knew from older Old English poetry what was the conventional dress for pagan soldiers —he is unconcerned that these particular ones are Romans. He merely tosses in such brief phrases where the earlier *Beowulf* poet describes in detail; although even the *Beowulf* poet's long descriptions are so impressionistic—a mere highlighting of one or two outstanding features of an object—that there is often difficulty in reconstructing it.

---

[12] *Beowulf and the Seventh Century* (London, 1935), p. 38.

[13] l. 76. It has usually been assumed that the reference here is to a boar-crested helmet, but since the emperor is asleep when he sees the vision this would seem a rather peculiar addition of Germanic local colour. However, the phrase could mean a boar-standard: this is a common meaning of *cumbol* [standard], and it is clear that the protective boar-image was known in this form; cf. *Beowulf*, l. 2152, *eafor heafodsegn* [boarhead-banner]. The OE. poet has then added point to the well-known story of the creation of the *labarum* [sign of the cross], by stressing that when the new standard of victory, the cross, was shown to the emperor, he was lying overshadowed by the old heathen symbol of protection.

Helmets

This poetic method of description is in fact the main stumbling-block in any attempt at reconstruction and can only be illustrated by detailed examples, of which some present difficulties that archaeologists can resolve, and some remain enigmas. Helmets are described in greater detail than any other item of war-equipment in the poem, and despite the paucity of archaeological material so far discovered, a study of their descriptions provides some interesting results.

The length of the poet's descriptions in ll. 303 ff. or 1448 ff. is a measure of the aristocratic importance of the helmet which Alföldi sees as a *Herrschaftssymbol* [power-symbol] [14] among the Germanic peoples. Certainly the all-metal helmet does not seem to have been common in the earliest Anglo-Saxon period, and even in the tenth century, when helmets and corslets seem to have been more widely worn,[15] laws and wills show that twice as many spears and shields as helmets, corslets and swords were to be paid for heriot.

In the sixth and seventh centuries—the period from which examples have survived—two types of helmets were known among the Germanic peoples. One type derived from late Roman prototypes with solid crown comb, and some form of face and neck protection, examples of which have been found in the Swedish graves of Vendel and Valsgärde, as well as at Sutton Hoo. This last example may be a Swedish import, but it was found in an English grave and so would have been seen, and no doubt copied, here.

The second is the ribbed helmet or *Spangenhelm* [strap-helmet] which may have been eastern in origin and introduced into western Europe by the Ostrogoths.[16] So far twenty examples of these elegant conical helmets are known (e.g., from Batajnica), dating from the

---

[14] "Eine spätrömanische Helmform," *Acta Archaeol.*, V (1934), 142–43.

[15] For example the will of Archbishop Aelfric (D. Whitelock, *Anglo-Saxon Wills*, XVIII. 52) bequeaths to the king his ship and sixty helmets and corslets for the marines who would man it. See, too, depictions of Vikings on gravestones and the fighters on the Bayeux Tapestry.

[16] For recent discussions see J. Werner "Zur Herkunft der Frühmittelalterlichen Spangenhelm," *Prähist. Zeitschr.*, XXXIV–XXXV (1949–50), 178 ff., and Z. Vinski, "Ein Spangenhelmfund aus dem ostlichen Sirmien," *Germania*, XXXII (1954), 176–82.

fifth to the seventh centuries.[17] These helmets, moreover, have a much longer life and history than the Roman derived type, the latest depictions of which, if one excludes the mysterious gravestone from Aberlemno, are seen on the Franks Casket. The conical type, which no doubt never died out on the continent, seems to have been adopted by the Scandinavians by the ninth century, since gravestones in Gotland and in England [18] have clear depictions of them. Whether this form of helmet was introduced into England by the Danes, or earlier, it is impossible to say, but by the time the Bayeux Tapestry was embroidered, it was the only form of helmet worn by both English and Norman alike. Now in *Beowulf,* although the poet concentrates on exceptional or noteworthy features of helmets and leaves more mundane points of construction unstated, it is quite clear that he describes the romanesque and not the continental *Spangenhelm* form. When mentioning the helmet Hroðgar gives to Beowulf the feature he chooses to describe in detail [19] is the comb, *wala,* which passes round the roof of the helmet, *ymb þæs helmes hrof,* and is wound round with a wire inlay, *wirum bewunden.* Bruce-Mitford's lucid note on this passage[20] has put this interpretation of the difficult word *wala* beyond doubt. Wire-inlay was an expensive technique and so it is easy to see why the poet singled out this as worthy of comment.

Similarly, in what is the fullest description of a helmet in *Beowulf,*[21] the poet tells how the helmet is shining *hwit* [white] and *befongen fraewrasnum* [circled with noble chains], a phrase that has given much difficulty to commentators. The form *wrasen* [chains] [22]

[17] The helmet from Benty Grange has sometimes been called a *Spangenhelm* [strap-helmet], but, though it is of a ribbed construction, it is a unique and strangely primitive form of helmet, not only because of the boar-image but also because of the plates of bone which covered the iron ribs, perhaps the remains of the primitive idea of wearing part of a totem animal so as to share its qualities.

[18] For example the little figure from Kirk Levington: W. G. Collingwood, "Anglian and Anglo-Danish Sculpture in the North Riding of Yorkshire" *Yorks. Archaeol. J.,* XIX (1907), fig. *y,* facing p. 352.

[19] ll. 1030–34. My quotations throughout are taken from *Beowulf,* ed. F. Klaeber (3 ed., New York and London, 1941).

[20] R. H. Hodgkin, *History of the Anglo-Saxons* (3 ed., 1952), pp. 752–54.

[21] ll. 1448 ff.

[22] For examples of this word in both the abstract and concrete sense in other Germanic languages see A. Johannesson, *Isländisches Etymologisches Wörterbuch,* p. 248: "Zu ureik."

occurs in glosses: *nodus* [knot]—*wrasen* [chain]; *ost* [knot] (Corpus 1387), and is the second element of a compound in *Andreas* l. 1107, *fetorwrasen* [fetter-chain]; ll. 63 and 946, *inwitwrasen* [malice-chain]. In the first quotation in *Andreas* the word is used in a concrete sense—the chains of the fetters with which a victim is bound—and in *Solomon and Saturn* (ll. 293 ff.) we find the compound *hilde-wrasen* [battle-chain]:

> *Yldo beoð on eorðan æghwæs cræftig;*
> *mid hiðendre hildewræsne,*
> *rumre racenteage, ræceð wide*
> *langre linan—*

> [Age is on earth powerful over everyone;
> with its plundering battle-chain,
> its broad fetter, it reaches wide
> with its long line—]

which has been explained by Bosworth and Toller (A.-S. Dict.) as "a chain used to secure those taken in war," but which probably should be taken in an abstract sense as "hostile chain."

In *Andreas*, ll. 63–64 and 941–47, *inwitwrasen* [malice-chain] refers to the toils of heathen malice,[22] but the use of the word *searonett* [armor-net] in the same context is interesting, since in *Beowulf*, l. 406, this word is used as a synonym for corslet.

This evidence is, I think, sufficient to indicate that the word *freawrasnum* in *Beowulf* could plausibly mean some sort of chain-mail protection on the helmet, and in fact "encircled with lordly[23] or noble chains" has been the usual translation of the phrase, although this has not been further amplified.[24]

In recent years, however, the find of the two helmets from Valsgärde graves has provided a full explanation. The first helmet

---

[23] The word *frea* [noble] here is not used in its normal prefix sense as an intensitive (see Bosworth and Toller), but may perhaps indicate the aristocratic nature of the helmet's appendage. Chain-mail was rare and costly among the Germanic peoples.

[24] S. J. Herben, "A note on the helm in *Beowulf*," *Modern Language Notes*, LII (1937), 34–36, compared the *Beowulf* description with the Valsgärde grave 6 helmet, but, as I had reached my conclusions independently and further archaeological evidence has been discovered, it has seemed profitable to give a more detailed discussion of the word.

to be found (in Valsgärde grave 6,[25]) is of a latticed construction, unlike the more normal Vendel type with a solid crown, but Miss Arwidsson sees a link with the Benty Grange type of helmet in the Valsgärde specimen. In most respects, however, this helmet conforms to the normal Vendel style, and has been dated *c.* 650–700, but in contrast to the slatted neck-protection of Vendel helmets discovered earlier it had neck- and cheek-guards of chain-mail. This mail curtain, which is cylindrical in shape, tapers from a depth of about thirty-four rings in front to about half that number behind. The mail was fastened on to the helmet by iron wire which ran through the upper rings. Another helmet with a cylindrical mail protector has been found in grave 8 at Valsgärde,[26] this time together with body armour consisting of a combination of chain-mail and staves, and it would seem that the Vendel XII helmet[27] and one from Vestre Englaug in Norway were also provided with mail curtains. In fact it would seem that such protection on Scandinavian helmets of the seventh century was "at least equally common as the plates suspended on hinges." [28] There is no archaeological evidence that such helmets were known in England during the Anglo-Saxon period,[29] but Sutton Hoo has shown that helmets of the Vendel type were known here, and when *Beowulf* tells us so unambiguously that Beowulf wore a shining helmet encircled with noble links or chains, it seems sufficient proof that this sort of truncated camail was meant.

The other feature of the helmet with the camail that the poet chooses to mention is the protective boar-image telling how the smith who made it *besette swinlicum,* "set it around with boar-images." Here the plural form of *swinlicum* [boar-images], where only one helmet is in question, seems to refer not to one figure set

[25] G. Arwidsson, "A new Scandinavian form of helmet from the Vendel-time," *Acta Archaeol.,* V (1935), 243–57; *id., Die Gräberfunde von Valsgärde, I: Valsgärde 6* (Upsala, 1942).

[26] G. Arwidsson, "Armour of the Vendel Period," *Acta Archaeol.,* X (1939), 31–59, pls. iii–iv; *id., Die Gräberfunde von Valsgärde, II: Valsgärde 8* (Upsala, 1954), pp. 22–28.

[27] *Acta Archaeol.,* V (1935), 255, fig. 11.

[28] *Acta Archaeol.,* V (1935), 254.

[29] The helmet with camail is, however, a popular type of post-conquest armour, and the warriors on the Bayeux Tapestry wear a combination of helmet over mail, although not attached together.

on the helmet's top as at Benty Grange, but to two or more little figures, perhaps set over the cheek-guards as at Sutton Hoo. This may also be what is meant in ll. 303 ff. where the boar-images on the helmets of Beowulf and his followers shine *ofer hleorberan*—over the cheek- or face-protectors. On the other hand in l. 1286 *swin ofer helme* [swine over the helmet], and the *swin ealgyldan, eofer irenheard* [swine all-golden, boar iron-hard] which are plainly to be seen, *eþgesyne,* on a funeral pyre in ll. 1111–12 more plausibly refer to the larger, free-standing type of figure. In fact it is a tempting supposition that the poet used *swin* [swine] or *eofor* [boar] uncompounded to indicate a boar-image on a helmet's crown, and the *-lic* [-like] compounds for the small stylized figures set elsewhere.

It is difficult now-a-days to know what would constitute a distinguishing term between one form of helmet and another, and perhaps the most one can say is that despite the limited archaeological evidence no feature of the poetic descriptions is inexplicable and without archaeological parallel. Moreover these features—ornamented comb, visors,[30] and chain-mail neck-protection—can most closely be paralleled by the type found at Sutton Hoo and related to Scandinavian graves.

Swords

If a discussion of helmets shows how very illuminating even a limited amount of archaeological material can be, descriptions of swords in the poem illustrate to the full the difficulties provided by the poetic technique even when there is a much larger body of material for illustration.[31] This is not, I think, because limited archaeological evidence gives a falsely clear picture, but because in describing swords the poet concentrates on rather generalized terms of ornament, and our knowledge of which of these may be technical

---

[30] I have not stressed this feature, which is mentioned in ll. 334, 2049, 2257, 2605 of *Beowulf,* since visored helmet is an epithet found elsewhere in OE. poetry, but here, in combination with the other evidence, it is an added pointer to the sort of helmet the poet means, since *Spangenhelmen* do not have the full visor.

[31] Standard reference books which provide full illustrations are E. Behmer, *Das zweischneidige Schwert der germanischen Völkerwänderungszeit* (Stockholm, 1939), and J. Petersen, *De Norske Vikingesverd* (Kristiania, 1919).

terms is hazy. This is particularly seen in compounds of the words
fah [decorated] and *mæl* [ornamented], which, as their dictionary
definitions show, seem to sum up the total effect of ornament.[32]
That is to say, such words do not always appear to have been used
solely with application to a play of light and shade or colour, to
shape or to texture—all these effects are simultaneously present, but
one or the other is made predominant by the addition of a prefix,
e.g. *wunden-mæl* [curve-decorated], *græg-mæl* [grey-marked].

The aesthetic sense shown here linguistically can be paralleled
from archaeology in the Anglo-Saxon preoccupation with techniques of ornament which produce an effect of light and shade, for
instance pierced or interlace work, or the setting of dark garnets
against a background of glittering gold or opaque white paste.
Precisely this combined effect of pattern and a play of light and
shade that gives the effect of colour contrast is what stirred the
admiration of Theodoric when he thanked the king of the Vandals
for his marvellous gift of pattern-welded swords:[33]

> Harum media pulchris alveis excavata, quibusdam videntur crispari
> posse vermiculis, ubi tanta varietatis umbra conludit (colludit), ut
> intentium (intextum) magis credas variis coloribus lucidam metallum.[34]
> [The middle of these (blades), which are engraved with beautiful
> marks, seem to be curled with some little worms, where such shading
> of variety plays that you might rather believe the bright metal to have
> been interwoven with various colors].

It is perhaps because of this aesthetic similarity in the patterning
of blades and other patterns that could occur on hilts that has

---

[32] As L. D. Lerner has pointed out in "Colour Words in Anglo-Saxon," *Modern
Language Review*, XLVI (1951), 246–49, we tend today to specialize our colour
perception of hue, but unlike the Anglo-Saxons, have not many words to describe
the effects of absorption or reflection of light; "we tend not to notice that different hues of similar brightness may give a very similar sensation." This is an important distinction for the terminology of AS. ornament.

[33] Cassiodorus, V (J. P. Migne, *Patrologia Latina*, LXIX), 645.

[34] Modern research on the construction of such blades can be found in the following works: H. Maryon, "A sword of the Nydam type from the Ely Field's
Farm," *Proc. Cambs. Antiq. Soc.*, XLI (1947), 73–76; *id.*, "A sword of the Viking
period from the River Witham," *Antiq. J.*, XXX (1950), 175–79; A. France-Lan-
ord, "La fabrication des épées damassées aux époques mérovingienne et carolin-
gienne," *Pays gaumais* 1–2–3 (1949), 1–27; A. Liestøl, 'Blodrefill og Mål', *Viking*,
XV (1951), 71–96.

caused the long wrangle about what part of the sword such terms as *sceadenmæl* [branch-patterned], or *wyrmfah* [worm-ornamented] referred to.[35] Only a detailed analysis can illustrate such linguistic difficulties, and the poet's description of the sword Beowulf finds under the mere is the best illustration, because the most complete (ll. 1557 ff.):

> *Geseah ða on searwum sigeeadig bil,*
> *ealdsweord eotenisc ecgum þyhtig,*
> *wigena weorðmynd; þæt (wæs) wæpna cyst,—*
> *buton hit wæs mare ðonne ænig mon oðer*
> *to beadulace ætberan meahte,*
> *god ond geatolic, giganta geweorc.*

> Then he saw among the weapons a victory-blest blade, an ancient giant-made sword, mighty of edge, a glory for warriors; it was a weapon of weapons,—but it was greater than any other man could bear into battle, serviceable and splendidly adorned, the work of giants.

There is a good artistic contrast here with the passage where Hroðgar examines the hilt in detail; in the above passage the epithets used are much more general—consistent with a first impression: when Beowulf first catches sight of it he sees it as a weapon that could save his life, *sigeeadig bil* [victory-blessed sword], an ancient mighty weapon, as were all the best swords, but differing from other such swords in that it was much larger, the sort of weapon only a hero like Beowulf could wield. It is also "the work of giants." In his reference to the *gigantas* [giants] the poet introduces a word that is much rarer than the other term meaning "made by giants," *eotenisc,* but the learned Latin word *gigant* occurs again later in the description of this sword's hilt, and it is typical of the poet to provide such a link.

Attention is now concentrated on the sword-hilt as Beowulf grasps at it, *gefeng þa fetelhilt* [he grabbed the belted hilt] (l. 1563). It has been assumed by some commentators[36] that *fetelhilt* [belted-hilt] and *hringmæl* [ring-ornamented] in the next line mean that the sword was a "ring sword" such as are found in Kentish graves

---

[35] For the latest contribution to this discussion see A. T. Hatto, "Snake-swords and Boar-helms in *Beowulf*," *English Studies*, XXXVIII, 4 (1957), 145–60.

[36] Stjerna, *op. cit.* in note 5, pp. 25–27.

of the late sixth century and Scandinavian graves of the seventh century,[37] and, because this type of sword has a limited life, that references to ring-swords in *Beowulf* could be used for dating the poem. In fact, the memory of such swords could have lingered on in Old English literature [38] (as it did in Norse) long after their type was superseded and in this particular *Beowulf* context the epithets do not seem to refer to this feature at all. The evidence of Old English wills show that a *fetel* is an appendage to a sword that could be considered in separation from it.[39] It therefore seems more reasonable to follow the suggestions of Falk[40] and Keller,[41] who connect the word with the Norse *fetill* and translate it as a sword-belt. "Belted hilt" would imply that the hilt was in some way attached to a belt, and not just that the belt was fixed in the more normal way to the sheath, and one is reminded of the Snartemo sword which has a small ring on the lower guard, no doubt to bind the sword into the sheath or to the sword-belt. Beowulf then would snatch at the sword and belt and draw out the sword, so *hringmæl gebrægd* would mean "he drew out the ring-patterned sword." Later (ll. 1612–16), the poet tells how Beowulf took away from the mere only the hilt of this sword, for the blade had melted away, corroded by Grendel's poisonous blood, *sweord ær gemealt/forbarn brodenmæl* [sword melted before/the wavy-ornamented (sword) burned up]. Here surely it is a question of the blade, but the latest commentator, whilst pointing out that *broden-* [wavy-] and *hringmæl* [ring-ornamented] are "near equivalents"—the former can refer to a woven or braided pattern and the latter to a coiled pattern—would see both these epithets as referring to the hilt.[42] Circular and interlacing patterns are certainly found on Anglo-Saxon sword-hilts throughout the period, but they are also found on blades. Moreover, as Liestøl points out,[43] weaving terms are used to describe

[37] For a full discussion of these swords and the possible significance of the ring see E. Behmer, *op. cit.* in note 31, pp. 135–37, pls. xxxviii–xlv.

[38] H. Falk, *Altnordische Waffenkunde* (Kristiania, 1914), pp. 27–29.

[39] D. Whitelock, *op. cit.* in note 15, XVI. 3 and II. 6.

[40] *Op. cit.* in note 38, p. 35.

[41] "The Anglo-Saxon weapon names," *Anglistische Forschungen,* XV (1906), 163–64.

[42] Hatto, *op. cit.* in note 35, pp. 146–47.

[43] A. Liestøl, *op. cit.* in note 34, English summary.

pattern-welding in Norse and this is appropriate since the patterns are built up in the blade by twisting, plaiting or pleating the bands of hard and soft iron. One does not, however, have to assume that the poet knew the manufacturing secrets of such swords; he merely described the finished effects most aptly.

The other passage where the Grendel sword is described is ll. 1687–98, when Beowulf has handed the treasure-adorned hilt (*since fage* [treasure-adorned], l. 1615) to Hroðgar. Again its mysterious giant manufacture is referred to (l. 1679). This idea no doubt arose because the best pattern-welded swords were imports—the products of inherited trade secrets. Hroðgar examines the hilt:

> on ðæm wæs or writen
> fyrngewinnes syðþan flod ofsloh
> gifen geotende, giganta cyn,
> frecne geferdon; þæt wæs fremde þeod
> ecean Dryhtne; him þæs endelean
> þurh wæteres wylm Waldend sealde.
> Swa wæs on ðæm scennum sciran goldes
> þurh runstafas rihte gemearcod
> geseted ond gesæd, hwam þæt sweord geworht,
> irena cyst ærest wære
> wreoþenhilt ond wyrmfah.

> On it was engraved the beginning of the ancient struggle when the Flood, the rushing tide, slew the giant race; they behaved insolently, they were people hostile to the eternal Lord; the Ruler gave them a last requital for this by the onslaught of the water. Also on the pure gold covering of the hilt was set out and made known, fittingly marked in runes, for whom that sword was made, that best of weapons with its hilt spirally adorned its blade glinting red.

The elaboration and detail of this description is quite different from any other sword description in Old English literature, and unless one assumes it to be a complete fantasy one is compelled to think that the poet is describing an elaborate weapon he had seen, or at least a type he had seen. Lines 1694–95 are of crucial importance for the interpretation of the whole passage: Falk[44] sees the word *scenna* [plates] as deriving from the Germanic form **skanjo* and cognate with other Germanic words which mean a skin or cover-

[44] *Op. cit.* in note 38, p. 30.

ing, so here *scenna* would refer to thin metal plates covering the sword-handle in part or in whole. If one translates *swa*, like Klaeber,[45] as "also," then not only the runes but the preceding material was on the pure gold plating of the hilt, and so it seems most likely that the whole hilt was overlaid with gold. On it then was *writen* [engraved] the beginning of primaeval strife and the overthrow of the giants by the flood, seemingly a reference to *Genesis*, vi. 4–7. This passage was perhaps stressed more in Anglo-Saxon biblical teaching than today—certainly Ælfric sees "the works of giants" as one of the four significant episodes in *Genesis*.[46] Here *writen* must, I think, be taken in the sense of engraved, since any sort of inscription or poem lengthy enough to give this information, such as Girvan suggests, would be highly improbable on such a small area as a sword-handle. One could, however, imagine a combat-scene such as the now unintelligible figure-groups on the Vendel or the Sutton Hoo helmets. The poet was, no doubt, influenced in his choice of subject-matter for the engraving less by the anomaly of showing the triumph of good over evil on a monster's sword, than by a desire to point the moral and make a striking analogy with Beowulf's achievement. There is a possibility that the account of the fight under the water is drawing on pagan folk-legend, where the sword had a more obviously magical part to play, and was engraved with some heathen device; but if this be so the poet has obviously changed his material as carefully as he has traced Grendel's descent from Cain.

Lines 1694 ff. tell us that on the gold plates of the hilt was also engraved in runes, *hwæm þæt sweord geworht* [for whom that sword was made]. The only Anglo-Saxon runic inscription on a hilt is on the Gilton sword, but that is unintelligible.[47] Klaeber points out that on grammatical grounds the *hwæm* should refer to the original owner's name, and this interpretation seems reasonable, although no hilt with an owner's name in runes has yet been found.

---

[45] *Beowulf* (3rd ed. 1941), p. 189 note.

[46] *Homilies of the Anglo-Saxon Church* (ed. B. Thorpe, London, 1844–46), II, p. 198: "*ærest be frumsceafte, þe nan eorðlic man ða nyste, and siððan be Adames ofspringe, and Noes flode, and þære enta getimbrunge, and swa forð*" [first of creation, of which no earthly man then knew, and afterward of Adam's offspring, and Noah's flood, and the building of giants, and so forth].

[47] G. Stephens, *Handbook of Runic Monuments* (1884), p. 115.

The one-edged dagger from Sittingbourne, however, has both the owner's and the maker's name set on the blade in Latin characters, and blades with the maker's stamp are known on Germanic weapons from sub-Roman to Viking times, as well as more rarely—in Viking times—blades with the owner's name.[48] The difficulties of the terms *wreoþenhilt* [bound-hilt] and *wyrmfah* [worm-decorated] are well illustrated by the conflicting conclusions reached by those who have discussed them.[49] *Wreoþen* means "bound or twisted" and Bosworth and Toller consider that it must refer to a hilt bound with wire; but this is impossible, since the hilt is said to be covered with gold plating on which the giant-combat is engraved. The word should therefore refer to some sort of spiral or twisted ornament on the pommel or guard. Such ornament is known on Anglo-Saxon and other Germanic swords from the migration period until the ninth century, and I think it is of little use to try to pin it down to ornament on any known sword.

Wyrmfah [Worm-decorated] could refer to ornamentation on the hilt or on the blade, for although Hroðgar is examining the hilt only, ll. 1697–98 could be taken as a sort of summary of the whole weapon, as *irena cyst* [choicest of irons] suggests. I have pointed out above (p. 123 f.) the difficulty of knowing when compounds with -*fah* [-ornamented] refer more specifically to colour or a play of light and shade as *hasufah* [ashen], *readfah* [reddish], *bleofah* [variegated], or when they are used to convey a more general ornamental effect as *goldfah* [gold-adorned], *stanfah* [stone-adorned], *banfah* [bone-adorned]. Now the epithet *wyrmfah* could be used in the latter sense and refer to serpentine interlace on the hilt, but in view of what is known about the effect of colour in pattern-welded blades, I prefer to think that this epithet refers to the blade. *Wyrm* could then, as Nora Kershaw suggests in her notes on the *Wanderer* (l. 98)[50] "come from *wurma, wyrma* as in *wyrmbasu* [scarlet], *coccus* [scarlet-dye]." The blade would be straked or variegated with red,

---

[48] *Ibid.*, p. 242, for what seems to have been the owner's name set in runic characters. The sword guard from Exeter, however, which is dated about 1000, has on it the maker's name in Latin characters, as opposed to the normal placing on the blade.

[49] See especially, Stjerna, *op. cit.* in note 5, pp. 22–24, 29; Girvan, *op. cit.* in note 12, p. 36.

[50] *Anglo-Saxon and Norse Poetry* (Cambridge, 1922), pp. 166–67, note.

and, no doubt, as in the letter of Theodoric, both the serpentine effect of the wriggling patterns and the play of colour of the pattern-welding would be present in the poet's image.

To sum up the description of the Grendel sword: it does not conform exactly to any example yet discovered, but it does not seem to be a fantastic type, and is at least comparable with such elaborate gold-hilted swords as that from Snartemo. This is a large and costly weapon with pommel, handle and guards completely covered with gold plating, and one could imagine similar plating engraved with the giant-combat scene. The Snartemo example has also spiral ornament on the pommel and guards, and so could be called *wreoþenhilt* [bound-hilt], and it has a little ring on the lower guard whereby it could be bound into a sheath or belt, but here the resemblance ceases. The Grendel sword was pattern-welded as English swords, unlike their Scandinavian counterparts, seem to have been from the migration period onwards, and it has a runic inscription which could be on the back of the pommel, as on the Gilton sword.[51] Perhaps, when other richly adorned English swords are found, a nearer analogy to the description in *Beowulf* will be forthcoming.

Houses

Descriptions of Hroðgar's palace in *Beowulf*—they are the only full-scale picture of a secular building in Old English literature— have in the past presented different problems. Our knowledge of Germanic grave-goods, such as swords or helmets, has been accumulating for a long time, but discoveries of habitation-sites are still comparatively few and recent. In 1936 Suse Pfeilstücker[52] gave a valuable summary of earlier reconstructions of Hroðgar's hall *Heorot* from evidence based on a few continental sites, manuscript illustrations and English churches and post-conquest buildings. At that time the only Anglo-Saxon houses known were the squalid huts such as Leeds found at Sutton Courtenay, Berkshire, or Dunning at Bourton-on-the-Water, Gloucestershire.

[51] G. Stephens, *l.c.* in note 47.
[52] *Spätantikes und germanisches Kunstgut in der frühangelsächsischen Kunst* (Berlin, 1936), pp. 42-54.

These may in fact have been the living as well as the working quarters of the lowest orders of Anglo-Saxon society, but an increasing mass of evidence from the continent has shown that there such huts are always found in association with longhouses of a more elaborate type,[53] and that they are in no way typical living quarters. As Tischler[54] says:

> Wir kennen die Grubenhütten seit der Goldberggrabung in Verbindung mit grössern Häusern und das gilt auch für die Befunde in Bärhorst/Nauen, Haldern Hodorf, Westick/Kamen, Hessens, Ziejen/Rhee, Warendorf, Burgheim, Gladbach. Diese Beispiele reichen von Hallstatt C-Periode bis in die Karolingerzeit und bezeihen geographisch einen Raum von Basel bis zur Nordsee ein.
>
> [We have known these pit-huts ever since the Goldberg excavation in association with larger houses, and this is also true for the findings in Bärhorst/Nauen, Haldern Hodorf, Westick/Kamen, Hessens, Ziejen/Rhee, Warendorf, Burgheim, and Gladbach. These examples extend from the "Hallstatt C" period to the Carolingian times, and geographically speaking they cover an area from Basel to the North Sea].

The typical Germanic house, then, was a long, rectangular building, which sometimes had the roof supported by two or more rows of internal pillars, as at Ezinge,[55] or external buttresses as at Warendorf,[56] sometimes with neither of these supports, but with a cruck-roof.[57] The commonest West-Germanic building material [58] from migration to Viking times was wattle-and-daub, although in parts

[53] Warendorf, for instance, has provided a clear and typical series of rectangular buildings of diminishing size and solidity of construction representing living halls, cattle-sheds, servants' quarters, sheds and outhouses, and there are others from Bärhorst; see also C. A. Ralegh Radford, *supra*, pp. 27 ff., for a discussion of recent English and continental evidence.

[54] "Der Stand der Sachsenforschung, archäologisch gesehen," *Bericht der Römisch-Germanischen Kommission*, XXXV (1954: Berlin, 1956), 137.

[55] Der Warf in Ezinge," *Germania*, XX (1936), 40–47.

[56] W. Winkelmann, "Eine westfälische Siedlung des 8. Jahrhunderts bei Warendorf," *Germania*, XXXII (1954), 189–213.

[57] J. Walton, "The Development of the Cruck-framework," *Antiquity*, XXII (1948), 68–77.

[58] That this was the normal building material in ninth-century England is proved by the extended simile of house building which King Alfred uses in the preface to his *St. Augustine's Soliloquies*. The ninth-century boat-shaped houses from Thetford were also built in this material.

of Scandinavia[59] stone-and-earth was used, as at Vallhagar. From the ninth century onwards, however, a more advanced form of building with upright or horizontal planks was introduced, the earliest continental example so far known being the small house from the late-eighth-century site, Visselhövede, Kreis Rothenburg.

The newly discovered site at Yeavering in Northumberland of the *villa regia* [royal villa] mentioned by Bede (*H.E.*, ii, 14), has, however, provided examples of this advanced planking construction of at least a century earlier than any so far known. A full report of this important site is still to be published, but what has so far been made public has shown the amazing building skill that a seventh-century English king could command. The excavator says:

> The focus of the township was the great hall of the palace. We have not found one such building but a great complex of seven structures, representing different phases. The most impressive are four halls each nearly a hundred feet long: two with a porch at each end; the others of a simpler plan but elaborately buttressed. Set about these main palace buildings were eleven smaller halls. Most were the private halls of noble retainers, but one appears to have been a native servants' house, and another a pagan temple later put to Christian purposes.[60]

All the halls were of heavy planks set in the Trelleborg manner[61] except for the presumed servants' quarters, which were of wattle-and-daub, and only one, the temple, had a double row of supporting inner pillars. These magnificent buildings, the grandest in the Germanic world before the Viking age, are worthy to be set beside descriptions of *Heorot* in *Beowulf,* although it is too much to expect that this site can answer all the problems posed in the poem. The difficulties of reconstructing the buildings arise here, as elsewhere, mainly because the poet naturally concentrates on their more interesting or unusual features, and we still have not enough knowledge of the norm. However, in view of the recent interest in Anglo-Saxon habitation-sites, it seems worth while to reconsider what the poet says.

---

[59] The most complete recent discussion of these Scandinavian longhouses is to be found in M. Stenberger and O. Klindt-Jensen, *Vallhagar; A Migration-period Settlement in Gotland, Sweden* (Copenhagen, 1955).

[60] Extract from a talk by Brian Hope-Taylor, *The Listener* (October 25, 1956), p. 650.

[61] P. Nørlund, *Trelleborg* (Copenhagen, 1948), p. 20.

Most of the poet's descriptions are lavished on the great hall of the palace, to which building alone it seems the name *Heorot* is given.[62] Here all public business such as the reception and feasting of visitors takes place, and here before the attacks of Grendel Hroðgar's *comitatus* [retainers] slept. There were other buildings, however, in the palace complex: the normal pattern of a royal Anglo-Saxon palace seems to have been hall, *buras* [chambers] and other, presumably domestic, buildings, *swa swa ælces cynges hama; beoþ sume on bure, sume on healle, sume on odene.*[63] The *buras* [chambers] in *Beowulf* were perhaps behind the hall,[64] and certainly at some distance from it, for after Grendel's attacks on the hall the poet ironically says (ll. 138–40):

> *þa wæs eaðfynde þe him elles hwær*
> *gerumlicor ræste (sohte)*
> *bed æfter burum.*

Then it was easy to find the man who sought out a resting-place elsewhere further off, a bed in the women's quarters.

A *bur* was a private room, as is stressed by such Old English glosses as *camera* [vaulted-chamber]—*bur*,[65] often a woman's or women's quarters. Thus Hroðgar and his queen retire to the *brydbur* [woman's apartment] for the night. However, the word could also refer to a guest-house or the private quarters of a young man in his father's household.[66] There is no evidence that such buildings would be anything more than small rectangular ones, and perhaps the eleven smaller "halls" found at Yeavering were the *buras* of the site.

The hall however was obviously the most impressive building in

[62] ll. 77–79.

[63] "So in all king's residences; some men are in his private room, some in the hall, some on the threshing-floor": *King Alfred's Old English Version of St. Augustine's Soliloquies,* ed. H. Hargrove (Yale Studies in English, New York, 1902), p. 44.

[64] This would be supported by the fact that visitors to the palace seem to follow a path that leads straight to the hall, and in Ælfric's description of St. Thomas building a palace for the King of India he builds first the hall and then the other buildings which include *wynsume buras* behind the hall: *Lives of the Saints,* IV (ed. W. Skeat), XXXVI, 404.

[65] *Anglo-Saxon and Old English Vocabularies* (ed. T. Wright and R. Wülker), 184. 25.

[66] *Beowulf,* ll. 2455–57; *op. cit.* in note 64, XXXV, 380.

the palace. A "stone adorned," *stanfah*, path leads up to it[67]—a feature that is known from several Germanic sites—and although the poet says (ll. 75–76) that the hall was "adorned by the skill of many nations," it is constructed in the native timber tradition, unlike the exotic stone buildings that are found in Old English religious poetry. *Heorot* is a *(s)æl timbred* [timbered hall] (l. 307), doomed to a future destruction by fire,[68] but the only clues to its type of timber construction are rather enigmatic: during Beowulf's bitter fight in the hall with Grendel the poet remarks that it was a wonder that the building did not fall to the ground with the impact, but (ll. 773–76):

> *he þæs fæste wæs*
> *innan ond utan irenbendum*
> *searoþoncum besmiþod*

[it was built sturdily inside and outside with iron-bands skillfully];

and again (ll. 997–98):

> *Wæs þæt beorhte bold tobrocen swiðe*
> *eal inneweard irenbendum fæste*

[That bright hall, all sturdy inside with iron-bands, was badly shattered];

while in l. 722 he also says that the doors were *fyrbendum fæst* [sturdy with fired-bands]. Now, it is easier to imagine doors strengthened by bands hardened by fire,[69] which is what this unique word *fyrband* seems to mean, than whole walls strengthened by iron bands, and so far nothing that could serve as an example has been found from the pre-conquest period. The nearest analogy are the small flat pieces of iron that were found lying around the line of the wooden superstructure over the Sutton Hoo burial.[70] Pfeilstücker supposes that the hall was built of split logs and that *innan ond*

---

[67] l. 320.

[68] ll. 82–83.

[69] These would be a more pretentious equivalent of the wooden cross-piece known from doors of migration-period farm-houses without necessarily being as elaborate as the iron work on late Viking or Saxon doors: D. Talbot Rice, *English Art, 871–1100* (Oxford, 1952), p. 237, pl. xci; see also *Christ*, ll. 309–10, *duru . . . wundurclommum bewripen* [doors wrapped with wondrous-bands].

[70] See plan of the deposit: *op. cit.* in note 2, pl. 24.

utan [in and out] meant that these logs were fastened in bundles with iron binders passing in and out.[71] It seems equally justifiable however to suppose that the phrase could mean "inside and out-side," in which case the clamps could be bolted through planking walls, in pairs with the bolt passing right through the wall into a plate on the other side, or the iron bands could be both inside and out without any conjunction. Whatever the poet means, he implies that the hall was built in the most outstanding technique that he knew of, and iron bands on timber work best fit a type of stave walling, which, as Yeavering has shown, appeared at an early date in England in buildings with an almost Roman solidity and pre-cision of structure.

As the building is approached from outside the striking features are its height, to which several references are made, and which seems to have been accentuated by the steep roof (ll. 926–27) *steapne hrof/golde fahne* [steep roof/gold adorned], and its wide gables (ll. 81–82):

> *sele hlifade*
> *heah ond horngeap*

[the hall towered high and horn-gapped].

This description reminds one of early Anglo-Saxon churches such as Bradwell or Escomb, and the steeply-gabled roofs of the Celtic world, that are known from their churches, and from crosses, such as Durrow and Muiredach, and the Book of Kells.[72]

The references to the gold or gilding of *Heorot* seem the most unreal and inexplicable thing about it. The poet is quite explicit, however; he mentions this feature three times,[73] and one hesitates to dismiss it as poetic fancy when this seems so alien to his style elsewhere. Moreover, this is not the only reference to buildings

---

[71] *Op. cit.* in note 52, p. 51. Pfeilstücker compares the *Beowulf* passages with l. 20 of *The Ruin*, where the Anglo-Saxon poet describes a Roman building where the stone blocks are clamped together with metal. It is not impossible that a similar technique could have been taken over by Anglo-Saxons into their timber architecture.

[72] I. A. Richmond, "Irish Analogies for the Romano-British Barn Dwelling," *J. Rom. Stud.*, XXIII (1932), pls. 22–23; F. Henry, *Irish Art in the Early Christian Period* (London, 1940), p. 78.

[73] See above, ll. 926–27, and ll. 308 and 715–16.

ornamented with precious metals in Anglo-Saxon times; Asser says of King Alfred, "how can it be told of *aedificiis aureis et argenteis incomparabiliter, illo edocente, fabricatis*" [incomparable buildings made of gold and silver by his instructions],[74] and Stevenson states,[75] on the doubtful authority of William of Malmesbury, that King Ine built a chapel of gold and silver at Glastonbury. It seems unlikely that archaeology will ever be able to resolve this problem, for it is too much to hope that if such an expensive item as a gold-adorned roof ever existed it would have remained for the present day excavator. If we accept the idea that the poet means real gold and not just a golden effect, then a gold-plated shingle roof is at least imaginable.

Compounds with *horn* such as *hornsele* [horn-hall] or *horngeap* [horn-gapped], which most commentators agree refer to the gables,[76] are found in other contexts in Old English poetry, but the unique epithet *banfag* [bone-adorned] to describe the hall is more controversial. It has been supposed that the term refers to a stag's head nailed over the door, but it seems more likely that this is a coinage on analogy with *horn*,[77] and that *fag* is used in its weakest sense, so that the phrase means adorned with gables.

It is not clear in the poem whether the main door of the hall was on the long or short side of the building; there were usually two or more doors in a large Germanic building, and the traditional placing of them varies; for example, the doors are in the gable walls in Gotland and Bornholm but in the long walls in Öland, Norway and Denmark. However, there seems to be an outer and an inner door at the main entrance to the hall, perhaps divided by a porch: when Grendel pays his last visit to *Heorot* (ll. 721–24):

> *Duru sona onarn*
> *fyrbendum fæst, syððan he hire folmum (æth)ran;*
> *onbræd þa bealohydig, ða (he ge)bolgen wæs,*
> *recedes muþan.*

[74] *Life of King Alfred* (ed. W. Stevenson, Oxford, 1904), chap. 91, p. 77.
[75] *Ibid.*, pp. 329–30.
[76] T. Miller, "The position of Grendel's arm in Heorot," *Anglia*, XII (1889), 396–400.
[77] For example the word *ban-helm* in the *Fight at Finnsburg*, 30, seems to mean "horned helmet."

> The door, fortified by iron bands, at once sprang open when he
> touched it with his hands; then intent on evil, for he was enraged,
> he flung open the entrance to the hall,

and immediately after that he stepped on to the hall floor. There is
a definite progression of events here, and the *recedes muþan* [hall's
mouth] does not seem to be the same as the iron-bound outer door.
It would be quite in keeping with Hroðgar's great public hall that
it should have a reception-room with two sets of doors, one leading
to the outside and one to the hall proper; and no doubt, like the
halls with porches at Yeavering or Bärhorst,[78] the doors would be
placed eccentrically to avoid draughts. Whether we are to assume
a basilican type of plan like the former, or a porch on the long side
like the latter, it is not possible to say.

Two other much discussed features of *Heorot* must be mentioned.
When Beowulf tears off Grendel's arm and shoulder in the fight, he
places this trophy *under geapne hr(of)* [under the spacious roof]
(l. 836), and in the morning many people come to look at it, including the king who comes with his queen and retainers from the
brydbur [woman's chamber] (ll. 925 ff.):

> he to healle geong
> stod on stapole, geseah stapne hrof
> golde fahne ond Grendles hond

[he went to the hall, stood on the step, saw the steep roof adorned with
gold, and Grendel's hand].

The word *stapol* seems to be something on which one steps or
stands, cf. *fot stap(p)el* [foot step], and although elsewhere *stapol*
can mean a pillar or support (see *Beowulf*, l. 2718), that cannot be
the meaning here, as Hroðgar is definitely outside the hall when he
sees at the same time Grendel's arm and the high, gilded roof.
Nevertheless, if this most reasonable placing of the hand is accepted,
and *stapol* is taken to mean a step, what exactly does this mean? Is it
the top step or landing of a flight of steps leading up to the hall, as
Miller, followed by Pfeilstücker, suggests; is it a reference to an
outside staircase leading to an upper room as Addy[79] suggests; or is

---

[78] *Prähist. Zeitschr.*, XXVIII–XXIX (1937–38), 299, fig. 11.
[79] S. O. Addy, "The meaning of *stapol* in Beowulf," *Notes and Queries*, May
1927, pp. 363–65.

it, as Earle thinks, "an erection in the open air in an area in front
of the hall"? [80]

The idea that Hroðgar has come down an outside staircase[81] in
Heorot can, I think, be ruled out. There is no other mention of
such a room in this poem, and ll. 920–25 give a clear impression of a
leisurely procedure towards the hall of the king, queen and at-
tendants from the *brydbur* [woman's chamber], which, as mentioned above, was probably some way from the hall. The idea of a
platform at some distance from the hall on which the king stood, is
tempting in view of the "grand stand" that has recently been found
at Yeavering,[82] but it certainly seems from the text as though
Hroðgar went right up to the hall until he could see the very nails
of the hand.

The best solution seems to be that the king stood on a step or
small landing at the entrance to the hall and looked directly up at
the monstrous hand and arm propped up under the overhanging
roof. Archaeological parallels are known for both these features:
heavy stone or wood thresholds raised above the ground level and
so forming a step are widely known from Germanic sites, and one
of the houses from the ninth-century site at Haithabu[83] has an
entrance on its gable end approached by two shallow steps and a
small landing.

The other controversial feature of *Heorot* is the poet's reference
(l. 725) to its *fagne flor* [decorated floor]. The difficulties of this
word in Old English have already been discussed above; in its
simplest form it could mean something as vague as "gleaming" or
as specific as "variegated." It is this latter sense which those who
interpret this passage as referring to a tessellated floor would see
here. In Anglo-Saxon glossaries *tessere* or *tessellae* [square] are explained pedantically with reference either to substance, *tesellis*
[squares]—*stanflorum* [paving-stones] (*Old English Glosses*, 14. 3),
or to their square shape, *tessellae—lytle feþerscite florstanas* [little

[80] See the note to this passage in Klaeber's edition of *Beowulf*.

[81] The occurrence of the word as a gloss for the Latin *patronus* (*petronus*)
[?foundation?] in a list of the parts of a house, Wright/Wülker, *op. cit.* in note
65, 126. 8, is further proof that the word did not mean a stair, for in the same
list appears *stæger* [stair] glossing *ascensiorum* [ascents].

[82] Brian Hope-Taylor, *op. cit.* in note 60.

[83] H. Jankuhn, *Haithabu* (Neumünster, 1956), p. 103, plan II.

four-cornered floor-stones] (Wright/Wülker, 150. 27), and not by the word *fah* [decorated] or any decorative term. Nevertheless, place-name evidence has shown that the Anglo-Saxons could use *fah* to describe mosaic work: a mosaic pavement has been discovered at Fawler in Oxfordshire, and other place-names may contain the same element.[84] This does not prove, of course, that the term *fah flor* [decorated floor] could not have been extended in sense, especially by a poet.

Stone flooring is found in Germanic building, but in the form of flags or cobbles. It seems, then, on the present evidence as though a mosaic floor in *Heorot* would either be a reused Roman one, or the work of foreign craftsmen, or a poetic fancy. There is as yet no evidence for Saxon superstructures over Roman flooring, and although foreign workmen might have been called in, as they were in Anglo-Saxon church building, it seems rather an exotic possibility. In fact a stone floor to which wooden benches were clamped seems odd anyway,[85] and perhaps the poet merely meant a gleaming wooden floor. All interpretations seem rather dubious and only further excavation of housing sites might give a solution to the problem.

What then is the final picture of *Heorot* that emerges? It was built of wood clamped together with iron bands, which seems to fit a heavy planking construction best, though of a variety not so far discovered. Its roof was high gabled, and covered in some way with gold: the steeply-gabled roof of a wooden building would perhaps be most easily supported by internal or external pillars, but these are nowhere mentioned; the roof, if it was really overlaid with gold, was probably of shingles. To enter the hall one went up a step or steps and passed through two sets of doors, i.e. presumably through an anteroom or porch, and inside, the floor of the hall was decorated or gleaming. Future archaeological discoveries may add more to this picture, but what emerges already is a not impossible description of

---

[84] A. H. Smith, "English Place-Name Elements," *Engl. Place-Name Soc.*, XXV (Cambridge, 1956), 164 and 176.

[85] Pfeilstücker, *op. cit.* in note 52, p. 50, assumes that the sides of the hall had a wooden flooring, but in the middle around the fire the flooring was of "gemustertem Stein" [patterned stone]. This would be an excellent safety precaution, but wooden floors are known from Trelleborg for example, and seem to be mentioned in *Finnsburg*, l. 30, *buruhðelu dynede* [castle-floor resounded]; while a similar phrase in *Beowulf*, *healwudu dynede* [hall-wood resounded] (l. 317) occurs in the description of Beowulf entering Hroðgar's *bur* [chamber].

a royal building that the poet takes care to tell us was the greatest of halls the children of men had ever heard of.

Conclusions

As W. P. Ker said:[86] "The poem of *Beowulf* has been sorely tried; critics have long been at work on the body of it to discover how it is made." It is a measure of the poem's strength that it emerges alive from this continual vivisection, but the newest archaeological evidence has transfused new vigour into the body. The recent analyses of literary critics have shown the careful artistry of the poem, its lack of empty statement and vain allusion, and archaeologists must equally have examined the work as a whole before criticising a unit of its statement.

What archaeology brings to the poem is not yet a solution of its date; there is not a sufficient body of relevant evidence to do this. If enough of such evidence is ever forthcoming to prove that the poet muddled together objects and conditions of widely different dates, then the latest of these might give a clue to the poet's own time. However, even if all the background could be closely fixed to one era, it would still be necessary to refute or support the undoubted historical sense he sometimes shows. The archaeological evidence that is now available, however, can enrich considerably the study of the poem; it can supply relevant illustrations so that simple words such as "hall" or "sword" conjure up a precise picture in the mind of the modern reader. Moreover a knowledge of the excellencies and refinements of Anglo-Saxon craftsmanship enables us to appreciate what governed the poet's choice of epithet in stressing the features that he did stress in more complicated passages of description.[87]

[86] *Epic and Romance* (1908: reprinted New York, 1957), p. 158.
[87] I should like to thank Professor D. Whitelock and Professor C. F. C. Hawkes for their kind help in the preparation of this work.

The Making of an Anglo-Saxon Poem

by Robert P. Creed

I

The diction of *Beowulf* is schematized to an extraordinary degree.[1] Roughly every fifth verse is repeated intact at least once elsewhere in the poem. An essential part of about every second verse—such a part as a whole measure, or a phrase which straddles both measures, or one which encloses the two measures of the verse—is repeated elsewhere in the poem. Many of these verses or essential parts of verses bear such a resemblance to certain others as to suggest that the singer "knew them"—in the late Milman Parry's words—"not only as single formulas, but also as formulas of a certain type." [2] In composing a line containing any one of these verses, therefore, he was guided by the rhythm, sound, and sense of other verses belonging to this type or "system." [3]

The degree of the schematization of his diction suggests that the

"The Making of an Anglo-Saxon Poem." From *ELH*, XXVI (1959), 445–54. Copyright © 1959 by The Johns Hopkins Press. Reprinted by permission of the publisher. For this reprinting, Professor Creed supplied the additional remarks at the end of his essay.

[1] The evidence for this statement is contained in Appendix A, "Supporting Evidence," of my *Studies in the Techniques of Composition of the Beowulf Poetry* . . . , Harvard University (unpublished doctoral dissertation), 1955, 200–385.

[2] Milman Parry, "Studies in the Epic Technique of Oral Verse-Making. I. Homer and Homeric Style," *Harvard Studies in Classical Philology*, XLI (1930), 85.

[3] Parry uses the term *system* to designate a group of formulas of similar construction (pp. 85–89). For a discussion of certain systems of formulas in Anglo-Saxon poetry, see Francis P. Magoun, Jr., "Oral-Formulaic Character of Anglo-Saxon Narrative Poetry," *Speculum*, XXVIII (July, 1953), especially 450–53, and also my "The *andswarode*-System in Old English Poetry," *Speculum*, XXXII (July, 1957), 523–28.

singer of *Beowulf* did not need to pause in his reciting or writing to consider what word to put next. His diction was one which, in Goethe's words, did his thinking and his poetizing for him, at least when he had completely mastered that diction and its ways. Precisely *how* that diction might have done his poetizing for the Anglo-Saxon singer is the subject of the present paper.

I cannot attempt to deal in so brief a study with the way in which the singer puts together the larger elements of his poem. I shall therefore take only a very small portion of *Beowulf,* eight verses (four lines), and attempt, by means of references to similar verses and lines in the rest of the poem and in other surviving Anglo-Saxon poems, to illustrate the thesis that the making of any Anglo-Saxon poem was a process of choosing rapidly and largely on the basis of alliterative needs *not* between individual words but between *formulas.*

A formula may be as large as those whole verses repeated intact to which I referred earlier, or even larger. There are whole lines and even lines-and-a-half repeated within *Beowulf.* At the other extreme a formula may be as small as those trisyllabic prepositional phrases which end certain A-verses, or even as small as a single monosyllabic adverb, *if* the adverb makes the whole spoken portion[4] of the measures and thus makes it possible for the singer to compose rapidly.

This last fact is important. The essential quality of the formula is not its memorable sound—although some formulas are, even for us, memorable—but its *usefulness* to the singer. To be useful to a singer as he composes rapidly a phrase or word must suggest to him that it belongs at only *one* point, or possibly only two points, in his verse or line; that is, it must be a significant segment of his rhythm. To be useful to the singer every phrase or word which is metrically significant should also be a syntactic entity, that is, if it is not a polysyllable which by itself makes a whole verse or whole "crowded" measure, it should at least be a phrasal group or a clause. It should be, for example, an article and its noun, or a noun or pronoun and its verb, or a verb and its object, or a preposition and its noun, *not*

---

[4] As opposed to that portion of the measure accounted for by a rest or harp-substitution. See John Collins Pope, *The Rhythm of Beowulf* (New Haven, 1942).

such syntactically meaningless groups as, for example, an adverb and a preposition.

The formula in Anglo-Saxon poetry is, then, to paraphrase and somewhat emend Milman Parry's definition of the formula in Homer, a word or group of words regularly employed under certain strictly determined metrical conditions to express a given essential idea.[5]

In a formulaic or traditional poem we are frequently able, because of this schematization of the diction, not only to examine the formula which the singer chose, but also to guess at with some measure of assurance, and to examine, the system or entire group of formulas from *among* which he chose at a given point in his poem. When we have studied his tradition with care we are able to appreciate his poetry in a unique way, because we can perform in slow motion the very process which he of necessity performed rapidly: we can unmake, and make in new fashion, each line according to the rules of the game, and thus approximate what the singer himself might have done in a different performance of the same tale.

II

At line 356 of his poem the singer has got Beowulf safely across the sea from Geatland to Denmark, and has placed him outside the hall Heorot. Wulfgar, Hrothgar's herald, has just learned from Beowulf who he is and what his mission is at Hrothgar's court.

> Hwearf þá hrædlíce   þǽr Hróþ-gár sæt,
> eald and unhár,   mid his eorla gedryht;
> éode ellen-róf   þæt hé for eaxlum gestód
> Deniga frêan;   cúðe hé duguðe péaw.[6]

---

[5] See Parry, p. 80.

[6] Quotations from *Beowulf* and other Old English poems are cited in the normalized spelling proposed by Francis P. Magoun, Jr., in "A Brief Plea for a Normalization of Old-English Poetical Texts," *Les Langues Modernes*, XLV (1951), 63–69, and adopted in Magoun's own classroom edition of the poem, *Béowulf and Judith, Done in a Normalized Orthography* . . . (Cambridge, Mass., 1959). [This edition is based primarily upon Charles Leslie Wrenn, *Beowulf with the Finnesburg Fragment* (London–Boston, 1953).]

Then he [that is, Wulfgar] turned quickly to where Hrothgar sat, old and very hoary, with his troop of men; famous for his courage [he, Wulfgar] went until he stood before the shoulders of the lord of the Danes; he knew the custom of the comitatus.

There are several different ways by which the singer could, in good formulas, have got Wulfgar or anyone else from one place to another. Not many lines before this passage the singer has got Beowulf out of Geatland with the following verse: *gewát þá ofer wǽg-holm* [he departed then over the wave-sea]. At line 720 the singer will get Grendel to Heorot with the following verse: *cóm þá to rećede* [he came then to the hall]. At line 1232 he will get Wealhtheow to her seat with *éode þá to setle* [she went then to the bench].

We can be sure that each one of the verb-adverb groups (*gewát þá, cóm þá, éode þá* [he departed then, he came then, she went then]) which begin these lines is a formula not only because it fits the conditions of usefulness and significance, but also because the singer has used each of these phrases in this same position more than once.

But at our point in the story the singer chose to say *hwearf þá* [he turned then], like these other verb-adverb groups a demonstrable formula since it appears at the beginning of line 1188, 1210 and 1573. We can find good reasons for his choice of *hwearf þá* [he turned then] in this passage. *Gewát þá* [He departed then] suggests a journey longer than the length of a hall, *cóm þá* [he came then] suggests a new arrival rather than a return. The singer might then have said *éode þá* [went then] as he will do at 1232 and 1626 (*éodon . . . þá* [they went . . . then]), or simply *éode* [he went] as he does at eight other places in his poem. That he said *hwearf þá* [he turned then] here suggests that he had already thought ahead not only to the adverb with which *hwearf* [he turned] incidentally alliterates, but to *Hróþ-gár* in the second verse of the line, which is the excuse for the adverb itself. The singer had no particular need to get Wulfgar from Beowulf to Hrothgar with haste; he *did* need to get him to Hrothgar with alliteration.[7]

---

[7] Quite by accident the study of this passage (which, by the way, I chose at random) led me to what seems to be a rather dramatic demonstration of this principle. In my reflections on what the singer *might* have said here it seemed to me that, had he chosen not to mention but rather to allude to Hrothgar in

In *Beowulf* 356, then, the singer has correctly established his alliterative bridge-head with *hrædlíce* [quickly] for an assault on the second verse of the line. That verse, *þǽr Hróþ-gár sæt* [where Hrothgar sat], does not divide neatly into two formulas each of which makes a single measure as does 356a. Verse 356b belongs to a type the pattern of which can be expressed by *þǽer x sæt* [where x sat], where *x* equals the subject of *sæt*. Eight hundred lines after this passage, at line 1190, the singer has composed another verse of this type, *þǽr se góda sæt* [where the good-one sat], in which the substitution for the sake of alliteration is perfectly straight-forward. Just seventy lines before our passage, however, the singer has apparently used the same container, *þǽr . . . sæt* [where . . . sat], with a different kind of alliterating content: *þǽr on wicge sæt* [there on his horse he sat]. Apparently the singer does not restrict himself to employing the same kind of substituting element within the framework of this simple substitution system. Or perhaps it would be more correct to say that he shows signs at such points as these of thinking in terms of two complementary types of formula which he can readily combine to make a single verse.

This verse, *þǽr Hróþ-gár sæt* [where Hrothgar sat], completes a line, and might, had the singer so chosen, have completed a thought. He does not so choose; he amplifies in the following line this brief mention of Hrothgar seated into a noble picture of the aged king surrounded by his retainers. But before we turn our attention to this picture in the next line of this passage, let us first observe how this

---

his second verse, he might have substituted for *Hróþ-gár* a vowel-alliterating noun or phase such as *se ealdor* [the prince]. In consequence he would probably have substituted for *hrædlíce* [quickly] the adverb *ofostlíce* [speedily] in the second measure of the first verse. The point is that the singer is likely to have regarded such synonymous and metrically equivalent polysyllables as interchangeable. As a matter of fact the singer of *Beowulf* uses at line 3130 *ofostlíc[e]* [speedily] exactly as he uses *hrædlíce* [quickly] here, that is, as the second measure of a C-verse which begins the line: *þæt híe ofostlíc[e]/út geferedon/díere máðmas . . .* [that they speedily carried out the precious treasures . . .]. But another singer, the singer of *Genesis,* at one point in his poem appears to have supplied *one* of these two adverbs where he intended the other. In "*Genesis* 1316," *Modern Language Notes,* LXXIII (May, 1958), 321–25, I discuss this fascinating slip of the singer more fully. Had I not been, in effect, performing the part of the apprentice singer by seeking here for a different polysyllabic adverb than *hrædlíce* [quickly], I should not have stumbled so soon across this slip, nor so quickly have grasped what I found in *Genesis* 1316.

line as a whole has helped to prepare the singer to make another
whole line later in his poem.

Some eight hundred lines after this passage the singer moved
Wealhtheow not into but across the hall with the following line:
hwearf þá be benće /þǽr hire byre wǽron . . . [she turned then
along the bench / where her sons were . . .] (1188). The design of
this line is very similar to that of the one we have just studied. Both
lines begin with the same formula; the second verse of both lines
is enclosed by a similar phrase (*þǽr* . . . *sæt, þǽr* . . . *wǽron*
[where . . . sat, where . . . were]). The singer requires, however,
a different alliteration in each line: he wishes to name Hrothgar in
the first and to refer to Wealhtheow's sons in the second, consequently he uses a different second measure (*hrædlíće, be benće*
[quickly, along the bench]). We shall return to this later passage in
a moment to indicate how the earlier passage has influenced even
further the construction of the later.

To sum up my rather extensive remarks on this single line: the
singer appears to have composed his line of at least three separate
formulas, *hwearf þá* [he turned then], *hrædlíće* [quickly], and *þǽr*
x *sæt* [where x sat]. He seems to have chosen the second formula,
which carries the important alliteration of the first verse, in order
that he might name Hrothgar in the second verse. He was, finally,
guided in the shaping of the line as a whole by the *association* in
his mind of these three formulas, as his later line 1188 seems to
prove.

Line 357 presents fewer problems. The first verse, *eald and unhár*
[old and very hoary], belongs to a type long recognized as a formula,
the so-called *reim-formel* [rhyme-formula]. Formulas of this kind
have sometimes been regarded as a particularly characteristic kind
of formula in Anglo-Saxon poetry or elsewhere.[8] Such formulas are

---

[8] Klaeber [Fr. Klaeber, *Beowulf* . . . , Third Ed., Boston, 1950] gives a promi-
nent place to *reim*-formulas (which he more accurately but also more ponder-
ously calls "copulative alliterative phrases") in his list of "formulas, set combinations of words, phrases of transition, and similar stereotyped elements" (lxvi).
John S. P. Tatlock, in "Lagamon's Poetic Style and Its Relations," in *The Manly
Anniversary Studies in Language and Literature,* Chicago, 1923, page 7, calls attention to these formulas in Lawman: "One *chief function* of his *shorter epic
formulas* was as expletives to fill in a half-line [a whole verse in Old English
poetry] for which he had no matter, that he might not be obliged to introduce
a new theme." (My italics.)

indeed distinctive and decidedly ornamental; in fact, so far as getting any real work done is concerned, they are more ornamental than useful. For this very reason they can hardly claim to be the type of formula *par excellence.*

In making this verse the singer was guided by its simple and rather pleasing A-rhythm. At three other places in his poem the singer was guided by the same play of sound and rhythm to link *eald* [old] with another alliterating word (*eald and infród* [old and experienced], 2449 for example).

The vowel-alliteration of *eald* [old] gets him easily to the second verse of this line. Had he wished to name Hrothgar in the first verse of this line, or, for any other reason to employ *h*-alliteration or even *s*-alliteration he would have been faced with no problem in making the second half of the line. *mid his eorla gedryht* [with his troop of earls] is an even better example than verse 356b of the simple sub-stitution system. For *h*-alliteration the singer replaces *eorla* [earls] with *hæleða* [heroes], as he does at line 662; for s-alliteration he replaces *eorla* [earls] with *secga* [men] as he does in line 633 and 1672.

The noble picture is complete with this fourth verse; the singer pauses momentarily, and editors punctuate accordingly. If, during that pause, we turn again to that later picture of Wealhtheow at which we have already glanced, we shall see even further similarities between these two passages. Line 1188, like 356, is followed by a *reim*-formula, *Hræþ-ríc and Hróþ-mund,* in this case a *reim*-formula which, like 357a, amplifies the alliterating core of the previous verse. Again like 357a, and probably to some degree because of 357a, 1189a is followed by the mention of the troop of warriors, "sons of heroes," seated around the two princes: *and hæleða bearn* [and sons of he-roes]. But this later passage does not end with the fourth verse; *hæleða bearn* itself is amplified by the following verse, *geoguþ ætgædere* [young-warriors together]. Thus the two passages are alike but not identical. We can only with increasing difficulty deny, how-ever, that the rhythms and ideas which governed the making of the first passage played some part in the making of the second when we note that *geoguþ ætgædere* [young-warriors together] is followed by the paradigm of 356b: *þǽr se góda sæt* [where the good-one sat]. *Se góda* [*The good-one*] in verse 1190b refers not to Hrothgar but to Beowulf, whose name and whose location *be þǽm gebróðrum twǽm* [by the two brothers] completes in eight verses a reflection of the noble picture we have seen condensed into four.

But perhaps it is not quite correct to say that the earlier picture is yet complete, since, in verse 358a, the singer returns to the idea contained in the first measure of 356a. The singer has made the second measure of the later verse not out of a single adverb but a single substantive, *ellen-róf* [famous for courage]. Eighteen lines before this he has made the entire second measure of a B-verse out of this word; twenty-eight hundred lines later in his poem he will again make *ellen-róf* [famous for courage] the second measure of a D-verse.

But to stop with these observations of the other appearances of this compound as a compound is to ignore an important and interesting point of the singer's technique. That point may be expressed as a kind of rule-of-thumb which runs something like this: the first element of any compound noun or adjective will more often than not exist for the sake of alliteration rather than for the sake of a more precise denotation. We can demonstrate the operation of this rule in the present case by noting that the singer has elsewhere combined *hige-* [mind-] with *róf* [famous] to mean something synonymous with *ellen-róf* [famous for courage] but having a different alliteration and a different metrical value. He has also combined *beadu-* [battle-], *brego-* [chief-], *gúþ-* [war-] *heaðu-* [battle-], and *sige-* [victory-], with this same adjective *róf* [famous] to obtain slightly different meanings and three more different alliterations.

Verse 358b, *þæt hé for eaxlum gestód* [until he stood before the shoulders], appears to be made of two such complementary formulas as appear in 356b. The container, *þæt hé . . . gestód* [until he . . . stood], is made in the same fashion as the container of 356b. Again, the container does the real work of the verse, that is, it functions syntactically as a complete clause with its subject pronoun and verb. The easily replaceable contained element, *for eaxlum* [before the shoulders], both carries the alliteration and delimits the action of the verb.

This verse might indeed be spoken of as a delimiting formula, or as a formula for indicating distance. Once the singer has learned to isolate the container from the alliterating content of the verse, as we have just done, he has learned a most useful technique. That

the singer of *Beowulf had* so isolated the container is evident from
the following verses in which he indicates, at various points in his
poem, different distances travelled by inserting a different prepositional phrase into this same container:

þæt hé on héorðe gestód   [until he stood on the hearth] (404)
þæt hit on wealle ætstód   [so that it stood fixed] (891)
þæt hit on hafolan stód   [so that it stood in the head] (2679)

Compare also

þæt him on ealdre stód   [so that in his vitals stuck] (1434).

The problem of indicating before whose shoulders it was that
Wulfgar came to a stop caused the singer little difficulty. He knew
several kinds of whole verse formulas for referring to Hrothgar.
The most numerous group of these formulas, or, to express it properly, the most useful group, is the x *Scieldinga* [x of the Scildings]
group, to which belong *wine Scieldinga* [friend of the Scildings],
which he employs in the poem seven times, *fréa Scieldinga* [lord of
the Scildings], which he employs four times, *helm* [protector] (three
times), *eodor* [prince], *léod* [prince], *þéoden* [prince] (each twice).
This group alone provides him with six different alliterative possibilities.

But before speaking 359a, the singer must have thought ahead to
the *duguðe* [retainers] with its *d*-alliteration in 359b. Hence he provided himself here with a *d*-alliterating epithet, *Deniga fréan,* [ruler
of the Danes], as he had done at line 271 and was to do at 1680.

359b, *cúðe hé duguðe þéaw* [he knew the custom of the comitatus],
has no very close analogues in *Beowulf.* If, however, we compare it
with verse 1940b, *ne biþ swelć cwænlíć þéaw* [such is not a queenly
manner (to behave)], we can observe some similarity between the
second measures of these two verses.

If the two second measures are derived from the same play of
sounds and ideas, the two first measures which accompany them are
not. *cúðe hé* [he knew], which appears nowhere else in *Beowulf,*
is quite unlike *ne biþ swelć* [such is not] in 1940b, which appears
again in line 2541. It has been suggested that, in such lightly stressed
first measures as these, the singer has a kind of escape valve, or a
measure into which he can cram, without worrying about allitera-

tion, needed but metrically annoying words and phrases. Perhaps this is so, but it is also true that the singer composed many of these lightly stressed measures out of formulas.[9]

III

At the beginning of this paper I noted that we can both unmake and make again each of the singer's lines if we are careful to follow the same rules which seem to have guided the singer. It might be amusing, and perhaps even instructive then, for such a novice singer as I—who have, however ridiculous this idea seems, been training myself and the careful reader to be a singer, and in a way not unlike that by which the singer trained himself—to attempt to do just that: to remake this passage from *Beowulf* which we have just unmade, attempting to say as closely as possible but with other formulas what the singer has said:

> Éode þá ofostlíĉe   þǽr se ealdor sæt
> hár and hige-fród   mid his hæleða gedryht;
> éode hilde-déor   þæt hé on héorðe gestód
> freân Scieldinga;   cúðe hé þæs folces þéaw.

[He went then speedily where the prince sat hoary and mind-wise with his troop of heroes; he went battle-brave until he stood on the hearth the prince of the Scildings; he knew the custom of the people].

There is my poem. If you analyze it properly you will find every single formula elsewhere in *Beowulf* or in other poems in the Anglo-Saxon corpus, and used exactly as I have used it here. I must however claim credit for combining *hár* [hoary] with *hige-fród* [mind-wise] and, I had thought, even for the manufacture of *hige-fród*. I needed a *reim*-formula with *h*-alliteration and hit upon *hige-fród* by following that rule-of-thumb I spoke of earlier. Only afterwards I discovered *Genesis* 1953, *hálig and hige-fród*, [holy and mind-wise], along with marginal notes indicating that I had been reading this portion of that poem not very long ago.

I don't like my poem nearly so much as I like the singer's.[10] Yet

[9] See my *Studies in . . . Beowulf* (note 1, above), Chapter VI, especially pp. 90–94 and the chart which accompanies this chapter on pp. 118–20.

[10] A close comparison of my poem with the *Beowulf* singer's seems to me to

my poem is composed of the same formulas out of which this singer and other Anglo-Saxon singers of ability created their poems. The diction of my poem is schematized to no greater degree than the diction of most other surviving old English poems. What my experiment helps to prove, then, is that the simple use of formulaic diction is no guarantee of aesthetic success. Conversely, the use of a formulaic diction does not make such success impossible. *Beowulf,* with its highly schematized diction yet continually marvelous subtlety, is sufficient proof to the contrary.

If my feeble attempt to compose formulaic poetry only serves to demonstrate once again the subtle art of the singer of *Beowulf* I shall be satisfied. I should be more than satisfied if the experiment should serve also to remind the reader that this subtle art is a traditional and formulaic art, and that it is possible to praise the four lines of *Beowulf* I have chosen to examine as, for their purposes, the best of all possible *combinations of formulas.*

Additional Remarks

In the years that have elapsed since the appearance of this article it has come under the scrutiny of a number of scholar-critics of Old English poetry. I should like to take the opportunity, generously offered by the editor of the present volume, to respond to some of these criticisms in the hope that by accepting and attempting to deal with just criticisms I can make the article somewhat more useful.

In "The Oral-Formulaic Analyses of Old English Verse," *Speculum,* XXXVII (1962), pp. 382–89, Robert D. Stevick points out that "memory of past performances will have a very large effect on any

---

show a sharp contrast between the ceremonial slowness with which the Anglo-Saxon gets Wulfgar in the D-verse *éode ellen-róf* [he went famous-for-courage] before his lord and the rather discourteous bump with which in the B-verse *éode hilde-déor* [he went battle-brave] I get him into the royal presence. Nor do I like for describing Hrothgar the jigging rhythm of my *hár and hige-fród* [hoary and mind-wise] so well as the singer's *eald and unhár* [old and hoary]. My *éode þá* [he went then] is also a vaguer introduction to the passage than the singer's more precise suggestion of Wulfgar's turning *away* from Beowulf in order to move *towards* Hrothgar in *hwearf þá* [he turned then]. But then this is where I've got by *trying* to be different from a great singer.

further performance; any familiarity at all with successive jazz performances suggests strongly that performers (and particularly professional ones) repeat earlier performances as entities, subject only
to such changes as faulty memory, momentary experiments, or effects
of audience reaction may produce. They do not build each performance merely a phrase at a time" (p. 386). I am grateful for this re-
minder of the complexity of the forces impinging upon any traditional performance. I should therefore modify my description of
the factors at work upon these eight lines from *Beowulf* to indicate
the possibility that not *all* the singer-poet's "decisions" that produced the recorded performance were made at the same time, that
is in a single performance. Yet some simplification of the complexity
of the interaction of tradition and the traditional singer-poet may
well be necessary if we are to try to understand something of the
nature of the singer as artist, that is as *shaper* of the tradition, and
not simply as performer, that is as *transmitter* of the tradition.

In "The Canons of Old English Criticism," *ELH*, XXXIV (1967),
pp. 141–55, Stanley B. Greenfield quotes with approval R. F. Lawrence's comment: " 'If [Creed] can effectively use the oral techniques
in the privacy of his study, then how much more effectively might
the Anglo-Saxon monk have done like-wise?' " (R. F. Lawrence,
"The Formulaic Theory and its Application to English Alliterative
Poetry," in Roger Fowler, ed., *Essays on Style and Language*, London, 1966, pp. 175–76.) I should point out that the "monk" who was
as much concerned as I was about possible substitutions of the sort
I have suggested above either performed the same elaborate and
painstaking operations I performed with the aid of his version of
Grein-Köhler-Holthausen's *Sprachschatz* or was a singer-poet thoroughly trained in the tradition.

Greenfield later quotes Lawrence again, though this time with
only grudging approval: "it may well be, as Lawrence says, 'that a
popular theme, or poem of several related themes, as it is progres-
sively developed and refined by a succession of oral poets [or, we
might add, by the same singer himself in successive performances]
could achieve a perfection of form and a density of utterance perhaps even beyond the capacity of written literature' " (p. 143). Lawrence's suggestion, particularly as modified by Greenfield's bracketed
insertion, seems to be worthy of ungrudging approval.

Greenfield's sharpest criticism focuses on my definitions of the formula and formulaic system in the article. (See his pp. 144–46, especially p. 145). From another point of view Donald K. Fry has recently attacked my definitions in "Old English Formulas and Systems," *ES*, XLVIII (1967), pp. 193–204. I am willing to announce my retreat from the position taken in the article that a formula can be as small as a measure to Fry's position that a formula can be no smaller than a whole verse (p. 203). Yet I must add that even under the new definition only two of the eight verses discussed in the article require special comment: verse 356a, I should now state, can be viewed as composed of the blending of the two formulaic systems *hwearf þá x* [turned then x] and *x hraedlíce* [x quickly]. Similarly verse 358a appears to be composed of the blending of the two systems *éode x* [went x] and *x ellenróf* [x famous-for-courage].

Point of View and Design for Terror
in *Beowulf*

by Alain Renoir

The theory that Old-English poetry was formulaic and composed orally at the time of recitation is all but generally accepted today. Among the scholars who have studied the principles of oral-formulaic composition in languages other than Homeric Greek,[1] Francis Peabody Magoun, Jr., has done pioneer work in analyzing formulas,[2] Robert P. Creed has demonstrated the validity of the theory by actually composing an oral formulaic poem in Old English,[3] and David K. Crowne has shown beyond doubt that certain topical formulas survived in Old English long after losing their significance as means of communication between the poet and his audience.[4] Contrary to what we might expect, oral-formulaic composition and recitation in front of an audience by no means result in the poet's necessary loss of control over the organization of his materials. Cedric Whitman's study of the *Iliad*, for instance, has

"Point of View and Design for Terror in *Beowulf*." From *Neuphilologische Mitteilungen*, LXIII (1962), pp. 154–67. Copyright © 1962 by *Neuphilologische Mitteilungen*. Reprinted by permission of the publisher.

[1] The initial principles of oral-formulaic composition were established in 1930 and 1932 by Milman Parry in respect to Homer, in "Studies in the Epic Technique of Oral Verse-Making," *Harvard Studies in Classical Philology*, XLI, 73 ff. and XLIII, 1 ff.

[2] Francis P. Magoun, Jr., "Oral-Formulaic Character of Anglo-Saxon Narrative Poetry," *Speculum*, XXVIII, 446 ff., and "The Theme of the Beast of Battle in Anglo-Saxon Poetry," *Neuphilologische Mitteilungen*, LVI, 81 ff.; see also Stanley B. Greenfield, "The Formulaic Expression of the Theme of Exile in Anglo-Saxon Poetry," *Speculum*, XXX, 200 ff., and Adrien Bonjour, "*Beowulf* and the Beasts of Battle," *PMLA*, LXXII, 563 ff.

[3] Robert P. Creed, "The Making of an Anglo-Saxon Poem." *ELH*, XXVI, 445 ff.

[4] David K. Crowne, "The Hero on the Beach," *Neuphilologische Mitteilungen*, LXI, 362 ff.

demonstrated that the structure of that poem has been carefully planned according to a preconceived geometric pattern.[5] This mode of composition, however, forces the poet to give constant heed to the reactions of his audience and to handle certain episodes in his narrative accordingly. He is at the same time a creator and a performer, and must act very much like the vaudeville comedian who keeps a close watch on the faces before him and shapes his performance so as to keep their interest at the highest pitch. In recent years studies by Tauno F. Mustanoja[6] and Albert B. Lord [7] have suggested the extent to which the poet is likely to follow the audience, and the recordings in the Milman Parry Collection of South-Slavic Songs at Harvard offer ample documentation in support of the theories advanced by these scholars. The oral-formulaic poet performing before an audience accompanies himself with a musical instrument and sings his composition in a rather monotonous tone from which he occasionally departs at appropriate points in the narrative. When the audience expresses approbation, he is likely to add a great many descriptive details which might be omitted from a less successful performance,[8] and the pitch of his voice may change according to the material.

Now it goes almost without saying that if the poet must hold the attention of his audience while recounting a tale of action, *he must make them visualize that action.* Furthermore, he must make them visualize it *as fast as they hear the words that describe it.* In this necessity to evoke immediate visualization lies a fundamental difference between the Old-English poet and his modern counterpart: whereas the latter *writes for readers* who may proceed through the text at their own leisure and go back over any passage as often as necessary, the former *sings for listeners* who will never have a second chance if they miss anything upon a first hearing. This relationship between the oral-formulaic performer and his audience may well

[5] Cedric H. Whitman, *Homer and the Heroic Tradition* (Cambridge, Mass., 1958), especially the chart at the end of the book.

[6] Tauno F. Mustanoja, "The Presentation of Ancient Germanic Poetry: Looking for Parallels," *Neuphilologische Mitteilungen,* LX, 1 ff.

[7] Albert B. Lord, *The Singer of Tales* (Cambridge, Mass., 1960), p. 16 ff. This book is the most authoritative study of oral-formulaic composition available at present.

[8] Lord, *Singer,* p. 17, describes the poet composing before a receptive audience as "savoring each descriptive detail."

account for the extreme care which the Old-English poets seem to have taken with visual description, as witnessed by such magnificently vivid passages as the battle scene in *Judith,* the picture of Satan at the bottom of hell in *Genesis B,* the crucifixion in *The Dream of the Rood,* and innumerable other instances.

The visual evocation of an action, if it is to prove effective upon a first hearing, requires not only a careful selection of details but also —and perhaps especially—the presentation of these details from an appropriate point of view. A given action visualized at close range is likely to assume in the beholder's mind a much greater importance than the same action visualized at a great distance. To illustrate from painting, when Vincent van Gogh wants to convey the significance which he attaches to his own suffering after cutting off his ear to spite a prostitute, he paints a self-portrait in which his bandaged head covers nearly the entire canvas; when, on the other hand, Pieter Bruegel wishes to convey the insignificance of human suffering, he paints the fall of Icarus from such great distance that only two tiny legs are seen sinking in the immensity of the sea.

Point of view, of course, can be emotional as well as visual: indeed, the two often go together, and the latter usually expresses the former. To take an example relevant to *Beowulf,* we need no great psychological insight to realize that a killing visualized from the killer's point of view will have a very different emotional effect than the same killing visualized from the victim's point of view, even if we disapprove of the action in both cases. In Emile Zola's *La Bête Humaine,* for instance, Jacques' killing of Séverine is narrated in the third person but from the killer's point of view, both emotionally and visually. The passage is too long for quoting here in its entirety, but a brief excerpt will illustrate both the method and the effect:

> Il fixait sur Séverine ses yeux fous, il n'avait plus que le besoin de la jeter morte sur son dos. . . . Elle renversait son visage soumis, d'une tendresse suppliante, découvrait son cou nu, à l'attache voluptueuse de la gorge. Et lui, voyant cette chair blanche, comme dans un éclat d'incendie, leva le poing, armé du couteau. Mais elle avait aperçue l'éclair de la lame, elle se rejeta en arrière, béante de surprise et de terreur. . . . Et il abattit le poing, et le couteau lui cloua la question

dans la gorge. En frappant, il avait retourné l'arme, par un effroyable besoin de la main qui se contentait.[1]

[His wild eyes glared at Séverine, he now felt only the need to throw her dead body over his shoulder. . . . She turned around, and her submissive expression betrayed a tender supplication, as it revealed her naked neck voluptuously attached to her throat. And he, at the sight of this white flesh, as in the sudden burst of flames, raised the fist that clenched the knife. As she noticed the flashing blade, she started backwards, paralyzed with terror and surprise. . . . And he brought down his fist, and the stroke of the knife prevented any word from emanating from her throat. In striking, he had twisted the weapon, out of a horrible need of the hand that dictated such a gesture.]

As I have said, the killing is visualized from Jacques' point of view, and the horror evoked by the passage comes from the fact that we are thus made to participate visually and emotionally in an act that is morally revolting to us.

In Virgil's *Aeneid*, on the other hand, Aeneas' killing of Turnus is seen predominantly from the victim's point of view:

> Tum pectore sensus
> uertuntur uarii; Rutulos aspectat et urbem
> cunctaturque metu telumque instare tremescit,
> nec quo se eripiat, nec qua ui tendat in hostem
> . . .
> Ille humilis supplex oculos dextramque precantem
> protendens . . . inquit.
> . . .
> . . . Ast illi soluontur frigore membra
> uitaque cum gemitu fugit indignata sub umbras.
> (XII, 914–52)[2]

[Then in his breast varied feelings revolved; he looked at the Rutulians and the city, hesitated in fear, and shuddered at the spear's menace; he found no way to save himself, nor the power to attack his foe . . . He, humbled and suppliant, entreating with his eyes and outstretched right hand, . . . said.

[1] Emile Zola, *La Bête Humaine,* ed. Eugène Fasquelle (Paris, 1928), pp. 334–35.
[2] This and the other quotation from the *Aeneid* are from the edition by René Durand (Paris, 1936).

. . . But his limbs relaxed and chilled, and his life, indignant and groaning, fled to the shades.]

Here, because the point of view does not make us participate actively in the action we are visualizing, we feel no horror. Because we are made to endure that action with Turnus, however, we share in his terror, so that what is said of him might almost be said of us as well: "genua labant, gelidus concreuit frigore sanguis" [his knees buckled, his chilled blood froze with cold] (XII, 905).

My argument is that, under the conditions of oral-formulaic composition and presentation, the *Beowulf* poet masterfully succeeds not only in selecting immediately effective details but also in presenting them from such points of view as are likely to arouse the most appropriate emotional reactions in the audience. In support of this argument I offer an examination of Grendel's approach of Heorot. I have chosen this particular passage, not only because it is one of the very most graphic passages in English literature and is highly representative of the descriptive technique of the poem, but also because it belongs to the first of what Friedrich Klaeber has called "the three great crises in the poem" [1] and has been selected for extensive discussion in Arthur G. Brodeur's monumental study, *The Art of Beowulf.* We may therefore assume that it is familiar to all professional students of English literature. In quoting the passage, I have arbitrarily divided it into four sections so as to emphasize the quadripartite organization:

1)   Com on wanre niht
       scriðan sceadugenga.   Sceotend swæfon,
       þa þæt hornreced   healdan scoldon,
       ealle buton anum.   Þæt wæs yldum cuþ
       þæt hie ne moste,   þa metod nolde,
       se scynscaþa   under sceadu bregdan;
       ac he wæccende   wraþum on andan
       bad bolgenmod   beadwa geþinges.

[He came in the dark night, the shadow-goer stalking. The shooters slept, they who should have guarded that horned-building, all except one. It was known to men that he might not, if the Lord did not wish

[1] Friedrich Klaeber, ed., *Beowulf and the Fight at Finnsburg,* 3rd ed. (Boston, 1941), p. l (i.e., 50 of introduction).

it, the phantom-fiend fling them under the shadows; but he lying awake, a vexation to his enemy, awaited swollen in spirit the outcome of the struggle.]

> 2) Þa com of more   under misthleoþum
>   Grendel gongan,   godes yrre bær;
>   mynte se manscaða   manna cynnes
>   sumne besyrwan   in sele þam hean.

[Then came from the moor under the cover of darkness Grendel stalking; he bore God's wrath; the evil-killer intended to ensnare one of the race of men in that hall so high.]

> 3) Wod under wolcnum   to þæs þe he winreced,
>   goldsele gumena,   gearwost wisse,
>   fættum fahne.   Ne wæs þæt forma sið
>   þæt he Hroþgares ham gesohte;
>   næfre he on aldordagum   ær ne siþðan
>   heardran hæle,   healðegnas fand.

[He strode under the clouds until the wine-hall, gold-hall of men, he might most eagerly perceive, adorned with gold-plates. Nor was that the first time that he sought Hrothgar's home; never had he in days of old before or after found harder luck or hall-retainers.]

> 4) Com þa to recede   rinc siðian,
>   dreamum bedæled.   (702b–21a)[2]

[He came then to the building, the warrior journeying, deprived of joys.]

In a chapter entitled "Design for Terror" Brodeur analyzes these lines as follows: "Grendel is first seen moving through the dark: four of the six words that announce him evoke fear: Com on *wanre niht scriðan sceadugenga* [He came in the dark night, the shadow-goer stalking.] (702b–3a). Tension is then somewhat eased with the assurance that God could, if he would, thwart Grendel's purpose, and that Beowulf holds faithful vigil. Then, all at once, the monster is closer: he moves down from the mist-shrouded moor. His advance is emphasized by the vigorous verb *wod* [he strode]: he strides with baleful haste and murder in his heart; he knows where

---

[2] This and all subsequent quotations from *Beowulf* are from the edition by Elliot van Kirk Dobbie (New York, 1953).

the hall stands, with the knowledge of murderous experience." [8] This incisive account of the passage is likely to remain unsurpassed, and whatever departures from it may be found in my own examination must be considered footnotes to Brodeur rather than disagreements. For instance, I have divided the passage into four sections instead of two simply because I am not nearly so concerned with Grendel's actual progression toward Heorot as with the points of view from which it is visualized.

The four sections, we must note, follow precisely the same rhetorical pattern. Each begins with a brief statement of Grendel's motion and of his position in respect to Heorot. Each is then followed by one or more longer considerations that tell us nothing about his approach but remind us of the reason for it and of the circumstances under which it takes place. Thus we learn in the first section that, with the exception of Beowulf himself—who seems to have taken the first watch, as may be expected from a young chieftain in search of glory—the Gautish guards are asleep, and that it was general knowledge that Grendel could not drag any of them in the open without God's permission. The second section tells us that Grendel is the object of God's wrath and that he firmly intends to catch a human prey in the hall. The third tells us that the hall is beautifully decorated, and that, although Grendel has visited it before, he has never yet found there the kind of reception that awaits him this time. The fourth simply reminds us that Grendel has no share in joy.

Although the passage is obviously designed to describe Grendel's approach of Heorot, only ten half-lines out of the total thirty-eight make the least contribution toward that end. These ten half-lines, however, are effective only because of the twenty-eight others, which seem expressly designed to make the monster's forward motion a truly terrifying event. In the first section, for instance, our initial sight of him is terrifying, not because he is coming to Heorot, but because the Gauts are asleep and therefore an easy prey for him; and the comment that he could not harm anyone against God's will is little comfort, for while divine will is at best a very unpredictable element, we have emphatically been told earlier in the poem, "Gæð

[8] Arthur G. Brodeur, *The Art of Beowulf* (Berkeley, 1960), p. 91.

a wyrd swa hio scel" [Fate always goes however it chooses] (455b). Indeed, immediately subsequent events suggest that God's will is that Grendel should gulp down at least one of the Gauts:

> ac he gefeng hraðe   forman siðe
> slæpendne rinc,   slat unwearnum,
> bat banlocan,   blod edrum dranc,
> synsnædum swealh;   sona hæfde
> unlyfigendes   eal gefeormod,
> fet ond folma.   (740a–45a)

[but he seized quickly the first time a sleeping warrior, tore greedily, bit the bone-locker, drank blood in streams, swallowed huge morsels; immediately he had the unliving one all eaten up, feet and hands.]

Conversely, what goes on inside Heorot acquires a terrifying quality only in the light of what goes on outside. This is particularly true of the statement that only Beowulf is lying in wait for Grendel. Of the protagonists in the drama we are witnessing, he alone is awake to endure the suspense; and we, because we know better than he does that Grendel is on his way, both share that suspense and respond to the mounting tension. The same argument may be made about the next two mentions of Grendel's approach and the considerations that immediately precede and follow them. The only difference is that the suspense increases with each new glimpse we get of the monster.

Examining the visual aspect only, we find that the first three sections of the passage adhere to a basic sequence of images: each alternates a picture of the scene outside Heorot with one of the scene inside it—or at least with an evocation of it. If, for the sake of clarity, we draw an analogy with the cinematograph, the first section may be analyzed as follows. First we have a long exterior shot dimly revealing an approaching destructive force; then we have a medium interior shot showing the helpless potential victims of the danger in question; and finally we have a close-up of the only potential opposition to the incoming destructive force: "ac he wæccende wraþum on andan / bad bolgenmod. . . ." [but he lying awake, a vexation to his enemy / waited swollen in spirit]. It is significant that with each successive section, we are asked to imagine Grendel a little closer. At first he is seen in the rather vague distance: "on wanre niht" [in the dark night]. With the second mention of his coming, the picture becomes more precise, and he specifically emerges "of more" [from the moor]. With the third mention he is close enough to distinguish the hall where we have just seen Beowulf lie in wait while the Gauts are asleep. With the fourth mention, he finally comes "to recede" [to the building].

As Brodeur has noted, the use of the verb *wod* [strode] at the beginning of the third section gives Grendel's advance a terrifying vigor. If we contrast it to the verb *com* [came], which describes Grendel's motion in the other three sections, we find that it does much more than add vigor. Although *cuman* occasionally means *to go* and *to happen,* its normal meaning is *to come;* used in the second or third person without any mention of specific geographic goal, it strongly suggests that its subject is seen *by the speaker* as moving toward him. Thus, when we hear that Grendel "com on wanre niht" [he came in the dark night] and "com of more" [he came from the moor] we necessarily visualize him as coming toward the speaker, with whom we are located by definition, and whose point of view in the context of the narrative is Heorot. We may thus say that the advance of the destructive force is first visualized at a great distance from the point of view of its prospective victims, and again at a shorter distance from the same point of view.

With the next mention of Grendel's approach, however, the poet uses the verb *wod* [he strode]. In contrast to *cuman* [to come], the verb *wadan* [to stride] contains no intrinsic implication of point of view. Thus, with the statement that Grendel "Wod under wolcnum to þæs þe *he winreced, / goldsele gumena gearwost wisse . . .*" [He strode under the clouds until the wine-hall, / gold-hall of men he might most eagerly perceive . . .], the point of view shifts 180 degrees; and, instead of looking away from Heorot with the poet, we are now made to look toward it and approach it with the monster. This is a masterstroke. If we have at all identified with the Gauts in the hall—and the original audience may surely be assumed to have done so to an even greater extent than the modern reader— then, we are suddenly made to move toward ourselves with the agent of our own prospective destruction. To return momentarily to the illustrations given at the outset of this paper, we have just been subjected to the kind of terror evoked by Virgil's account of the death of Turnus, and we are now suddenly subjected to the kind of horror evoked by Zola's account of the death of Séverine: this shift in point of view constitutes, to say the least, a formidable bill of fare.

With the final mention of Grendel's advance, the poet returns to the verb *com* [came] and to the previous point of view. In contrast with the first three sections of the passage, however, this last section makes no attempt to turn our attention inside the hall. The omission bears witness to the poet's acute sense of dramatic timing, for as Grendel finally reaches his goal—"Com þa to recede" [He came then to the building]—the period of suspence must come to an end and make place for brutal action. The very next line brings to an end the slow deliberate motion of the passage, and the first climactic scene of the poem opens as Grendel shatters the door with a single blow of his hand:

> Duru sona onarn,
> fyrbendum fæst, syþðan he hire folmum [æthr]an;
> onbræd þa bealohydig, ða he [ge]bolgen wæs,
> recedes muþan. Raþe æfter þon
> on fagne flor feond treddode,
> eode yrremod; him of eagum stod
> ligge gelicost leoht unfæger. (721b–27b)

[The door immediately sprang open, fast with fire-(forged) bands, after he touched it with his hands; then the evil-intending one swung it open, (he was enraged) the mouth of the building. Quickly after that on the shining floor the fiend trod, he went wrath-minded; from his eyes stood forth most like a flame a fearsome light.]

If we contrast Grendel's entry into Heorot to his approach thereof, we note three significant changes. In the first place, the point of view changes once again: in order to see the monster *from the front,* we have to be *inside* the hall ourselves. We are thus made to visualize his entry from the point of view of the only protagonist awake to see it, that is to say, from Beowulf's point of view. Just as Heorot has been earlier visualized from the point of view of its attacker, so Grendel is now visualized from the point of view of the only man brave enough to engage in dubious battle against him. We have come full circle both visually and emotionally. It is worth noting that this shift in point of view is emphasized by the only sound we are asked to imagine during the entire sequence: the crash of the hall door under Grendel's demoniac blow. In the second place, Grendel is seen at much closer range than ever before. Again in cinematographic terms, we may say that he has been made with each successive picture to occupy a greater portion of the screen: whereas he was at first only an uncertain entity lost in the vastness of the night, the entire screen is now occupied by his eyes alone. It is difficult to imagine a sequence better designed to inspire terror in the audience. In the third place, the illumination of the scene is considerably dimmer than previously, or, more accurately, there is no illumination at all. Outside, the night we have been asked to imagine is obviously light enough for us to distinguish Grendel and for him to distinguish Heorot; but inside, the pitch-blackness is momentarily so dense that only the burning eyes are visible to tell us where destruction stands.

The last image evoked here—two dots of fire against a veil of blackness—is probably the simplest in English literature; it is also one of the very most effective. That the monster's onslaught should take place in utter darkness makes it more terrifying because more mysterious. There is also the fact that, as Harry T. Levin has reminded us in his impressive critical study, *The Power of Blackness,* darkness has been associated with evil from Homeric times to the present.[4] More specifically, we recall that in the Old-English *Genesis,* the evil angels are explicitly hurled from Heaven "on þa *sweartan helle*" [into the darker hell] (312b).[5] Since the *Beowulf* poet introduces Grendel as a "feond on helle" [fiend in hell] (102b), the darkness in which the action takes place may well have provided the audience with an expected occasion for titillating terror. We cannot say that it helped them exercise their willing suspension of disbelief, because there was no need for it: Dorothy Whitelock has demonstrated that, even if Anglo-Saxon England did not actually swarm with live monsters, the testimony of the *Liber Monstrorum* suggests that their existence was certainly never considered outside the realm of possibility.[6]

---

[4] Harry T. Levin, *The Power of Blackness* (New York, 1958), e.g. on p. 30.
[5] Ed. George P. Krapp, *The Junius Manuscript* (New York, 1931), p. 12.
[6] Dorothy Whitelock, *The Audience of Beowulf* (Oxford, 1951), p. 46 ff.

That only the eyes of the monster should show further illustrates the poet's genius. Antoine de Saint-Exupéry once wrote, "When Joseph Conrad described a typhoon he said very little about towering waves, or darkness, or the whistling of the wind in the shrouds. He knew better. Instead, he took his reader down into the hold of the vessel, packed with emigrant coolies, where the rolling and the pitching of the ship had ripped up and scattered their bags and bundles, burst open their boxes, and flung their humble belongings into a crazy heap." [7] The same argument applies to the *Beowulf* poet. When he describes Grendel's entrance into the hall, he says nothing of the claws and teeth, the gigantic stature and the murderous looks: he knows better. Just as Conrad shows us only such details as are symbolic of the tragedy he wishes to convey, so the *Beowulf* poet shows us only the one detail that is most symbolic of the mysteriously destructive force which he wishes to suggest. Though we cannot see the monster himself, the sight of his eyes gives us the distressing sensation that *he* can see us; and then, under the circumstances the light that glows in these eyes is of a terrifying nature: "him on eagum stod / ligge gelicost *leoht unfæger*" [from his eyes stood forth/ most like a flame a fearsome light]. Furthermore, the eyes of humanlike monsters in early Germanic times were more often than not endowed with weird and evil powers. One remembers how, in the Old-Icelandic *Grettis Saga*, the troll Glámr was able to bring about Grettir's eventual undoing with a single glance:

> . . . en Glámr hvesti augun up í móti. Ok svá hefir Grettir sagt sjálfr, at þá eina sýn hafi hann sét svá at honum brygði við. Þá sigaði svá at honum af ollu saman, moeði ok því, er hann sá at Glámr gaut sínum sjónum harðliga, at hann gat eigi brugðit saxinu, ok lá náliga í milli heims ok heljar. En þvi var meiri ófagnaðarkraptr með Glámi en flestum oðrum aptrgongumonnum, at hann mælti þá á þessa leið: ". . . þá legg ek þat á við þik, at þessi augu sé pér jafnan fyrir sjónum sem ek ber eptir, ok mun þér erfitt þykkja cinum at vera; ok þat mun þér til dauða draga." [8]

[7] Antoine de Saint-Exupéry, *Wind, Sand, and Stars,* trans. Lewis Galantière (New York, 1939), p. 77. The quotation is given in English because it is taken from one of the two chapters added by the author to the American edition and not readily available in the French.

[8] *Grettis Saga,* in E. V. Gordon, ed., *An Introduction to Old Norse,* 2nd ed. (Oxford, 1957), p. 104.

[. . . and Glám stared up at it. And Grettir himself has said that that was the only sight he had ever seen which made him afraid. Then he grew faint from the combination of exhaustion and the sight of Glám's fiercely-gleaming eyes, so that he could not draw his short sword and lay almost between the living and the dead. Glám had greater demonic power than most other ghosts because he then said this: ". . . Then I lay this curse on you that you shall always see these eyes of mine and you shall hate being alone, and that will drag you to your death."]

No wonder, then, that the *Beowulf* poet should want to focus on Grendel's eyes and force us to visualize the evil in them!

If we accept the validity of the foregoing analysis, we must also accept the conclusion that Grendel's approach and entry in Heorot is surely one of the most effective presentations of terror in English literature. If we recall that the entire passage contains only one suggestion of sound, whose effect is to emphasize a transition in the otherwise purely visual account, we must further conclude that the terror which the scene so powerfully evokes in the audience is entirely the result of masterfully selected visual details consistently presented from the most immediately effective point of view. Such complete control over descriptive technique would be admirable in any work of literature; in the work of an oral-formulaic singer, it truly becomes a literary *tour de force*.

Classics Revisited—IV: *Beowulf*

by Kenneth Rexroth

Like the more hardy and noble fish, the kinds of men that we heirs of the Anglo-Saxon tradition think most heroic thrive best amidst the colder seas. The figures of the Norse, Welsh, and Irish Heroic Ages possess a magnanimity, courage, and contempt for triviality that we do not find in the heroes of Homer. Nor do our heroes come to their doom because they have pushed their normal endowment of great pride to the point of existential conceit; nor are they haunted by irresponsible fate or plagued by the frivolities of the gods.

For these reasons *Beowulf* seems essentially heroic in a way that the epics of the Mediterranean do not; its hero fulfils our insistence upon a moral heroism. His legend is one with those of Gordon, Florence Nightingale, Wellesley, or of Jesse W. Lazear and other martyrs of public health. Modern criticism has devalued our nineteenth-century heroes, but Beowulf is far away; all we know of him is a single document, so he stands as a mythic paradigm of the brave, generous, self-sacrificing aristocrat.

Beowulf, nephew of Hygelac, king of Geatas in Southern Sweden, sails to Denmark with fourteen companions and offers to rid the hall of Hrothgar, King of the Danes, of a devouring monster in human shape called Grendel. After a feast, the Danes withdraw. Grendel enters and kills one of the Swedes. Beowulf wrestles with the monster and tears off its arm. Grendel, mortally wounded, escapes to die at the bottom of the aweful mere which is his home. The next night Grendel's mother kills and carries off one of the Danish nobles. In

"Classics Revisited—IV: *Beowulf*." From *Saturday Review* (April 10, 1965), p. 27. Copyright © 1965 by Saturday Review, Incorporated. Reprinted by permission of *Saturday Review* and the author. The final paragraph, which deals with translations, has been omitted with the permission of the author.

full armor Beowulf plunges into the water and, after a terrible fight, kills her with a mysterious sword which he finds under the waves. After the death of Hygelac and his son, Beowulf becomes king of the Geatas. In extreme old age a dragon ravages his country and Beowulf destroys it but dies of his wounds. The poem ends with his funeral. Hrothgar and Hygelac were historical persons and Beowulf may have actually existed.

The most unexpected quality in *Beowulf* is its abiding communication of joy. In contrast with the Mediterranean glitter of the *Odyssey,* plagued by fatigue and melancholy, *Beowulf* takes place in an atmosphere of semi-darkness, the gloom of fire-lit halls, stormy wastelands, and underwater caverns. It is full of blood and fierceness. Its rhythms have the tone of pre-emptory challenge and the clang of iron. Men exult in their conflict with each other and the elements. The sea is not a jealous, cantankerous, senile deity. It is a cold, thrilling antagonist. Even Grendel and his mother are serious in the way Greek demons never are. They may be horrors survived from the pagan Norse world of frost giants, wolf men, and dragons of the waters, but nobody would ever dream of calling them frivolous. They share Beowulf's dogged earnestness; what they lack is his joy, which suffuses the book in spite of a counter-suffusion—a doom that haunts the far background of the narrative, like a few drops of ink and milk spreading into water from opposite directions.

Though they glory in themselves as successful animals, always we feel that *Beowulf* is a tale of men at the end of their tether. Not only do life and splendor fall to ruin but a hand is writing, "Mene, mene tekel upharsin" in the firelight on the walls of Hrothgar's banqueting hall. This civilization is almost over. The onrushing twilight of the gods is ominous in the distance. The refrain of another great Anglo-Saxon poem: *"Thaes ofereode, thisses swa maeg!"* (That passed away, this will too.) might as well have occurred every twenty lines or so in *Beowulf* or again, "Mood be the more as our might lessens." This sense of doom we can feel by simply reading the poem in adequate translation. If we read the notes or introduction, we learn not only that *Beowulf* takes place against the imminent end of the Heroic Age of the Teutonic peoples, but in addition a specific tragedy is unfolding in the background. The immediate personal future of Hrothgar's family was filled with treachery and disaster. The author knew this and so did his audience. Foreboding echoes as a counterpattern of rhythm and symbolism against all the poem's exultation.

This is a specifically northern epic theme. Arnold Toynbee, quoting John Knox, calls it "the monstrous regimen of women." Both Helen and Penelope determine the Homeric epics only by the passive exercise of their femininity. The queens and enchantresses of the North interfere actively. It is their machination that brings disaster.

Grendel and his mother, devourers of men, inhabitants of subterranean depths, embody the demonic past whose claims can be destroyed with the facility only of courage and strength—but the future cannot be destroyed. Its doom depends on the deliberate evils of its participants, not on karma, not on myth, not on the unconscious. It will be played out in treachery, the murder of kinsmen, and civil war. All through the poem the poet inserts carefully muted ambiguous references to the dynastic ruin that is about to overwhelm all the participants except Beowulf himself. It is this tension between the easily subjugated occult and the inchoate and ungovernable overt fact of human destiny that gives the poem its irony, its pathos, and its structure. Once this tension is understood, *Beowulf* ceases to seem a folkloristic collection of Scandinavian legends and emerges as a strictly organized but muted tragedy—an elegiac drama.

Beowulf dies and is buried "above the battle," overlooking the pale, cold sea, the perfect example of heroic transcendence. His grave must have been much like the ship burial discovered in our own generation at Sutton Hoo in England on the western shore of the same sea of adventure. Among the surviving treasures of that anonymous hero are the enameled clasps of his sporran, ornamented with a figure of a man strangling two beasts—the Gilgamesh motif come to the far North across 4,000 years.

A Note on Chronology

No definite date for the composition of *Beowulf* is known, and estimates range from 600 to 1000 A.D. Most scholars would place it in the first half of the eighth century. The events described take place between about 450 and 550 A.D. The manuscript itself can be dated about the year 1000 on paleographical evidence.

The first surviving mention of the poem comes in 1705 in Humphrey Wanley's catalogue of Anglo-Saxon manuscripts, where he describes it as an epic poem on the wars between the Danes and Swedes, a not unlikely impression for one who probably only read as far as line 73. In 1805 Sharon Turner translated about 165 lines of it into English verse. The first edition was published in 1815 by Grímur Jonsson Thorkelin, a Dane who had seen to the transcription of the poem in 1787. The first complete translation into English was by John M. Kemble in 1837. The first American edition was published in 1882 by James A. Harrison, and the first American translation was by James M. Garnett in that same year.

Notes on the Editor and Authors

DONALD K. FRY, the editor, is Assistant Professor of English at the University of Virginia. His book-length bibliography of *Beowulf* and the *Finnsburg Fragment* will be published by the Bibliographical Society of the University of Virginia in 1969.

JOAN BLOMFIELD (MRS. G. TURVILLE-PETRE) is a Research Fellow of Somerville College, Oxford.

MORTON W. BLOOMFIELD, Professor of English at Harvard University, is the author of *Piers Plowman as a Fourteenth-Century Apocalypse*.

ROSEMARY CRAMP is Lecturer in Anglo-Saxon Antiquities and Archaeology at the University of Durham.

ROBERT CREED, Associate Professor of English at the State University of New York at Stony Brook, is currently writing a book on the Old English oral formula.

ROBERT M. LUMIANSKY, Professor of English at the University of Pennsylvania, is the author of a study of the dramatic principle in Chaucer, *Of Sondry Folk,* and of translations of Chaucer's major works.

FRANCIS PEABODY MAGOUN, JR., Professor of English Emeritus at Harvard University, has edited numerous Old English poems in normalized orthography, and has recently translated the Finnish *Kalevala*.

ALAIN RENOIR is Professor of English and Comparative Literature at the University of California at Berkeley. He is the author of *The Poetry of John Lydgate*.

KENNETH REXROTH, poet and critic, is author of the "Classics Revisited" series in *Saturday Review*. He has recently published his collected shorter poems.

J. R. R. TOLKIEN, Merton Professor Emeritus of English Language and Literature in the University of Oxford, has edited the *Wanderer* and *Sir*

Gawain and the Green Knight. He is currently at work on a sequel to his trilogy, *The Lord of the Rings.*

RICHARD WILBUR, Professor of English at Wesleyan University, is the author of four books of poetry and winner of the Pulitzer Prize and the National Book Award.

Selected Bibliography

An extensive bibliography of *Beowulf* and *The Finnsburg Fragment* will be published by the Bibliographical Society of the University of Virginia in 1969. The editions cited below contain the most extensive bibliographies currently in print.

Editions

Dobbie, E. V. K. *Beowulf and Judith* (London and N. Y., 1953).

Klaeber, F. *Beowulf and the Fight at Finnsburg.* Third edition with supplements (Boston, 1950).

Wrenn, C. L. *Beowulf, with the Finnesburg Fragment.* Second edition (London, 1958).

Translations

Donaldson, E. T. *Beowulf* (N. Y., 1966).

Hall, J. R. C. *Beowulf and the Finnesburg Fragment: A Translation into Modern English Prose.* Revised by C. L. Wrenn, with preface by J. R. R. Tolkien (London, 1950).

Kennedy, C. W. *Beowulf: The Oldest English Epic* (Oxford, 1940).

Morgan, E. *Beowulf: A Verse Translation into Modern English* (Aldington, Kent, 1952; N. Y., 1953). Reprinted Berkeley and Los Angeles, 1962.

Raffel, B. *Beowulf* (N. Y., 1963).

Critical and Historical

Bliss, A. J. *The Metre of Beowulf* (Oxford, 1958).

Bonjour, A. *The Digressions in Beowulf* (Oxford, 1950).

————. "Monsters Crouching and Critics Rampant: or the *Beowulf* Dragon Debated," *PMLA*, LXVIII (1953), 304–12.

Brodeur, A. G. *The Art of Beowulf* (Berkeley and Los Angeles, 1959).

Campbell, A. "The Old English Epic Style," in *English and Medieval Studies Presented to J. R. R. Tolkien*, edited by N. Davis and C. L. Wrenn (London, 1962), pp. 13–26.

Chadwick, N. K. "The Monsters and *Beowulf*," in *The Anglo-Saxons*, edited by P. Clemoes (London, 1959), pp. 171–203.

Chambers, R. W. *Beowulf: An Introduction to the Study of the Poem, with a discussion of the Stories of Offa and Finn.* Third edition, with supplement by C. L. Wrenn (Cambridge, 1959).

————. "*Beowulf* and the Heroic Age in England," in his *Man's Unconquerable Mind* (London, 1939), pp. 53–69.

Clark, G. "Beowulf's Armor." *ELH*, XXXII (1965), 409–41.

DuBois, A. E. "The Unity of *Beowulf*," *PMLA*, XLIX (1934), 374–405.

Fry, D. K. "Old English Formulas and Systems," *English Studies*, XLVIII (1967), 193–204.

Gang, T. M. "Approaches to *Beowulf*," *Review of English Studies*, New Series 3 (1952), 1–12.

Girvan, R. *Beowulf and the Seventh Century* (London, 1935).

Greenfield, S. B. "*Beowulf* and Epic Tragedy," *Comparative Literature*, XIV (1962), 91–105.

————. "Geatish History: Poetic Art and Epic Quality in *Beowulf*," *Neophilologus*, XLVII (1963), 211–17.

Haber, T. B. *A Comparative Study of the Beowulf and the Aeneid* (Princeton, 1931).

Hulbert, J. R. "*Beowulf* and the Classical Epic," *Modern Philology*, XLIV (1946), 65–75.

Kaske, R. E. "*Sapientia et Fortitudo* as the Controlling Theme of *Beowulf*," *Studies in Philology*, LV (1958), 423–57. Reprinted in Nicholson (below), pp. 269–310.

Kellogg, R. L. "The South Germanic Oral Tradition," in *Franciplegius*, edited by J. B. Bessinger and R. P. Creed (N. Y., 1965), pp. 66–74.

Ker, W. P. *Epic and Romance*. Second edition (Oxford, 1908).

Lawrence, W. W. *Beowulf and Epic Tradition* (Cambridge, Mass., 1928).

Leake, J. A. *The Geats of Beowulf* (Madison, 1966).

Lindquist, Sune. "Sutton Hoo and *Beowulf*," *Antiquity*, XXII (1948), 131–40.

Malone, K. *"Beowulf," English Studies,* XXIX (1948), 161–72. Reprinted in Nicholson (below), pp. 137–54.

Metcalf, A. "Ten Natural Animals in *Beowulf," Neuphilologische Mitteilungen,* LXIV (1963), 378–89.

Nicholson, L. E. *An Anthology of Beowulf Criticism* (South Bend, 1963).

Pope, J. C. *The Rhythm of Beowulf.* Second edition (New Haven, 1966).

Quirk, R. "Poetic Language and Old English Metre," in *Early English and Norse Studies,* edited by A. Brown and P. Foote (London, 1963), pp. 150–71.

Renoir, A. "The Heroic Oath in *Beowulf,* the *Chanson de Roland,* and the *Nibelungenlied,"* in *Studies in Old English Literature in Honor of A. G. Brodeur,* edited by S. B. Greenfield (Eugene, 1963), pp. 237–66.

Rosier, J. L. "Design for Treachery: the Unferth Intrigue," *PMLA,* LXXVII (1962), 1–7.

Schaar, C. "On a New Theory of O. E. Poetic Diction," *Neophilologus,* XL (1956), 301–5.

Schücking, L. L. "Das Königsideal im *Beowulf* [The Ideal of Kingship in *Beowulf*]," *Englische Studien,* LXVII (1932), 1–14. Translated in Nicholson (above), pp. 35–49.

Sisam, K. "Beowulf's Fight with the Dragon," *Review of English Studies,* New Series 9 (1958), 129–40.

———. "The Compilation of the *Beowulf* Manuscript," in his *Studies in the History of Old English Literature* (Oxford, 1953), pp. 65–96.

———. *The Structure of Beowulf* (Oxford, 1965).

Van Meurs, J. C. *"Beowulf* and Literary Criticism," *Neophilologus,* XXXIX (1955), 114–30.

Whitelock, D. *The Audience of Beowulf* (Oxford, 1951).

Woolf, H. B. "On the Characterization of Beowulf," *ELH,* XV (1948), 85–92.

Wrenn, C. L. "Sutton Hoo and *Beowulf,"* in *Mélanges Fernand Mossé* (Paris, 1959), pp. 495–507. Reprinted in Nicholson (above), pp. 311–30.